THE ESSENTIALS OF BUDDHIST PHILOSOPHY

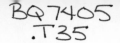

THE ESSENTIALS OF BUDDHIST PHILOSOPHY

JUNJIRŌ TAKAKUSU

EDITED BY

WING-TSIT CHAN AND CHARLES A. MOORE

University of Hawaii, Honolulu, T. H.

GREENWOOD PRESS, PUBLISHERS
WESTPORT, CONNECTICUT

Library of Congress Cataloging in Publication Data

Takakusu, Junjirō.
    The essentials of Buddhist philosophy.

    Reprint of the 1956 ed.
    1. Mahayana Buddhism. 2. Buddhist doctrines--East
(Far East) 3. Buddhist sects--East (Far East)
I. Title.
BQ7405.T35 1973   181'.04'3   72-10701
ISBN 0-8371-6619-5

This edition originally published in 1956 by the Office
Appliance Co., Ltd., Honolulu

Reprinted with the permission of Office Appliance Company, Ltd.

Reprinted by Greenwood Press, Inc.
First Greenwood reprinting 1973
Second Greenwood reprinting 1974
Third Greenwood reprinting 1975
Fourth Greenwood reprinting 1976
Paperback edition 1976

Library of Congress Catalog Card Number 72-10701

ISBN 0-8371-6619-5 Cloth edition
ISBN 0-8371-8990-X Paper edition

Printed in the United States of America

EDITORS' PREFACE

For several decades prior to Professor Takakusu's death in June, 1945, the English-speaking world knew him as an author, editor, and translator of monumental works on Buddhism. In this book, Dr. Takakusu's only major work in English, the summation of his lifetime study of Buddhist philosophy is presented. Dr. Takakusu prepared the material in Tokyo and in 1938-39 delivered it as a series of lectures at the University of Hawaii, where he was a visiting professor. In the summer of 1939, philosophers from several parts of the world gathered at the University of Hawaii for an East-West Philosophers' Conference, and they used this text as one of the books in their discussions. The results of this conference are presented in *Philosophy—East and West,* published in 1944 by the Princeton University Press.

Before Professor Takakusu returned to Tokyo, he authorized us to publish this text and to make minor alterations without consulting him. We have made some revisions, but, in order to avoid the possibility of altering the meaning, we have revised the English only where we felt that a change was essential. The text gives basic Buddhist terms in English, Chinese, and Sanskrit, and the index gives the diacritical marks of the Pali and Sanskrit. Dr. Takakusu employs irregular Sanskrit forms at times in order to avoid confusion on the part of the reader. As an aid to students, we have inserted references to important texts of all major Buddhist philosophical systems.

This work represents the conclusions of a Buddhist scholar whose renown is attested by the academic and honorary degrees and other honors conferred upon him. Among these were: M.A., D. Litt. (Oxon.), Dr. Phil. (Leipzig), D. Litt. (Tokyo), Ehren Dr. Phil. (Heidelberg), Member of the Imperial Academy (Japan), Fellow of the British Academy. At the time of his death he was Professor Emeritus of Sanskrit at Tokyo Imperial University.

Some readers may believe that Japanese Buddhism has been overstressed in this volume, but, as Professor Takakusu states, it is justified—or necessitated—by the fact that in Japan "the whole of Buddhism has been preserved," as well as the fact that, in Japan, Buddhism is the living and active faith of the mass of the people.

As Director of the University's Oriental Institute (now the School of Pacific and Asiatic Studies), Mr. Gregg M. Sinclair arranged for Dr. Takakusu's engagement as visiting professor at the University of Hawaii, and as President of the University since 1943 he has kept alive the plan for publishing this book at an appropriate time.

The project has received generous financial assistance from Professor Takakusu's friends in Hawaii, especially through the cooperation of Mr. Eimu Miake and the Reverend Kenju Ohtomo.

Thanks are also due to Professor Yukuo Uyehara for his assistance in planning and effecting publication of the volume, to Professor Johannes Rahder for invaluable assistance on the proofs and index, and to the Reverend Iwasaburo Yoshikami for help on the index. Special appreciation is hereby expressed to Mr. Richard A. Gard for his very generous assistance in checking the entire manuscript with Professor Takakusu after the latter's return to Japan from Hawaii in 1939, and working out with the author many important changes in the text. Mr. Gard deserves thanks also for similar assistance in connection with Professor Takakusu's chapter in *Philosophy—East and West,* which includes, in essence, the same material as found in Chapter III of this volume.

W. T. CHAN
CHARLES A. MOORE

EDITORS' PREFACE TO SECOND EDITION

The enthusiastic reception of Dr. Takakusu's presentation of the basic principles and schools of Buddhist Philosophy led to the early depletion of the first edition and has been interpreted to mean that the book fills a substantial need in the field of technical secondary literature on the subject. A second edition, therefore, seemed desirable to the editors and to those who first published the book, namely, the University of Hawaii and friends of Dr. Takakusu in Hawaii.

In presenting this second edition, the editors have maintained the policies stated in the preface to the first edition; that is, they have not considered it their privilege to change the text materially. A few changes have been made for the sake of greater clarity, however, and minor errors have been corrected.

The editors wish to express their great appreciation for generous assistance in making these revisions to Professor Johannes Rahder, Yale University; Professor Sitaram Tripathi, Banaras Hindu University; Professor Yukuo Uyehara, University of Hawaii; and Mr. Richard A. Gard, Ontario, California.
May 1, 1949

W. T. CHAN
CHARLES A. MOORE

PREFACE TO THIRD EDITION

In all essentials this edition is merely a reprint of the second edition, that is, no major revisions have been made. However, a few doubtful points and a small number of mistakes have been revised for the sake of clarity and accuracy.

Perhaps it should be noted especially that the charts on pages 150 and 151 have been transposed from the positions they occupied in earlier editions. Scholars differ concerning the precise form in which these charts should be presented and described, but it is felt that the transposition which has been made is the best available solution of a difficult problem.

C. A. M.

CONTENTS

I. INTRODUCTION

(1) How to Depict Buddhism

A discourse on Buddhist Philosophy is usually begun with the philosophy of Indian Buddhism, and in this respect it is important to trace the development of Buddhist thought in India where it thrived for 1500 years. It should be remembered, however, that before Buddhism declined in India in the eleventh century, its various developments had already spread far into other countries. Hinayana Buddhism, or the Small Vehicle, which emphasizes individual salvation, continued in Ceylon, Burma, Siam and Cambodia. Mystic or esoteric Buddhism developed as Lamaism in Tibet. Mahayana Buddhism, or the Great Vehicle, which emphasizes universal salvation, grew in China where great strides in Buddhist studies were made and the different thoughts in Mahayana schools were systematized.

In Japan, however, the whole of Buddhism has been preserved— every doctrine of both the Hinayana and Mahayana schools. Although Hinayana Buddhism does not now exist in Japan as an active faith, its doctrines are still being studied there by Buddhist scholars. Mikkyō,[1] which we may designate as the Esoteric Doctrine or Mysticism, is fully represented in Japan by Tendai[2] mysticism and Tōji[3] mysticism. The point which Japanese mysticism may be proud of is that it does not contain any vulgar elements, as does its counterpart in other countries, but stands on a firm philosophical basis.

The schools which were best developed in China are Hua-yen[4] (Kegon, the 'Wreath' School) and T'ien-t'ai[5] (Tendai, the 'Lotus' School). When the Ch'an[6] (Zen) School is added to these two, the trio represents the highest peak of Buddhism's development. These three flourished in China for a while and then passed away, but in Japan all three are still alive in the people's faiths as well as in academic studies.

A rather novel form of Buddhism is the Amita-pietism. It is found to some extent in China, Tibet, Nepal, Mongolia, Manchuria and

---

[1] 密教　[2] 天台　[3] 東寺　[4] 華嚴　[5] 天台　[6] 禪

Annam; but it flourishes most in Japan where it is followed by more than half of the population.

I believe, therefore, that the only way to exhibit the entire Buddhist philosophy in all its different schools is to give a résumé of Buddhism in Japan. It is in Japan that the entire Buddhist literature, the Tripitaka, is preserved and studied.

The great Tripitaka Literature,[7] which is chiefly in Chinese translation, was brought to Japan from China in the T'ang (618-907) and Sung (960-1279) periods. It consisted then of 5048 volumes, all of which have been preserved in Japan although many were lost in China. In Japan, the Tripitaka Literature has been published at least four times, *each edition adding new volumes.* Recently it became my responsibility to complete its latest publication, which contains the Chinese and Korean compilations as well as texts newly discovered in Central Asia and Japan—a work of thirteen years—comprising 13,520 *chüans* [8] or parts in 100 bound volumes of 1000 pages each.[9]

There is little need of describing the numerous monasteries in Japan, which are seats of Buddhist learning. But I should mention the fact that there are six strong universities of Buddhist affiliations which make the philosophy of Buddhism their chief subject of study. There are also many colleges and schools of Buddhist support, and in five of the governmental universities Buddhist philosophy, Sanskrit and Pali are studied.

In the present study of Buddhist philosophy the subject will not be presented in its historical sequence but in an ideological sequence. This ideological sequence does not mean a sequence in the development of ideas; it is rather the systematization of the different schools of thought for the purpose of easier approach.

Because of my peculiar approach to the subject, I am going to present a classification of Buddhist thought different from that of Professor Stcherbatsky, who made a very masterful presentation of

---

[7] 大藏經   This constitutes the basic literature of Buddhism comprising the three divisions of Buddhist doctrine: the Buddha's discourses; disciplinary rules; and philosophical treatises.

[8] 卷   [9] *Taishō Shinshū Daizōkyō* 大正新修大藏經 (Taishō Edition of the Tripitaka in Chinese). Edited by J. Takakusu, K. Watanabe, and G. Ono. 100 volumes. Tokyo, 1929—. Hereafter cited as *Taishō.*

Buddhist ideas in his *Buddhist Logic*.[10] He divided the first 1500 years of Buddhist history, dating back to 500 B.C., into three periods of five hundred years each, as follows:

First	Middle	Concluding
Pluralism	Monism	Idealism
Pudgala-sunyata	Sarva-dharma-sunyata	Bahya-artha-sunyata
(Denial of individuality)	(Denial of all elements)	(Denial of the external world)

In his table, Professor Stcherbatsky indicated the extreme and moderate schools in each period.

Historically, Professor Stcherbatsky's table is more accurate, and I am conscious of the fact that the Idealism of Asanga and Vasubandhu [11] arose in reaction against the extreme passivity of Nagarjuna's Negativism.[12] However, it being impossible to place Harivarman's Negativism [13] after Nagarjuna; I have taken the liberty of assuming the following table with the great thinker and writer Vasubandhu as the starting point of the development of all Buddhist thought:

[10] Th. Stcherbatsky: *Buddhist Logic*, two volumes (*Bibliotheca Buddhica* Vol. XXVI). Leningrad, 1932; Vol. I, p. 14.

[11] 無著 c. 410-500 A.D.; 世親 c. 420-500 A.D.

[12] 龍樹 c. 100-200 A.D. See 4th column of the following table.

[13] 訶梨跋摩, 師子鎧 c. 250-350 A.D. See 2nd column of the following table.

(1) REALISM*	(2) NIHILISM*	(3) IDEALISM*	(4) NEGATIVISM*
Hinayanistic	Hinayanistic (Nihilism)	Semi-Mahayanistic	Mahayanistic (Nihilism)
Sarvāsti. School 説一切有 (holding that everything exists)	*Satyasiddhi School* 成實 (holding that truth is attainable by antithetic negation)	*Vijnaptimatra School* 唯識 (holding that ideation alone exists)	*Madhyamika School* 中論 (holding that truth is attainable by synthetic negation)
Pudgala-sunyata (denying individuality)	*Sarva-dharma-sunyata* (denying the reality of all—matter and mind)	*Bahya-artha-sunyata* (denying the reality of all external things)	*Sarva-dharma-sunyata* (denying the reality of all—matter and mind and all attachments of living beings; thereby striving to reach the "highest" truth [Middle Path] which can be conceived only by synthetic negation or the negation of negation)
Doctrine of *Ens* (being)	Doctrine of *Non-ens* (non-being)	Doctrine of *both Ens and Non-ens*	Doctrine of *neither Ens nor Non-ens*
Middle Path as the ideal way in practical life; neither optimistic nor pessimistic.	Middle Path or Truth attainable by the recognition of nonentity, admitting neither individuality (*Pudgala*) nor reality of matter and mind (*Dharma*). All end in *Nirvana* (Void). Nihilism as opposed to Realism.	Middle Path or Truth lies neither in recognizing the reality of all things because outer things do not exist, nor in recognizing the non-reality of all things because ideations do exist.	Middle Path or Truth attained by either reciprocal negation or repetitional negation; reciprocal negation being the eightfold denial of phenomena of being, and repetitional negation being the fourfold serial denial of the popular and the higher ideas.
Vasubandhu (c. 420-500 A.D.)	Harivarman (c. 250-350 A.D.) Chinese translation 407 A.D.	Vasubandhu (c. 420-500 A.D.)	Nagarjuna (c. 100-200 A.D.)

12

---

* Each of these schools will be explained in detail later. See Chapters IV (Realism), V (Nihilism), VI (Idealism) and VII (Negativism).

According to my scheme, Nagarjuna, the earliest Buddhist philosopher, is placed after Harivarman and Vasubandhu, as may be seen in the table. However, when the development of ideas is to be fitted into a simple pattern, such a discrepancy is inevitable. In China when a philosopher-priest engages in philosophical studies, he does not usually take up the history of ideas, but he at once goes into the speculation of whichever thought attracts his interest. Therefore, there is little advantage in studying Buddhist ideas according to the historical sequence.

(2) BUDDHISM IN THE HISTORY OF CHINA

The history of Buddhist activities in China covers about 1200 years (A.D. 67-1271) and is practically identical with the history of the Chinese translation of the Buddhist scriptures. During those years 173 Indian and Chinese priests devoted themselves to the laborious work of translation, and the result was the great literature of the Chinese Tripitaka.

Careful studies of these translations were continued, and many schools of thought, or religious sects, were established. The most notable of them (fourteen in number) may be picked out for our purpose. Almost all of them were introduced to Japan. But we shall not trouble ourselves with minute accounts of them here, for we shall have to return to them when we study the philosophical tenets of each.

We must remember, however, that the Sui (A.D. 581-618) and the T'ang (A.D. 618-907) dynasties are the age when the sectarian schools were completed and that these schools were founded or originated some time earlier by those able men who translated or introduced the texts. We shall now examine the list of these schools founded and completed on Chinese soil. This list indicates the vast development and systematization of Buddhism in China.

13

LISTS OF CHINESE SECTS*

A. Foundation (Before Sui and T'ang Dynasties, A.D. 67-581)	B. Final Completion (In the Sui and T'ang Dynasties, A.D. 581-907)

Western Tsin Dynasty (A.D. 265-317)

1. P'i-t'an Tsung (毘曇宗)
(Abhidharma)
Hinayana
Formalistic
(Transl. Sanghadeva A.D. 383-390)

Eastern Tsin Dynasty (A.D. 317-420)

2. **Chêng-shih Tsung (成實宗)**
(Satyasiddhi)
Hinayana Sautranta
Nihilistic
(Transl. Kumarajiva A.D. 417-418)

3. San-lun Tsung (三論宗)
(Madhyamika)
Mahayana
Negativistic
(Found. Sêng-chao 僧肇, pupil of Kumarajiva 鳩摩羅什; transl. c. A.D. 384-414)

(3) **San-lun Tsung (三論宗)**
Madhyamika
Negativism systematized by Chi-tsang, 吉藏 A.D. 549-623.

4. Lü Tsung (律宗)
(Vinaya)
Hinayana
Disciplinary
(Found. Hui-kuang 慧光, pupil of Kumarajiva; transl. c. A.D. 402-412)

(4) Lü Tsung (律宗)
Dharmagupta Discipline completed by Tao-hsüan, 道宣 A.D. 596-667.

---

* Those sects in **Bold Face** were introduced into Japan.

14

LISTS OF CHINESE SECTS* (Continued)

Northern Liang Dynasty (A.D. 397-439)

5. **Nieh-p'an Tsung** (涅槃宗)
(Nirvana)
Mahayana
Noumenological
(Transl. Dharmaraksa A.D. 423)

Northern Wei Dynasty (A.D. 386-535)

6. Ti-lun Tsung (地論宗)
(Dasabhumi)
Mahayana
Idealistic
(Transl. Bodhiruci, c. A.D. 508)

Eastern Wei Dynasty (A.D. 534-550)

Western Wei Dynasty (A.D. 535-557)

7. **Ching-t'u Tsung** (淨土宗)
(Sukhavati)
Mahayana
Pietistic
(Transl. Bodhiruci, A.D. 529. Found. T'an-luan (曇鸞, A.D. 476-524)

Southern Liang Dynasty A.D. 502-557

8. **Ch'an Tsung** (禪宗)
(Dhyana)
Mahayana
Contemplative

11. **T'ien-t'ai Tsung** (天台宗)
(Pundarika—The 'Lotus' Doctrine)
Mahayana
Phenomenological
Phenomenology completed by Chih-i 智顗, A.D. 531-597.

12. **Hua-yen Tsung** (華嚴宗)
(Avatansaka, the 'Wreath' Doctrine)
Mahayana
Totalistic
Totalism completed by Fa-tsang 法藏, A.D. 643-712.

(7) **Ching-t'u Tsung** (淨土宗)
(Sukhavati)
Mahayana
Pietistic
Amitabha Pietism completed by Shan-tao 善導, d. A.D. 681.

(8) **Ch'an Tsung** (禪宗)
(Dhyana)
Mahayana
Contemplative

---

* Those sects in **Bold Face** were introduced into Japan.

Ch'ên Dynasty
(A.D. 557-589)

(Found. Bodhidharma, 菩提達摩.
c. A.D. 470-534)

The system of meditation flourished under Hui-nêng (慧能 A.D. 638-713), northern school, and Shên-hsiu (神秀 A.D. 605-706), southern school.

9. Shê-lun Tsung (攝論宗)........
(Mahayana-samparigraha)
Mahayana
Idealistic
(Transl. Paramartha, c. A.D. 563)

13. Fa-hsiang Tsung (法相宗)
(Vijnaptimatrata)
Quasi-Mahayana
Idealistic
Idealism translated and completed by Hiüen-tsang (Hsüan-tsang, 玄奘 A.D. 596-664) and Kuei, his pupil (K'uei-chi, 窺基 A.D. 632-682).

10. Chü-shê Tsung(俱舍宗)
(Abhidharmakosa)
Hinayana
Realistic
Similar in tenet to 1 above
(Transl. Paramartha, A.D. 563-567)

Chü-shê Tsung (俱舍宗)
(Abhidharmakosa)
Hinayana
Realistic
Kosa Realism transmitted byHiüen-tsang and completed by Kuei, his pupil.

14. Chên-yen Tsung (真言宗)
(Mantrayana)
Mahayana
Mystic
Mysticism transmitted by Subhakarasimha, 菩無畏 A.D. 637-735, Vajrabodhi, 金剛智 A.D. 663-723, and Amoghavajra, 不忍, A.D. 705-774.

* Those sects in Bold Face were introduced into Japan.

16

Of the above sects, ten (2, 3, 4, 7, 8, 10, 11, 12, 13, 14) were transmitted to Japan, and of them three, i.e., the realistic Chü-shê (10), the nihilistic Ch'êng-shih (2), and the negativistic San-lun (3) schools did not remain in Japan as active sects but are preserved for the purpose of training and preparing the Buddhist mind for higher speculation and criticism.

(3) JAPAN AS THE LAND OF MAHAYANA

Buddhism was officially introduced into Japan in A.D. 552 from Paikche,[14] a kingdom in Korea, but thirty years earlier Buddhist images had been brought to Japan. In 594 the Prince Regent, Shō-toku Taishi (574-622) declared Buddhism the state religion.

Buddhism at this time was quite devoid of the distinction of sects or schools, although the difference of Mahayana and Hinayana was clearly recognized. The Prince himself strictly adhered to Mahayana and wrote commentaries upon three Mahayana texts. The fame of these excellent annotations spread abroad, and one of them was chosen as a subject of commentaries by a Chinese savant.

The particular type of Mahayana that was adopted by the Prince may be seen from a consideration of the texts which were chosen. The first is the *Lotus of the Good Law,* a text devoted to the Eka-yana (One Vehicle) doctrine, indicating the idea of the good law. The second is the *Discourse on the Ultimate Truth* by Vimalakirti,[15] a lay Bodhisattva of Vaisali, while the third is the *Book of the Earnest Resolve* by Srimala, a lady Bodhisattva, the Queen of Ayodhya.[16] The central idea of this non-sectarian period was the doctrine of the Great Vehicle (Mahayana) as expressed in these three texts. This idea has remained the dominating feature of Buddhism throughout its history in Japan.

(4) JAPANESE BUDDHISM PHILOSOPHICALLY CLASSIFIED

To depict the whole of Buddhism it will be better, as I have already emphasized, to treat it according to its philosophical development. For the sake of clarity, I shall group the schools under two heads: the Schools of Negative Rationalism, i.e., the Religion of

---

[14] 百済   [15] 維摩詰

[16] *Saddharma-pundarika* 妙法蓮華經 *Taishō* No. 262; *Vimalakirti-nirdesa* 維摩詰經, *Taishō* No. 475; *Srimala-devi-simhanada* 勝鬘師子吼一乘大方便方廣經, *Taishō* No. 353.

Dialectic Investigation; and the Schools of Introspective Intuitionism, i.e., the Religion of Meditative Experience.

It is well known that Buddhism lays stress on the Threefold Learning (*siksa*) of Higher Morality, Higher Thought, and Higher Insight. That is to say, without higher morals one cannot get higher thought and without higher thought one cannot attain higher insight. Higher Thought here comprises the results of both analytical investigation and meditative intuition. Buddhism further instructs the aspirants, when they are qualified, in the Threefold Way (*marga*) of Life-View, Life-Culture, and Realization of Life-Ideal. In other words, without a right view of life there will be no culture, and without proper culture there will be no realization of life. Life-Culture here again means the results of right meditation.

The twofold inheritance of the Buddha was Right Reasoning (*nyaya*) and Right Meditating (*dhyana*). One set of the Buddhist Schools which chiefly dwells on the former method I classify here as Negative Rationalism. It may seem a misnomer to group Realism under Negative Rationalism. However, when we see that it holds the doctrines of selflessness, impermanence, blisslessness, and momentariness of life we cannot assume much of its positive features. As to the rest of the schools, no explanation will be necessary.

The other set of schools I classify as Introspective Intuitionism, because all these are taught according to the result of meditative or introspective activity of the mind and not by dialectical reasoning or simple perception of the senses. The Intuitive Schools are of two kinds: the Undifferentiative and the Differentiative. According to my idea, Buddhism may be classified as follows:

I.
SCHOOLS OF NEGATIVE RATIONALISM

1. Realism (Sarvastivada, Abhidharmika), Abhidharmakosa, Chü-shê, or Kusha [17] School [Ens School]
2. Nihilism (Sarvasunyavada, Sautrantika), Satyasiddhi, Ch'êng-shih, or Jōjitsu [18] School [Non-ens School]
3. Idealism (Vijnaptimatravada), Yogacara, Fa-hsiang, or Hos-sō [19] School [Both Ens and Non-ens School]
4. Negativism (Sarvasunyavada), Madhyamika, San-lun, or San-ron [20] School [Neither Ens nor Non-ens School]

---

[17] 俱舍宗　　[18] 成實宗　　[19] 法相宗　　[20] 三論宗

II.
SCHOOLS OF INTROSPECTIVE INTUITIONISM

(A)
Undifferentiated Intuitionism

5. Totalism (Avatansaka), Hua-yen, Kegon [21] or 'Wreath' School
6. Phenomenology (Saddharmapundarika, Ekayana), T'ien-t'ai, Tendai [22] or 'Lotus' School
7. Mysticism (Mantra), Chên-yen, Shingon [23] or 'True Word' School
8. Pure Intuitionism (Dhyana), Ch'an, Zen [24] or Meditation School
   Four divisions:
   a. Rinzai Sect [25] founded by Eisai [26]
   b. Sōtō Sect [27] founded by Dōgen [28]
   c. Fuke Sect [29] founded by Kakushin [30] in 1255; abolished after 1868
   d. Ōbaku Sect [31] founded by Ingen [32]

(B)
Differentiated Intuitionism

9. Amita-pietism (Sukhavati), Ching-t'u, Jōdo [33] or 'Pure Land' School [Objectively Differentiated Intuitionism]
   Four divisions:
   a. Jōdo Sect founded by Hōnen [34]
   b. Shin Sect [35] founded by Shinran [36]
   c. Yūzūnembutsu Sect [37] founded by Ryōnin [38]
   d. Ji Sect [39] founded by Ippen [40]
10. Lotus-pietism, Nichiren [41] or 'New Lotus' School founded by Nichiren [42] [Subjectively Differentiated Intuitionism]
11. Disciplinary Formalism (Vinaya), the New or Reformed Ritsu (Lü) [43] founded by Eison [44] [Subjectively Experienced Intuitionism]

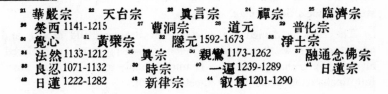

[21] 華嚴宗 [22] 天台宗 [23] 眞言宗 [24] 禪宗 [25] 臨濟宗
[26] 榮西 1141-1215 [27] 曹洞宗 [28] 道元 [29] 普化宗
[30] 覺心 [31] 黃檗宗 [32] 隱元 1592-1673 [33] 淨土宗
[34] 法然 1133-1212 [35] 眞宗 [36] 親鸞 1173-1262 [37] 融通念佛宗
[38] 良忍 1071-1132 [39] 時宗 [40] 一遍 1239-1289 [41] 日蓮宗
[42] 日蓮 1222-1282 [43] 新律宗 [44] 叡尊 1201-1290

II. INDIAN BACKGROUND

(1) BUDDHIST INDIA

The Buddha may or may not have been 'the greatest Aryan of all the Aryans,' or 'the greatest of all philosophers,' as some would call him. It is difficult to determine how such a man as the Buddha, who is so different from the other philosophers and religious men of India, could have appeared there, for he denied entirely the traditional gods, religious beliefs, institutions and customs.

When the Aryans conquered India, they pushed southward in their march of victory until they entered the tropical zone. Then, because of the severe heat, they chose to select their abode among the cool forests of the Black Mountains, which form the smaller range along the foot of the great Himalaya. Gradually they came to regard the forest as their ideal abode, and in time they acquired the habit of meditating with the great Himalaya as the object of their thoughts. For, there was Himalaya, eternally magnificent, eternally unapproachable. During mornings and evenings the snows would glow in changing splendor as the rays of the sun struck them; in winter the glaciers in the valleys were frozen solid, but in summer the glaciers flowed along the winding valleys like giant dragons come to life after a year's sleep. Finally, the Aryans, who had conquered India by force, in turn came to be completely conquered by the mysterious influence of Nature.

In very few words, Brahmanism, the old Indian religion, was a pantheism with Brahman (the eternal, absolute, unchanging principle) as the first cause of the universe. The manifestation of this Brahman is sometimes personified and is called Brahma (God, or the Great Self). Every human being has *atman* (little self). Brahman and *atman* are one, and of the same substance. Brahmanism, therefore, is an effort to seek the ultimate principle, Brahman, by studying one's Self, *atman*.

The Buddha denied the existence of Brahman and *atman,* and advanced a new theory of *anatman* (no-self), for, he declared, all things are changing and it is unreasonable to look for an absolute unchanging principle or an eternal self.

It is appropriate to speak of the Indian civilization as the civilization of the Forest. Religion, philosophy and literature were all products of the forest. Education was carried on in the sacred depth of the forest. Music, medicine and other branches of civilization were, without exception, cultivated in the forest.

Such theories as those which contend that city life produces civilization or that the origin of civilization is the triumph of man over Nature cannot be acceptable in India. The Indian people believe that the struggle for life is a hindrance to higher civilization. To them civilization means the assimilation of man into Nature; hence city life is simply the breeding-place of crime.

Brahmanism, the Indian philosophy, and Buddhism may both be called the product of self-culture [1] under Nature. The result of the custom of meditating morning and evening reverently before Nature was *yoga* (concentration of mind) in Brahmanism, and *dhyana* or *zen* (meditation) in Buddhism. There might be a sect in Brahmanism which does not require *yoga,* but in Buddhism no sect can be without *dhyana.* At present certain sects in Buddhism do not practice *dhyana* daily. However, it is a well-known fact that even those sects have their origin in *dhyana.* This is true with both Hinayana and Mahayana. For instance, the Three Learnings of Buddhism (*trisiksa*) are discipline, contemplation and wisdom; and one of the Six Perfections (*paramita*) is *samadhi* or concentration. Without *samadhi* the attainment of Buddhist knowledge is impossible. In Buddhism to act righteously is to think deeply.

(2) THE BUDDHA AS A DEEP THINKER

The Buddha (c 566-486 B.C.) was not satisfied with the ideas of his contemporary thinkers. Those who regard this earthly life as pleasant (optimists) are ignorant of the disappointment and despair which are to come. Those who regard this life as a life of suffering (pessimists) may be tolerated as long as they are simply feeling dissatisfied with this life, but when they begin to give up

---

[1] 'Anatman' denies the self as permanent substance or entity. However, Buddhism retains the self as a combination of matter and mind in continuous change. This 'self' is perfected by cultivation. This is what is meant by 'self-culture' or 'self-creation.' See also Section 3 of this chapter.

this life as hopeless and try to escape to a better life by practicing austerities (self-mortification), then they are to be abhorred. The Buddha taught that the extremes of both hedonism and asceticism are to be avoided and that the middle course should be followed as the ideal. This does not mean that one should simply avoid both extremes and take the middle course as the only remaining course of escape. Rather, one should transcend, not merely escape from, such extremes.

The Buddha's doctrine, in fine, rests on the idea of "knowing and regarding reality as it is." That means one should know the true facts about this earthly life and look at it without making excuses, and regulate one's daily conduct of life according to this knowledge and standpoint.

This idea that there is nothing but hardship in this world—even pleasures end in hardship—is one of the significant points of Buddhism. Someone might say that this idea of recognizing this life as hardship cannot be anything but pessimism. But that is not right. The idea is this: in this present life there are both pleasures and hardships. It is shallow to try to regard it as entirely of pleasure; what one regards as pleasure will cause suffering when it ceases to exist. In other words we may call it a kind of hardship which appears in the guise of pleasure. Therefore this life must be regarded as consisting entirely of hardship. Yet one must not lament over it. If one is ignorant of the fact that pleasures can cause hardships, one will be disappointed when that fact presents itself. The Buddha teaches that one should regard hardship as hardship, accepting it as a fact and opposing it. Hence his emphasis on perseverance, fortitude, and forbearance, the latter being one of the Six Perfections.

In short, there are both pleasures and hardships in life, but one must not be discouraged when hardship comes, or lose oneself in rapture of joy when pleasure comes. Both pleasure and hardship must be taken alike with caution, and one must attack them with all one's might. For this reason bravery and diligence (*virya*) were included among the Six Perfections.

The middle course does not mean escaping from life but it means invading life, and yet not to become a prisoner of life.

When the Buddha's idea on reality develops further and further along its path, it becomes the Buddhist philosophy. To realize it in the actual life of living men is the religious side of Buddhism.

Apart from Buddhism, however, there are efforts on the part of many thinkers to build up their respective thoughts on optimism and pessimism. Ever since before the time of the Buddha there had existed both schools of thought. The optimistic thought has developed into naturalism, hedonism, materialism, mechanism, etc. During the lifetime of the Buddha there existed even stronger materialism than that we see today. Pessimism developed along the line which may be described as more religious. They reasoned that since our organism (body and mind) is imperfect, we should overcome it by austerities (self-mortification); then in the next life we shall attain a perfect heavenly existence. Thus they invented various methods of self-mortification and practiced them. The Buddha abhorred this practice.

Because the Buddha's idea on both optimism and pessimism was very clear, there has never been anyone in Buddhism who strayed into materialism nor has there been anyone who went into the practice of self-mortification. In short, the extremes of both optimism and pessimism were prevented by the moderate doctrine of Buddhism. In a way Buddhism was a scheme against the ravages of both materialism and asceticism.

(3) WHAT IS SELF?

The Buddha regarded this world as the world of hardship, and taught the ways to cope with it. Then, what are the reasons which make it a world of hardship? The first reason, as given by the Buddha is that *all things are selfless or egoless,* which means that all things—men, animals and inanimate objects, both living and not living—do not have what we may call their original self or real being. Let us consider man. A man does not have a core or a soul which he can consider to be his true self. A man exists, but he cannot grasp his real being—he cannot discover his own core, because the existence of a man is nothing but an "existence depending on a series of causations." Everything that exists is there because of causations; it will disappear when the effects of the causations cease.

The waves on the water's surface certainly exist, but can it be said that a wave has its own self? Waves exist only while there is wind or current. Each wave has its own characteristics according to the combination of causations—the intensity of the winds and currents and their directions, etc. But when the effects of the causa-

23

tions cease, the waves are no more. Similarly, there cannot be a self which stands independent of causations.

As long as a man is an existent depending on a series of causations, it is unreasonable for him to try to hold on to himself and to regard all things around him from the self-centered point of view. All men ought to deny their own selves and endeavor to help each other and to look for co-existence, because no man can ever be truly independent.

If all things owe their existence to a series of causations, their existence is a conditional one—there is no one thing in the universe that is permanent or independent. Therefore, the Buddha's theory that selflessness is the nature of all things inevitably leads to the next theory that *all things are impermanent (anitya)*.

Men in general seem to be giving all of their energy to preserving their own existence and their possessions. But in truth it is impossible to discover the core of their own existence, nor is it possible to preserve it forever. Even for one moment nothing can stay unchanged. Not only is it insecure in relation to space but also it is insecure in relation to time. If it were possible to discover a world which is space-less and time-less, that would be a world of true freedom, i.e., Nirvana.

If, as the modern physicists assert, space is curved and time is relative, this world of space and time is our enclosed abode from which there is no escape—we are tied down in the cycles of cause and effect.

As long as men cannot discover a world which is not limited by time and space, men must need be creatures of suffering.

To assert that such a state, unlimited in time and space, is attainable by man is the message of Buddhism.

Of course there is no such thing as a limitless space or limitless time. Even modern physical science does not recognize infinity in time and space. However, the Buddha brought forward his ideal, Nirvana (extinction), following his theories of selflessness and impermanence. *Nirvana means extinction of life and death, extinction of worldly desire, and extinction of space and time conditions.* This, in the last analysis, means unfolding a world of perfect freedom.

Selflessness (no substance) and *impermanence* (no duration) are the real state of our existence; *Nirvana* (negatively extinction; positively perfection) is our ideal, that is, perfect freedom, quiescence.

24

(4) THE IDEAL OF BUDDHISM

The special community established by the Buddha was called the *Arya-sangha* (The Assembly of the Nobles), intended to be the cradle of noble persons. Since the Brahmanical tradition had been firmly established, the race distinction was strictly felt. On that account the Buddha often asserted that in his own community there would be no distinction between Brahmans (priests) and warriors or between masters and slaves. Anyone who joined the Brotherhood would have an equal opportunity for learning and training.

Against the asserted superiority of the Aryan race and the appellation of *anarya* (non-Aryan) given to the aborigines or some earlier immigrants, the Buddha often argued that the word 'Arya' meant 'noble' and we ought not call a race noble or ignoble for there will be some ignoble persons among the so-called *arya* and at the same time there will be some noble persons among the so-called *anarya.* When we say noble or ignoble we should be speaking of an individual and not of a race as a whole. It is a question of knowledge or wisdom but not of birth or caste. Thus the object of the Buddha was to create a noble personage (*arya-pudgala*)—in the sense of a noble life.

The noble community (*arya-sangha*) was founded for that very purpose. The noble ideal (*arya-dharma*) and the noble discipline (*arya-vinaya*) were set forth for the aspiring candidates. The path to be pursued by the noble aspirant is the Noble Eightfold Path (*arya-astangika-marga*) and the truth to be believed by the noble is the Noble Fourfold Truth [2] (*catvari arya-satyani*). The perfections attained by the noble were the four noble fruitions (*arya-phala*) and the wealth to be possessed by the noble was the noble sevenfold wealth (*sapta arya-dhana*), all being spiritual qualifications. The careful application of the word 'arya' to each of the important points of his institution must not be overlooked by a student of Buddhism. The Buddha thus seemed to have endeavored to revive the original meaning of *arya* in personality and the daily life of his religious community.

Whether the Buddha was an Aryan or not we cannot say. Some consider him to be an Indo-Scythian while others consider him to

---

[2] See next section.

25

be an Indo-Sumerian. The question of race has nothing to do with him, who in his idea transcends all racial distinctions.

The ideal set forth by him must be taken to be purely personal. As a man, he teaches men to be perfect men, i.e., men of perfect enlightenment.

(5) WHAT IS TRUTH? WHAT IS THE WAY?

The Buddha organized these ideas into the Fourfold Truth as follows:

1. That life consists entirely of suffering;
2. That suffering has causes;
(The above two are the description of reality.)
3. That the causes of suffering can be extinguished;
4. That there exists a way to extinguish the causes.
(The last two express the ideal.)

These constitute the Fourfold Truth to be believed by the *ariya* or those who pursue the way toward Nirvana. (Hereafter the word *ariya* or *arya* will be used in preference to its English equivalent 'the noble.' *Ariya* as used in Buddhism includes both those who aspire to become noble and those who are already noble.)

In explanation of the fourth Noble Truth the Buddha taught the Eightfold Way to be pursued by the *ariya* as follows:

1. Right View, by which to see the real state of all things.
2. Right Thought
3. Right Speech
4. Right Action
(Right Thought, Right Speech, Right Action are the elements of human character.)
5. Right Mindfulness
6. Right Endeavor
7. Right Livelihood
(These three are the elements of human life or the dynamic aspects of human character.)
8. Right Concentration, which is the motive power to carry one through all the worlds—this human world of desire, the heaven of (bodily-) beings, the higher heaven of formless (bodiless) beings and holy beings (*arhats*)—finally to reach the state of *Parinirvana* (Highest Nirvana), the Buddhahood.

The Eightfold Way may be regarded as the practical ethics of Buddhism for the purpose of building up the human character and improving it, but at the same time it is the way of the holy religion for attaining the highest enlightenment—the Buddhahood.

The Worlds of Beings attainable by Progressive Meditation

	Dharma-dhatu-samapatti			
	(Abstract-meditation on the universal principle, i.e., world)			V.
	Buddha			
	Nirodha-samapatti (Extinction)			
	Arhats			IV.
	Neither conscious nor unconscious state of the heaven			
Arupya-Samapatti	The heaven of nothingness	Heaven without Form		III.
	The endlessness of mind			
	The endlessness of space			
Rupa-Samapatti	Fourth Dhyana heaven	Heaven with Form		II.
	Third Dhyana heaven			
	Second Dhyana heaven			
	First Dhyana heaven			
	The world of living beings.			I.

The Eightfold Way should not be regarded as a combination of eight different ways. It is a unitary way—the Path of Insight (*Darsana-marga*)—to lead the *ariya* toward perfection.

The next stage [3] of the path is the Path of Practice and is described as the Seven Branches of Enlightenment (*Bodhi*) as follows:

    1. Thorough investigation of the Principle
    2. Brave effort
    3. Joyous thought
    4. Peaceful thought
    5. Mindfulness

---

[3] The Buddha taught a Threefold Path: the Path of Insight (Meditation), the Path of Practice or Culture, the Path of No-More-Learning.

6. Concentration

7. Equanimity

Thus the *ariya* proceeds to the last stage: i.e., the Path of No-More-Learning. Then the firm conviction that he has realized the Four-fold Truth will present itself.

The above three stages are to be passed through in the study of the Fourfold Truth. The Truth is studied and conceived in the first stage by the application of the Eightfold Way (Life-View); in the second stage it is investigated more fully and actualized by the practice of the Seven Branches of Enlightenment (Life-Culture); and in the last stage the Truth is fully realized in the Path of No-More-Learning (Realization of Life-Ideal).

When the *ariya* reaches this last stage, he becomes an *arhat*. According to the Hinayanistic view this is the perfect state of enlightenment, but according to the Mahayanistic view an *arhat* is thought to be only partially enlightened. The purpose of Buddhism is to perfect a man's character, or to let him attain Buddhahood on the basis of perfect wisdom and right cultivation, i.e., the highest personality. Such are the characteristics of Buddhism.

III. FUNDAMENTAL PRINCIPLES OF BUDDHIST PHILOSOPHY

The usual procedure would be to explain the general principles which are common to all the schools of Buddhism. In this section I will not refer to those doctrines which are made the basic principles of the existing sects in Japan, because we shall study them in detail when we come to Buddhism in Japan. At present I will bring out six general principles, common especially to all schools of Mahayana:

a. The Principle of Causation
b. The Principle of Indeterminism of the Differentiated
c. The Principle of Reciprocal Identification
d. The Principle of True Reality
e. The Principle of Totality
f. The Principle of Perfect Freedom

(1) THE PRINCIPLE OF CAUSATION

Buddhism does not give importance to the idea of the Root-Principle or the First Cause as other systems of philosophy often do; nor does it discuss the idea of cosmology. Naturally such a branch of philosophy as theology did not develop in Buddhism. One should not expect any discussion of theology from a Buddhist philosopher. As for the problem of creation, Buddhism is ready to accept any theory that science may advance, for Buddhism does not recognize any conflict between religion[1] and science.

According to Buddhism, human beings and all living things are self-created or self-creating. The universe is not homocentric; it is a co-creation of all beings. Buddhism does not believe that all things came from one cause, but holds that everything is inevitably created out of more than two causes.

The creations or becomings of the antecedent causes continue in time-series—past, present and future—like a chain. This chain is divided into twelve divisions and is called the Twelve Divisioned Cycle of Causations and Becomings. Since these divisions are inter-

---

[1] In Buddhism religion is understood as the practical application of the philosophical doctrine, making no reference to such ideas as God, creation and final judgment.

dependent, they are called Dependent Production or Chain of Causation. The formula of this theory is as follows: From the existence of *this, that* becomes; from the happening of *this, that* happens. From the non-existence of *this, that* does not become; from the non-existence of *this, that* does not happen.

There are several theories of causation which combine to give a complete explanation of things and events:

(a) CAUSATION BY ACTION-INFLUENCE [2]

There is law and order in the progress of cause and effect. This is the theory of Causal Sequence.

In the Twelve Divisioned Cycle of Causations and Becomings, it is impossible to point out which one is the first cause, because the twelve make a continuous circle which is called the Wheel of Life. It is customary to represent the Wheel of Life in the following manner:

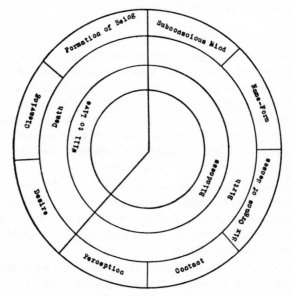

---

[2] The Sanskrit original of 'action' is '*karma,*' but the term *karma* is avoided in this study because it is often confused with the idea of soul and thus leads to misunderstanding of the Buddhist doctrine. *Karma* simply means action and action means its influence. That influence determines the subsequent existence.

The explanation of the principle of the Twelve Divisioned Cycle of Causations and Becomings is as follows:

People are accustomed to regard time as progressing in a straight line from the infinite past through present to infinite future. Buddhism, however, regards time as a circle with no beginning or end. Time is relative.

The death of a living being is not the end; at once another life begins to go through a similar process of birth and death, and thus repeats the round of life over and over again. In this way a living being, when considered in relation to time, forms an endless continuum. It is impossible to define what a living being is, for it is always changing and progressing through the Divisions or Stages of Life. The whole series of stages must be taken in their entirety as representing the one individual being. Thus, a living being, when regarded in relation to space, forms a complex of five elements. The Wheel of Life is a clever representation of the Buddhist conception of a living being in relation to both space and time.

The Wheel of Life is a circle with no beginning, but it is customary to begin its exposition at Blindness (unconscious state). Blindness is only a continuation of Death. At death the body is abandoned, but Blindness remains as the crystallization of the effects of the actions performed during life. This Blindness is often termed Ignorance; but this Ignorance should not be thought of as the antonym of knowing; it must include in its meaning both knowing and not knowing—Blindness or blind mind, unconsciousness.

Blindness leads to blind activity. The 'energy' or the effect of this blind activity is the next Stage, Motive, or Will to Live. This Will to Live is not the kind of will which is used in the term 'free will'; it is rather a blind motive toward life or the blind desire to live.

Blindness and Will to Live are called the Two Causes of the Past. They are causes when regarded subjectively from the present; but objectively regarded, the life in the past is a whole life just as much as is the life of the present.

In the life of the present the First Stage is Subconscious Mind. This is the first stage of an individual existence which corresponds, in actual life, to the first moment of the conception of a child. There is no consciousness yet; there is only the Subconscious Mind or the

Blind Will toward life. When this Subconscious Mind advances one step and takes a form, it is the Second Stage of the present, Name-Form. The Name is the mind, because mind is something we know by name but cannot grasp. Name-Form is the stage of prenatal growth when the mind and body first come into combination.

In the Third Stage a more complex form is assumed and the six sense organs are recognized. They are the eyes, ears, nose, tongue, body (organ of touch) and mind.

The Fourth Stage corresponds to the first one or two years after the birth of the child. The six sense organs reach the state of activity, but the sense of touch predominates. The living being begins to come into contact with the outside world.

Now that the living being is able to manifest its consciousness, it begins to take in the phenomena of the outside world consciously. This is the Fifth Stage called Perception, representing the growth-scale of a child three to five years old. Here the individuality of the living being is definitely recognized; in other words, the status of the present life has been formed.

The above five Stages are called the Five Effects of the Past appearing in the Present. In these Stages the individual is formed, but the individual is not entirely responsible for its own formation because the causes of the past have effectuated the development of these Stages. From here on, the individual begins to create causes on his own reponsibility, or in other words, enters the proper sphere of self-creation.

The first of the Three Causes in the Present is Desire. Through Perception the individual experiences sorrow, pleasure, suffering, enjoyment, or neutral feeling. When the experience is sorrow, suffering, or neutral feeling nothing much will happen. But when it is pleasure or enjoyment, the individual will endeavor to make it his own. This effort is Desire; it produces attachment. The first step of this attachment is the next Stage, Cleaving, the effort to retain the object of Desire. The last state of this attachment is Formation of Being. The term Existence is often used for this Stage, but as it is a link between the present and future, and the preliminary step for Birth, I believe that 'Formation of Being' is a more fitting term.

Desire, Cleaving and Formation of Being represent the three stages of the activities of an adult, and together constitute the Three

Causes in the Present. While an individual is enjoying the effects of the past, he is forming the causes for the future. While the plum fruit is ripening on the tree, the core in the fruit is being formed. By the time the fruit is ripe and falls to the ground, the core too is ready to bring forth a new tree of its own to bear more fruits in the future.

As to the Future there are two Stages—Birth and Old age-Death, or in short, Birth and Death. When viewed from the Three Causes in the Present, Birth and Death may be termed the effects. But when viewed in the light of the continuous Wheel of Life, we may regard the future as the time when the Causes in the Present open out and close. Also, the Effects of the Future contain in themselves causes for the life still further in the future.

The present is one whole life, and so is the future. Past, Present and Future are each a whole life. In this Wheel of Life, the present is explained particularly minutely with eight stages, but in truth Blindness and Will to Live of the past and Birth and Death of the future have the same constituent stages as those of the present.

Because we human beings are accustomed to make the present the starting point of consideration, naturally the future is regarded as effects of the present. Therefore the life in the future is given descriptively as Birth and Death. And because the past is regarded as the cause of the present, it is given as causal principles, Blindness and Will to Live.

It is quite possible to reconstruct the Wheel of Life in the following manner in which Birth and Death are to be regarded as merely an abbreviated description of a whole life and Blindness and Will to Live are to be regarded as an ideological description of a round of life. Past, Present and Future are relative terms.

It is clear that the Causation Theory of Buddhism is not like the theory of causality of classical physical science which is a fixed theory. In Buddhism every Stage is a cause when viewed from its effect; when viewed from the antecedent cause, it is an effect. It may be also said that there is a cause in the effect, and an effect in the cause. There is nothing fixed in this theory.

The Blindness, which remains after the death of a living thing, is the crystallization of the actions (karma) which the living being performed during its life, or in other words, the 'energy' or in-

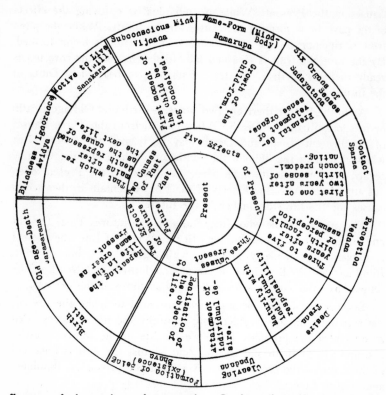

fluence of the actions that remain. One's action (*karma*) is the dynamic manifestation of mental and physical energy. This latent energy may be called action-influence or potential energy. Action-influence remains after the action ceases, and this is what makes the Wheel of Life move. As long as there is energy, it has to work, and the Cycles of Causations and Becomings will inevitably—subconsciously or blindly—go on forever.

In other words, a living being determines its own nature and existence by its own actions. Therefore we may say the living being is self-created. The act of self-creation has continued in the past for thousands and millions of lives, and the living being has gone around the circle of Twelve Divisioned Cycle of Causations and Becomings over and over again.

According to the nature of the preceding actions, the next Wheel of Life may be of a higher order or of a lower order. That is, a

34

living being may assume any form of life—human form, or animal form or even the form of a heavenly being (*deva*) according to the nature of the actions which caused its becoming. The repetition of the change from one form of life to another is called *sansara* (undulation of life).

Often *sansara* ('constant flow') is translated as 'transmigration of soul,' but that is a very misleading translation, for the idea is not that a soul lives after the death of the body and moves into another body. *Sansara* means the creation of a new life by the influence of the actions of the former living being. In the first place, Buddhism denies the existence of the soul. Life is like the waves on water; the vibration of one particle causes the vibration of the next particle and thus the waves are transmitted a long distance. One wave is one life, and the series of lives is *sansara*. In Buddhism the series of lives do not go on infinitely as in a straight line. They turn in a circle and repeat the circle over and over again. The Wheel of Life is a small circle of one life, while the great circle (the series of the Wheel of Life) is *sansara*.

Since this self-creation is regulated by the actions of the individual being, it does not depend upon the authority of another—for instance, God. Nor is there any confusion among the action-influence of different individuals. 'Self-acted, self-rewarded,' 'For a good cause, a good result; for an evil cause, an evil result,'—these are the rules.

Sometimes action is divided into two kinds, 'drawing action' and 'fulfilling action.' Drawing action causes a being to be born as a man, as a *deva,* or as a beast; no other force can draw a living being into a particular form of life. After the kind of life has been determined, the fulfilling action completes the formal quality of the living being so that it will be a thorough specimen of the kind.

There are two kinds of action-influence: individual action-influence and common action-influence. Individual action-influence creates the individual being. Common action-influence creates the universe itself. This is the meaning of the words 'individual effect' and 'common effect' as used in Buddhism.

From another point of view action may be classified into three groups: good action, evil action and neutral action. Also, according to the way its retribution is received, action may be classified into four, as follows: action to receive retribution immediately, action to receive retribution in the present life, action to receive retribution in the life to come, and action to receive retribution in one of the lives following the next.

There are two ways of viewing the process of becoming. The order of cause and effect is usually regarded as arising in sequence in relation to time. However, when all the factors of the Twelve Divisioned Cycle of Causation are considered as belonging to one being, we see that it possesses all at the same time. (One does not abandon the Six Organs of Senses to gain Contact.) Therefore we may regard all factors as mutually interdependent as if in a ring, developing simultaneously, none being purely a cause nor purely an effect.

Buddhism regards all things in the universe as 'existence depending upon series of causes.' Only when there are causes, is there existence. Without causes there can be no existence. No existence is permanent nor conclusive. In Buddhist terminology, such an existence is called 'conditional existence.' Such a way of regarding all things is called 'knowing and perceiving reality as such.' To regard all things in the universe as dynamic becoming is a characteristic doctrine of Buddhism.

Of the Twelve Stages of Causation, Blindness, Desire and Cleaving are called Delusions, while Will to Live and Formation of Being are called Effect-causing Actions. The rest of the cycle—the five effects in the Present and the two in the Future—are called Suffering or the effects which result in Suffering.

Delusion is the illness of the mind while Effect-causing Action is its physical manifestation, and the result is Suffering. For instance, one may be angry in mind and act accordingly, striking or killing, and later suffer retribution. From the suffering of retribution one will get into more delusions and act and suffer, thus repeating the same wandering again and again. Such is the Chain of Causation by Action-influence. Who or what is responsible for the progression of the Chain of Causation by Action-influence? To explain this question clearly we pass on to a discussion of Causation by the Ideation-store.

(b) CAUSATION BY THE IDEATION-STORE (*Alaya-vijnana*)

Actions (*karma*) are divided into three groups, i.e., those by the body, those by speech and those by volition. When one makes up one's mind to do something, one is responsible for it and is liable to retribution, because volition is a mind-action even if it is not expressed in speech or manifested in physical action. But the mind being the inmost recess of all actions, the causation ought to be attributed to the mind-*store* or Ideation-*store*.

The Buddhist ideation theory divides the mind into eight faculties: the eye-sense, the ear-sense, the nose-sense, the tongue-sense, the body-sense, the sense-center (the 6th, *mano-vijnana*), the individualizing thought-center of egotism (the 7th, *manas-vijnana*), and the storing-center of ideation (the 8th, *alaya-vijnana*)—Ideation-store.

Of these eight faculties the seventh and the eighth require explanation. The seventh, the Individualizing Center of Egotism is the center where all the selfish ideas, egotistic opinions, arrogance, self-love, illusions and delusions arise. The eighth, the Storing Center of Ideation, is where the 'seeds' of all manifestations are deposited and later expressed in manifestations. Buddhism holds that the origin of all things and events is the effect of ideation. We shall return later to the subject when we come to the theory of cognition in the Idealistic School. Let it suffice at present to say that the Storing Center of Ideation is the 'seed bed' of all that exists. Every seed lies in the Storing Center and when it sprouts out into the object-world, a reflection returns as a new seed. That is, the mind reaches out into the outer world and, perceiving objects, puts new ideas into the mind-store. Again, this new seed sprouts out to reflect back a still newer seed. Thus the seeds accumulate and all are stored there together. When they are latent, we call them seeds, but when active we call them manifestations. The old seeds, the manifestations and the new seeds are mutually dependent upon each other, forming a cycle which forever repeats the same process. This is called the Chain of Causations by Ideation.

That which makes the seed or subconscious thought sprout out into actual manifestation, that is, the motive force which makes the chain of causation move, is nothing but ideation. It is easy to see from this theory of Causation by Ideation that Delusion, Action and Suffering originate from mind-action, or ideation.

The Storing Center of Ideation is carried across rebirth to determine what the next form of life will be. This Storing Center might be regarded as similar to the soul in other forms of religion.

37

According to the Buddhist doctrine, however, what is reborn is not the soul, but is the result of the actions performed in the preceding life. In Buddhism the existence of the soul is denied.

One may ask from where this Storing Center of Ideation comes. To explain this question we must study the third theory of Causation.

(c) CAUSATION BY THUSNESS (*Tathata*)

Thusness, or suchness, is the only term which can be used to express the ultimate indefinable, the unnameable reality. It is otherwise called the Matrix of Thus-come. Thus-come is Buddha-nature hidden in ordinary human nature. 'Thus-come' is a designation of the Buddha employed by himself instead of 'I' or 'we,' but not without special meaning. After he had attained Enlightenment, he met the five ascetics with whom he had formerly shared his forest life. These five ascetics addressed him saying "Friend, Gotama." The Buddha admonished them, saying that they ought not treat the Thus-come (thus enlightened I come) as their friend and their equal, because he was now the Enlightened One, the Victorious, All-wise One. When he had 'thus come' in his present position as the instructor of all men and even of *devas,* they should treat him as the Blessed One and not as an old friend.

Again, when the Buddha went back to Kapilavastu, his former home, he did not go to the palace of his father, but lived in the banyan grove outside the town, and as usual went out to beg daily. Suddhodana, his king-father, could not bear the idea of his own son, the prince, begging on the streets of Kapilavastu. At once, the king visited the Buddha in the grove and entreated him to return to the palace. The Buddha answered him in the following words: "If I were still your heir, I should return to the palace to share the comfort with you, but my lineage has changed. I am now a successor to the Buddhas of the past, all of whom have 'thus gone' *(Tathagata)* as I am doing at present, living in the woods and begging. So your Majesty must excuse me." The king understood the words perfectly and became a pupil of the Buddha at once.

Thus-come and Thus-gone have practically the same meaning. The Buddha used them both and usually in their plural forms. Sometimes the words were used for a sentient being who thus comes, i.e., comes in the ordinary way. Thus-come and Thus-gone can therefore be used in two senses: 'The one who is enlightened but comes in an ordinary way' or 'The one who comes in an ordinary way simply.' The phrase 'Son of man' in Christianity has somewhat the same meaning.

Now, Thusness or the Matrix of Thus-come or Thus-gone means the true state of all things in the universe, the source of an Enlightened One, *the basis of enlightenment*. When static, it is Enlightenment itself (with no relation to time or space); but when dynamic, it is in human form assuming an ordinary way and feature of life. Thusness and the Matrix of Thus-come are practically one and the same—the ultimate truth. In Mahayana the ultimate truth is called Suchness or Thusness.[3]

We are now in a position to explain the Theory of Causation by Thusness. Thusness in its *static* sense is spaceless, timeless, all-equal, without beginning or end, formless, colorless, because the thing itself without its manifestation cannot be sensed or described. Thusness in its *dynamic* sense can assume any form; when driven by a pure cause it takes a lofty form; when driven by a tainted cause it takes a depraved form. Thusness, therefore, is of two states. The one is the Thusness itself; the other is its manifestation, its state of life and death.

There are therefore three series of causations to be considered: (a) Causation by Action-influence as depicted in the Wheel of Life; (b) To explain the origin of action, Causation by Ideation-store; (c) To explain the origin of the ideation-store, Causation by Thusness. The ideation-store of a human being is determined by his nature as a human being and this nature is a particular dynamic form of Thusness. One should not ask where Thusness or the Matrix of Thus-come originates, because it is the noumenon, the ultimate indescribable Thusness.

Next we must consider the wholesale causation of the universe, the universe being the dynamic manifestation of Thusness.

(d) Causation by the Universal Principle (*Dharma-dhatu*)

We have now penetrated the depth of the origin of causation, but it is still necessary to consider the mutual relationship of the

---

[3] For explanation see p. 45.

becomings of all things, and thus we pass on to the idea of universal causation.

The universe (all things) is the dynamic manifestation or expression of the static principle. All things are mutually dependent, mutually permeating without giving any hindrance to one another.

Dharma-dhatu means 'the elements of the principle' and has the two aspects of (1) the state of Thusness or noumenon and (2) the world of phenomenal manifestation. In this Causation Theory it is usually used in the latter sense, but in speaking of the ideal world as realized, the former sense is to be applied.

Buddhism holds that nothing was created singly or individually. All things in the universe—matter and mind—arose simultaneously, all things in it depending upon one another, the influence of each mutually permeating and thereby making a universal symphony of harmonious totality. If one item were lacking, the universe would not be complete; without the rest, one item cannot be. When the whole cosmos arrives at a harmony of perfection, it is called the 'Universe One and True,' or the 'Lotus Store.' In this ideal universe all beings will be in perfect harmony, each finding no obstruction in the existence and activity of another.

Although the idea of the interdependence and simultaneous rise of all things is called the Theory of Universal Causation, the nature of the rise being universal, it is rather a philosophy of the totality of all existence than a philosophy of origination.

According to this theory, four states of the universe are to be distinguished: (1) the real, or the world of actual life—the factual world; (2) the ideal, or the world of law or principle; (3) the ideal realized, or the world in which the principle is applied in actual life, or the fact and the principle harmonized; (4) the real harmonized, or the world in which actuality attains harmony in itself. The first, second and third states are easily understood, for those are the ideas often discussed by thinking men. But the fourth may be somewhat difficult to understand, because in these individualistic modern times it is usually thought that one individual is inevitably opposed to another, that classes in a society are opposed among themselves, that a business concern is in competition with another.

The idea of Universal Principle, on the other hand, demonstrates that all things in the real world ought to have harmony among themselves, and it advances the following reasons: (1) Because of the simultaneous rise of all things; (2) Because of the mutual permeation of the influence of all things; (3) Because of the necessity of reciprocal identification between all beings (mutual self-negation to agree with each other) for the realization of harmony; (4) Because of the necessity of unity, or harmony, between the leaders and the followers for the attainment of a purpose; (5) Because all things have their origin in ideation—therefore a similar ideal ought to be expected of all; (6) Because all things are the result of causation and therefore are mutually dependent; (7) Because all things are indeterminate or indefinite in character but mutually complementary —therefore they are free to exist in harmony with all things; (8) Because of the fact that all beings have the nature of Buddha dormant in them; (9) Because of the fact that all beings, from the highest to the lowest, are parts of one and the same *Mandala* (circle); (10) Because of mutual reflection of all activities—as in a room surrounded by mirrors, the movement of one image causes the movement of the thousand reflections. Buddhist writers enumerate twenty reasons, but for our purpose the above ten will suffice.

(2) THE PRINCIPLE OF INDETERMINISM AND INDETERMINATION

Determinism means the theory of being determined by Fate, Nature, God or the like. Mechanism generally takes a similar attitude towards the question of free will of man. Some of the modern physicists have proposed the theory of indeterminism because it is experimentally impossible to determine the conditions for determinism; the theory generalized is said to be that of 'uncertainty relation.' According to this idea, the nature of things or substances can in no way be determined by reason, experiment or science. This theory can be called 'indeterminateness,' which is opposed to the old theory that everything can be determined by experiment. Generally speaking, Buddhism has no concern with either determinism or determinateness because it is a religion of self-creation: it holds the theory of free will (not absolute) within the sphere of human beings.

Buddhism, therefore, has nothing to do with fatalism, for it does not admit the existence of anything like destiny or the decree of fate. According to Buddhism all living beings have assumed the present life as the result of self-creation, and are, even at present, in the midst of creating themselves. In other words, every being is a stage

41

of dynamic becoming. Although the grade and form of life vary in each birth, one should not think of the strict distinction of time as past or future. In truth there is present only. That is to say, we have a long continuity of existence, birth and death being simply the rise and fall of the waves in the ocean of life. Birth and death are not the predestined fate of a living being but a 'corollary of action (*karma*),' as it has been called by some. One who acts must sooner or later reap the effect; while experiencing an effect, one is sowing seeds anew, thus causing the next wave of life to be high or low according to the nature of one's preceding actions.

Now, by way of contrast, let us examine other Eastern schools of thought. Confucianism is determinism in so far as it maintains that Heaven's decree is the basic principle of human life. The same is true of Taoism in that it holds Tao to be the source of all things. With Brahmanism of India, too, Brahman is made the creative principle or a personified god. Similar ideas of determinism can be found among many of the Western schools of thought.

Buddhism, on the other hand, has quite a different method of approach. While practically all the schools of thought begin with a static first principle, Buddhism begins with the actual, dynamic world, and the individual, by cultivating oneself, strives to realize the ideal in the end. *Sansara* (the rise and fall of life) is not an onward flow, but a 'wavicle' circle, each wave being a cycle of life appearing on the great orbit of *Sansara*. It has no beginning nor end, just as one cannot point out the beginning of a circle.

There is, therefore, no room for the idea of a First Cause or Creation which might determine things. In the *Dhamma-pada* (Book of Religious Verse) the idea is described as follows: "All that we are is the result of what we have thought; it is founded on our thoughts; it is made up of our thoughts." We must remember, however, that though the will is free or undetermined in the human world, it may appear as abstract energy-instinct or animal desire which is not un-determined among the beasts and lower forms of life which are the lesser waves in the continuity of self-creation. The individual is self-creating and freely so, largely because he has no determinate nature or character.

The motion of the mind-action which defines the form of an individual life is like the motion of a corpuscle in the physical world. All things, matter and mind, have no substratum, no soul, no abiding self-reality, no such thing as absolute self or ego. What appears to be real is a temporary existence, an instant in a causal sequence, one ripple in the long line of waves, the effect of two or more causes combined.

If you do not insist on the existence of a central principle or absolute ego, you may define yourself in any way you please. When speaking roughly, it is quite correct to say that you exist and to describe yourself. But in minutely definite and exact language, it is impossible to define your own self or to describe yourself. However, there is no danger of losing yourself, for no one can extinguish the influence of your action, or latent energy. A particular manifestation of that energy in human form is yourself and the *whole* of you—for the present.

A substance may become energy and energy may become substance, but one must not think that the energy is preserved always in one and the same substance. By virtue of your own action you will get your next life and so on along the long line of lives. Having no permanent center, a living being changes itself as time goes on, sometimes for better, sometimes for worse. Your self does not exist apart from the changing manifestations, but the cycles of the changing manifestations as a whole constitute yourself. Therefore there is no possibility of the disappearance of your identity.

The idea of indetermination which has been seen as the basis of the idea of indeterminism is expressed by many terms: 'Having no special nature,' 'Having no definite nature,' 'All things are emptiness,' 'Having no special state,' 'All are of temporary existence,' 'All are existence by combination of causes.' 'No substance, no duration' is a root idea of Buddhism.

(3) THE PRINCIPLE OF RECIPROCAL IDENTIFICATION

Hinayana Buddhism is generally satisfied with analysis and is rarely inclined to synthesis. The Mahayana, on the other hand, is generally much inclined to the reciprocal identification of two conflicting ideas. If one party adheres to his own idea while the other party insists on his own, a separation will be the natural result. This is what happens in the Hinayana. The Mahayana teaches that one should put one's own idea aside for a moment and identify one's own position with that of the other party, thus mutually synthesizing the opposed positions. Then both parties will find themselves perfectly united. This is really a process of self-denial which is minutely taught in the dialectic method of the School of Negativism (*Sunyata,* Void).[4]

The word for 'reciprocal identification' is more literally 'mutual' and 'regarding,' that is, 'mutually viewing from each other's point,' 'mutual identification,' which is as much as to say an 'exchange of views.' It is indispensable to bring about a reconciliation of conflicting opinions or to effect a syncretism among opposing speculative systems. This trend of thought, in fact, served greatly to restore the original idea of tolerance which was revealed in the Buddha's teaching but was almost entirely lost in the various schools of Hinayana which resulted from differences of opinion.

Among the reasons which justify such identification of opposing views are the following: (1) Identity is assumed because two distinct factors are united into one as copper and zinc are mixed together to form one alloy, bronze. This identity in form is the explanation common to all Buddhist schools. (2) Identity is assumed because one's front and one's back may appear differently but in reality they are one. There are opposing views as are the front and back of the same house. In the same way, if life is looked at from an illusioned view, it is life, but if it is looked at from an enlightened view, it is Nirvana. The two views simply refer to one thing. Some Mahayana schools hold this explanation of identity in substance. (3) Identity is assumed because the whole entity is entirely one, as water and wave, the whole of water being manifested as wave.

These three aspects or connotations of identity may be summarized as: (1) Identity in form as two different elements combining to form unity. (2) Identity in substance although there may be opposing angles. (3) Identity in form and substance as water and wave (phenomenology).

Reciprocal identification by mutual self-negation, when realized, has a great practical value in smoothing out conflicting opinions or in creating sympathy among opposing parties. Through one or more of these methods diversity can be brought to union, and illusory existence is synthesized with the enlightened life. Such ideas as seeing noumenon in phenomenon, regarding motion as calm or calm as motion, identifying action and inaction, purity and impurity, perfection and imperfection, one and many, the particular and the general, per-

---

[4] To be discussed in detail later.

44

manence and impermanence, are all attainable by this theory. It is one of the most important ideas of Mahayana and is indispensable for a clear understanding of the Buddhist doctrine as taught in the Mahayana.

The most important application of this doctrine concerns the identification of life and Nirvana. Life itself is Nirvana, just as water and wave are identical. Life is one thing and Nirvana is another lifeless thing. If one attains Nirvana while yet living, life becomes identified with Nirvana but only in the sense of a state of mind because the body still exists. But perfect or complete Nirvana is attained at death. The extinction of the body is the *sine qua non* of perfect Nirvana, just as the cessation of the wave results in the perfect quiescence of the water.

(4) The Principle of True Reality (Thusness)

Many of the problems concerning Thus-come, Thus-gone, Thusness or Suchness have been studied in connection with the Causation theory. Thusness is the ultimate foundation of Buddhist thought concerning the real state of all that exists.

It is natural for people to seek first the innermost essence among the outward appearance of all things or to seek an unchanging fact among many changing things. Failing in this, people try to distinguish the unknowable from the knowable, the real from the apparent, or the thing-in-itself from the thing-for-us. This effort, too, will end in failure, for what they select as the real or the thing-in-itself is utterly beyond human knowledge. Such efforts may be called the search for the world-principle or for the life-principle. The method of search and the resulting theories are various. Some are monistic or pantheistic, while others are dualistic or pluralistic.

Against all these views Buddhism stands aloof by itself. Buddhism is atheistic—there is no doubt about it. When questioned about the First Cause or Principle, the Buddha always remained reticent. As to the life-principle, he denied the existence of an ego or soul or any kind of thing which one may call the real self, as we have discussed before. To see the true nature or the true state of all things is not to find one in many or one before many, nor is it to distinguish unity from diversity or the static from the dynamic. *The true state is the state without any special condition.* It is, in fact, 'the true reality without a reality,' i.e., without any specific character or nature. It is very difficult for the human mind to understand this idea of a reality in which there is no 'sub-stance' at all.

The idea of an abiding substance with changing qualities is very deeply rooted in our habits of thought. Buddhist schools, no matter what they are, Hinayana or Mahayana, realistic or idealistic, are utterly free from such a habit of thought and all maintain the theory of pure change without substratum. When any Buddhist speaks of the true state of reality he means the state without a specific nature. According to the general views of the Hinayana, the state without any special condition is Nirvana, because Nirvana is perfect freedom from bondage. The Realistic School (the Sarvastivada), belonging to the Hinayana, goes a step further and assumes that selflessness, impermanence and Nirvana (flamelessness) are the true state of all things. The Nihilistic School (the Satyasiddhi) holds that all things, matter and mind, are void or unreal and that nothing exists even in Nirvana.

The Mahayana teaches, on the one hand, that the truth can be discovered only by negative views of becoming,[5] and, on the other hand, holds that true perfection can be realized negatively in the denial of the illusory and causal nature of existence.[6] The 'Wreath' School[7] of the Mahayana thinks that the ideal world, or the World One-and-True, is without any independent individual. The 'Lotus' School[8] identifies the manifested state as it is and the true entity immanent-in-nature.

On the whole, to see only the fact that a flower is falling is, after all, a one-sided view according to the theory of impermanence. We ought to see that immanent in the fact of a flower's falling there lies the fact of a flower's blooming, and also immanent in the blooming of the flower there is the fact of its falling. Thus the opposition of falling (extinction) and blooming (becoming) is synthesized and we form the view of reciprocal identification which is an unbiased view of the mean, or Middle Path.

This amounts to saying that we see inaction in action and action in inaction, immotion in motion and motion in immotion, calm in

---

[5] Madhyamika, the Negativistic School.
[6] Vijnaptimatra, the Idealistic School.
[7] Avatansaka, the Totalistic School.
[8] Pundarika, the Phenomenological School.

wave and wave in calm. We thus arrive at the true state of all things, i.e., the Middle Path. And this is what is meant by Thusness or Suchness.

When the view is negatively expressed it indicates the true negation or Void, because any special state of things is denied altogether. Such is considered to be the ultimate idea of Buddhist philosophy. When the ultimate principle is considered from the universal point of view, it is called *'Dharma-dhatu'* (the Realm of Principle), but when it is considered from the personal point of view, it is named *'Tathagata-garbha'* (the Matrix of Thus-come or Thus-gone). Other ways of expressing this same idea are: *'Buddha-ta'* or *'Buddha-svabhava'* (the Buddha Nature), and *'Dharma-kaya'* (the Spiritual- or Law-body). These are all practically synonymous.[9] Without knowing the principle of Thusness or Void in the highest sense of the word, one can in no way understand the Mahayana doctrine. The word 'void' in its highest sense does not mean 'nothingness,' but indicates 'devoid of special conditions,' 'unconditioned.'

(5) THE PRINCIPLE OF TOTALITY (*Dharma-dhatu*)

Concerning the principle of Totality much has been said already in connection with the discussion of the Principle of Universal Causation. We have seen that there were four kinds of universe to be considered, namely; (1) the world of actual life, (2) the world of ideal principles, (3) the world of the ideal principles realized, (4) the world of actual life harmonized. The first, second and third can be easily understood, but the fourth is a rather uncommon idea. In the actual world individualism is apt to predominate, and competition, conflict, dispute and struggle too often will disturb the harmony. To regard conflict as natural is the way of usual philosophies. Buddhism sets up a world in which actual life attains an ideal harmony.

The reasons brought forward to prove the possibility of such a world have already been shown.[10] According to this principle no one being will exist by itself and for itself, but the whole world will move and act in unison as if the whole were under general organization. Such an ideal world is called 'the World One-and-True' or 'the Lotus-store.'

---

[9] Some of these will be encountered later in detail in studies of the special schools of Buddhism.

[10] See section I (d).

47

The principle is based upon the universal causation of *Dharma-dhatu* (Realm of Principle) which we may regard as the self-creation of the universe itself. One should not forget that it is nothing but a causation by the common action-influence of all beings, and that the principle is also based on the theory of selflessness. In the Buddhist terminology, the principle of totality is called 'the Avatansaka' ('Wreath'), and will be discussed in Chapter VIII.

(6) THE PRINCIPLE OF NIRVANA OR PERFECT FREEDOM

To understand Buddhism properly we must begin at the end of the Buddha's career. The year 486 B.C. or thereabouts saw the conclusion of the Buddha's activity as a teacher in India. The death of the Buddha is called, as is well known, 'Nirvana'—'the state of a fire blown out.' When a fire is blown out, nothing remains to be seen. So the Buddha was considered to have entered into an invisible state which can in no way be depicted in word or in form.

Just prior to his attaining Nirvana, in the Sala grove of Kusinagara, he spoke to his disciples to the following effect: "Do not wail saying 'Our teacher has passed away, and we have no one to follow.' What I have taught, the *Dharma* (ideal) with the *vinaya* (disciplinary) rules, will be your teacher after my departure. If you adhere to them and practise them uninterruptedly, is it not the same as if my *Dharma* body[11] (*Dharma-kaya*) remained here forever?"

In spite of these thoughtful instructions some of his disciples were expressing a dissenting idea even before his funeral. It was natural, therefore, for the mindful elders to think of calling a council of elders in order to preserve the orthodox teaching of the Buddha. They consulted King Ajatasatru who at once ordered the eighteen monasteries around his capital to be repaired for housing the members of the coming Council of Rajagriha.

When the time arrived five hundred selected elders met together. Ananda rehearsed the *Dharmas* (*Sutras*) while Upali explained the origin of each of the *Vinaya* rules. There was no necessity of rehearsing the *Vinaya* rules themselves since they had been compiled during the Buddha's lifetime for the weekly convocation for confessions. At the council a fine collection of the *Dharma* and the *Vinaya*

---

[11] By '*dharma* body' the Buddha meant that his physical body would pass away but that his teaching would remain as his ideal 'body.' This is the interpretation by Hinayanists.

was made, the number of *Sutras* was decided, and the history of the disciplinary rules was compiled.

The result of the elders' activity was acknowledged as an authority by those who had a formalistic and realistic tendency. There were, however, some who differed from them in their opinion—Purana, for instance, who was skilled in preaching. Purana was in a bamboo grove near Rajagriha during the council, and being asked by some layman, is said to have answered: "The council may produce a fine collection. But I will keep to what I heard from my teacher myself." So we may presume that there were some who had idealistic and free-thinking tendencies.

(a) The Unwritten Sacred Literature

The whole collection of the sacred literature authorized by the council was not written on paper or palm leaf during a period of about four hundred years. It is well known that Brahmanism has never written down its Vedic literature even to this day—especially those revealed texts called '*s'ruti*' ('hearing'). We may imagine that Buddhism simply followed the example of the older religion, but there were other reasons as well: First, they dared not desecrate the sweet voice and kindly words of the Blessed One by putting them down in the profane letters of a foreign origin. The Buddha had once forbidden the translation of his words into the Vedic Sanskrit. How much less would it please him to write his words in the foreign Accadian alphabet, which was used only for commercial and popular purposes? Secondly, the language they adopted in the council was, in all probability, a commingled one, something like the Pali language, that is, the language of Pataliputra. It was not advisable that their sacred language and literature should be open to the public, especially when there were some dissenting elders of a free-thinking tendency. Thirdly, to put the Buddha's holy words to letters might have seemed to them a sacrilege just as much as depicting his sacred image in painting or sculpture of which I shall speak immediately. At any rate the whole literature was kept in memory and was not committed to writing for about four centuries.

The Buddhist community, quite different from that of the Brahmans, was an assortment of all four castes coming from all quarters, and was not fit for a serious recital of the holy words. The result was an imperfect transmission. Fearing the loss and distortion of

49

the original teachings, King Vattagamani of Ceylon gave orders to commit the whole literature to writing in Sinhalese characters, about the year 80 B.C.

(b) THE UNREPRESENTED SACRED IMAGE

All the earlier sculptures of Sanchi and Barhut do not represent the Buddha in human figure. It is remarkable to us that the principal events of the Buddha's life have been fully given in sculpture without a figure of the hero. How was that possible? The Buddha at birth is represented by a full blooming lotus; the Buddha in Enlightenment by the bodhi tree with a rail around it; the Buddha in his first preaching by a wheel, above which a *tri-ratna* mark is sometimes added; the Buddha in his begging round, or mendicancy, by a bowl; and the like. If suggestion be a means of true art, the early Buddhist artists understood it perfectly and utilized the idea skillfully for practical purposes.

However, all this does not necessarily mean that the elders did not represent the Buddha at all during his lifetime, for there is a legend which tells of their making an image for the purpose of offering veneration during the Brother's absence. They were formalistic and realistic as mentioned above, and so if the Buddha was actually before them, they had a right to depict him in painting or sculpture. Now that he had passed into Nirvana, however, it was improper to represent the one who no longer existed in reality. It was after a considerable development of the Gandhara arts that the southern school of Buddhism began to have images of Buddha. This was, I believe, about the same time when the Buddha's teachings were committed to writing, i.e., 80 B.C.

The elders of idealistic and free-thinking tendencies, whom we might regard as the forerunners of the Mahayana, would not hold any meetings for the rehearsal of the Buddha's sermons, nor would they enlarge upon their *Vinaya* rules beyond what was laid down by the Buddha himself. They would commit those sacred words to memory or to writing as they pleased. They did not hesitate in using their talents in painting or sculpture to depict the Buddha's image according to their own ideal of beauty and perfection, as they did in the Gandhara art.

The trend of the free-thinking mind can also be seen in the metaphysical treatises of the Vaibhasikas (Optionalists), in which several opinions about *dharmas* or *abhidharmas* (higher *dharma*) are gathered together and some optional ones have been selected and recommended for study. Though the Vaibhasika School belonged to the Hinayana, it already betrayed a tendency toward the free-thinking school. Such free-thinking people would be bold in exegesis, erudition, annotation, or in forming and expressing any opinions. This, however, does not mean that they departed from the original teachings of the Buddha.

As to Nirvana, the free-thinking group among the early Buddhists took greatest liberty in interpretation, because the Buddha did not say much about it during his lifetime although it is sometimes touched upon and glorified in his poetic verses, as in the *Dhammapada*. Whenever he was asked by a questioner whether he was to live after death or what sort of world he was to enter after Nirvana, he always remained silent. When the Buddha remained silent to a question requiring an answer of 'yes' or 'no,' his silence usually meant assent. But his silence on the question concerning Nirvana was due to the fact that his listeners could not understand the profound philosophy involved.

One day a certain man said to the Buddha that he would join the band of his disciples if the Buddha would give clear answers to the questions: Would the Buddha ever die, and if so, what would become of him after death? What was the first cause of the universe, and what was the universe going to be like in the future? Why do men live and what becomes of them after death? The Buddha's answer was to the following effect: Suppose you were shot by a poison arrow and a physician came to draw the arrow from your body and to dress the wound, would you first ask him questions as to what the arrow was made of, what the composition of the poison was, and who shot the arrow, and if the physician did not dress the wound, what was going to happen, and such blissful questions, and refuse the treatment until the physician answered all the questions to your satisfaction? You would be dead before you obtained the answers.[12]

In this parable the Buddha advised the questioner to become his disciple without wasting his time on problems which were too profound to be understood by an ordinary man—probably after a long cultivation as a disciple of the Buddha, he might come to understand.

---

[12] See *Majjhima-Nikaya*, 144.

After his departure most of the metaphysical discussions and speculations centered around the subject of Nirvana. The *Mahaparinirvana Sutra,* the Sanskrit fragments of which were discovered recently—one in Central Asia and another in Kōyasan—indicates a vivid discussion on the questions as to what is 'Buddha-nature,' '*Dharma*-nature,' 'Thusness,' 'the Realm of Principle,' '*Dharma*-body,' and the distinction between the Hinayana and Mahayana ideas. All of these topics relate to the problem of Nirvana, and indicate the great amount of speculation undertaken on this most important question.

The main problem of Buddhism, either formalistic or idealistic, was concerning the extinction of human passion, because this distorted state of mind is considered to be the source of all the evils of human life. Human passion can be extinguished even during one's lifetime. Therefore liberation from such disorder of mind is the chief object of Buddhist culture. The extinction (Nirvana) of passion, of desire, of sense, of mind, and even of individual consciousness are often spoken of.

To the Buddhist mind Nirvana did not contain any idea of deification of the Buddha. It simply meant the eternal continuation of his personality in the highest sense of the word. It meant returning to his original state of Buddha-nature, which is his *Dharma*-body [13] but not his scripture-body [14] as the formalists take it to be. *Dharma* means the 'ideal' itself which the Buddha conceived in his perfect Enlightenment. The idealists hold that the Buddha has *Dharma*-body —the body identical with that ideal. The ideal was expressed in the Buddha's preachings but these preachings were always restricted by the language and the occasion and the listeners. Therefore the idealists hold that the scripture is not the Buddha's ideal itself. This ideal 'body' without any restricting conditions whatever is Nirvana.

The formalists, on the other hand, hold that the scripture is the perfect representation of the ideal of the Buddha. Hence their opinion that the Buddha lives forever in the scripture-body, Nirvana being his entire annihilation and extinction otherwise.

---

[13] In Mahayana, 'Dharma-body' refers to the pure ideal conceived in his Enlightenment, not merely to his teachings, i.e., his ideal as expressed in words.

[14] 'Scripture-body' means, for the Hinayanist, the Buddha continues to live as scripture or teaching.

Now, let me further illustrate the principle of Nirvana (the state of a fire blown out) in the light of space and time. It was an illusion on the part of philosophers, especially some of the Indian philosophers, to believe that space and time were infinite. Buddhism, however, has never treated space and time as infinite, for Buddhism takes them to be physical matters. Space is considered one of the five elements—earth, water, fire, air and space—and it is sometimes represented to be of round shape.

Time is treated as real in some schools while in other schools it is treated as unreal. But it is to be particularly noted that time has never been considered to exist separately from space. That is to say, every being or thing has time of its own. Space and time are always correlative. Men have an average wave-length, or lifetime, of fifty years. But a crane is said to live for a thousand years, and a tortoise even ten thousand years. And with the heavenly beings, their one day and night is said to be as long as the whole fifty years of the earthly men. A day-fly and a morning-glory, on the other hand, live a short wave-length of only one day.

The theory that space is curved, set forth by modern physicists, has considerably facilitated the elucidation of the doctrine of Nirvana. The universe, or the *Dharma-dhatu* (Realm of Principle) as it is technically called, is the region which is occupied by space and time and in which they control all the waves of existence. So, in practice, the space-time world is the ocean of the waves of life and death. It is the sphere of *sansara* (flowing cycles of life), the world of creation, of energy, of action, of causation and ideation, of self-creation, and of dynamic becoming. It is the sphere of desire, form (matter) and mind.

In opposition to such a world let us assume theoretically that there must be a sphere that is spaceless and timeless, of no creation, of no causation, and not disturbed by the waves of life and death. There will be no *Dharma-dhatu* in the dynamic sense of the word, i.e., the manifested world. But there will be the *Dharma-dhatu* in the static sense of the word, i.e., as it is in itself; that is, Thusness or Suchness, the ultimate state of Nirvana, the *Mahaparinirvana,* or *Samyak Sambuddha* (The Properly and Perfectly Enlightened One).

Dharma-dhatu in the sense of the phenomenal world is an encircled and restricted world which may be represented as follows:

53

The sphere of matter-mind.

The sphere of space-time.

Life-death, action, causation,
creation, becoming.

Sansara (life-flux)

The world of desire, form and mind.

Action-influence.

Nirvana with life conditions
remaining.

The realm of phenomena

Aside from the *Dharma-dhatu* in this sense there is the unrestricted
world to be described as follows:

Spaceless-timeless
Nirvana without life-conditions.
Lifeless-deathless.
No creation, no causation, no becoming.
Perfect Enlightenment, perfect freedom.
Thusness, Suchness, the state of
Thus-come, Thus-gone.

Among the Buddhist texts which have come down to us we do
not find passages expressly indicating these points. Howeyer, we
have one text—though its Indian original has not as yet been discovered—which contains the idea much as I have expressed it here.

It says: "In the *dharma-dhatu* (phenomenal world), there are three worlds of desire, form and mind. All created things or beings, both noble and ignoble, both cause and effect, are within the *dharma-dhatu*. Only the Buddha is outside the *dharma-dhatu*." The idea in this text is practically identical with the diagram given above.

The Mahayana text of the *Mahaparinirvana Sutra,* not being satisfied with all the negative elucidations, explains Nirvana in affirmative terms as permanency (against worldly impermanence), as bliss (against human suffering), as self (against the selflessness of all beings), and as purity (against the pollution of human life). However, as they are all transcendental qualities of the Buddha, these terms ought not be taken in the ordinary sense of the words. For instance, one must not picture to himself a special location, a world of Nirvana, where the Buddha lives in peace and joy, for the Buddha's Nirvana is the 'Nirvana of No Abode.'

An ordinary *arhat* (partially enlightened one) will cut off all the obstructions caused by passion or desire, thereby attaining his goal of annihilation. He finds satisfaction in the destruction of his intellectual life, because he thinks that the source of distinction, opposition or differentiation in things lies in consciousness. He thinks his state of annihilation is the ideal Nirvana. But in truth he has returned to the original blindness (*avidya*—ignorance) in leaving the obstruction of intellect. He himself may be thinking that he has done away with blindness. But blindness is the basic principle of existence which cannot be simply cut off, just as darkness cannot be destroyed without a light. The only way to get rid of darkness is to bring a light into the room. By virtue of enlightenment the darkness that bars intellect will be removed.

As a technical term the extinction of human passion is called the 'Nirvana with the condition of being still remaining' or, in a more literal expression, 'the Nirvana with the *upadhi* remnant,' *upadhi* being the material and immaterial condition of being. Plainly, this means becoming a person without passion while yet alive.

Then the next question will be: What is the Nirvana without the *upadhi* remnant? It is the total extinction of the conditions of being as well as of passion. One may call it the annihilation of being. This is Nirvana or 'Perfect Freedom,' the death of Sakyamuni the Buddha.

The formalistic view of Buddhism here comes to an end with the annihilation of being. But the speculative views of the idealistic standpoint have a fresh start with the passing of the visible Buddha into the invisible state. Even in his lifetime the Buddha had a perfect freedom in intellectual activity, and while he was a person, he had been super-personally enlightened. How much more free must he be when he passed into the thoroughly unconditioned state of Nirvana? He had now returned to his 'ideal' body. It is called the Body of His Own Nature, 'Self-natured Body' in contradistinction to the 'Body Manifested for All Beings.' All the incarnation theories entertained in later years have their origin in this interpretation of Nirvana.

The Buddha in Nirvana has a perfect freedom to live anywhere he pleases; he can act in whatever way he wishes and, on that account he has no fixed abode and; his Nirvana is called the 'Nirvana of No Abode.' The Blessed One may reappear in this world when he feels the necessity of saving all beings as the historical Sakyamuni did. Therefore, the Buddha, according to the idealistic view, does not live in the world of life and death as he is not bound by causation. However, at the same time he does not rest at ease in Nirvana, because he is the sufferer of others' suffering.

IV. THE KUSHA SCHOOL
(THE ABHIDHARMA-KOSA SCHOOL)[1]
(Sarvastivada, Abhidharmika)

(Realism: *Ens* School)
[Hinayanistic]

(1) Preliminary

The Japanese name of the School, Kusha, is an abbreviation of
Abhidharma-kosa[2] (*kosa=Kusha*) which is the title of Vasu-
bandhu's[3] work on realism and may be translated 'The Story of the
Higher Special Dharma.' To the text we shall return soon.

First of all let us consider what the word *'dharma'* means in Buddhism. It is derived from the verb *dhri* (to hold, or to bear), and its
noun form, *dharma,* would mean 'that which is held to,' or 'the ideal'
if we limit its meaning to mental affairs only. This ideal will be different in scope as conceived by different individuals. In the case of
the Buddha it will be Perfect Enlightenment or Perfect Wisdom
(Bodhi). Secondly, the ideal as expressed in words will be his Sermon, Dialogue, Teaching, Doctrine. Thirdly, the ideal as set forth for
his pupils is the Rule, Discipline, Precept, Morality. Fourthly, the
ideal to be realized will be the Principle, Theory, Truth, Reason,
Nature, Law, Condition. Fifthly, the ideal as realized in a general
sense will be Reality, Fact, Thing, Element (created and not created),
Mind-and-Matter, Idea-and-Phenomenon. In the Realistic School of
the Abhidharma teachers the word *dharma* is mostly used in the fifth
and last meaning.

Now we are in a position to understand what *Abhidharma* means.
The prefix *'Abhi-'* gives the sense of either 'further' or 'about.' There-
fore, *Abhidharma* would mean 'The Higher or Special Dharma' or
'The Discourse of Dharma.' Both will do for our purpose. While the
Dharma is the general teaching of the Buddha, the *Abhidharma* is a
special metaphysical discourse brought forward by certain elders.

---

[1] Chü-shê 俱舍
[2] *Taishō*, No. 1558. French translation by L. de la Vallée Poussin:
L'abhidharmakosa de Vasubandhu, 6 Volumes; Paris, 1923-31. 阿毘達磨俱
舍論 [3] 世親 c. 420-500 A.D.

Most of the Abhidharma schools probably arose after the Council of Asoka (c. 240 B.C.), because the Abhidharma literature, seven texts in all, was for the first time recognized as one of the Tripitaka (three baskets or collections) in this council.[4] At the time of the first and the second councils there were only two Pitakas *(Sutra* and *Vinaya).*[5] In this Asoka Council *Abhidharma* was added to make the Tripitaka.

While the orthodox Elders' School (Theravada)[6] was flourishing in the south, chiefly in Ceylon, a more avowed Realistic School was getting a stronghold in the north, mostly in Kasmira and Gandhara.

The existence of this Sarvastivada School[7] can be seen in Indian history from the time of the Buddhist Council held during King Asoka's reign (240 B.C.) down to the time of I-tsing's[8] travel in India (671-695 A.D.).[9] In the *Kathavatthu Controversy* compiled in the time of King Asoka, Sarvastivada seems to have occupied a strong position among the disputing parties.[10] The principal seat of this school was in Kasmira where its doctrine was taught in its purity and it was finally developed into an elaborate system known as the Vaibhasika.[11]

In time another branch of the Vaibhasikas was established in Gandhara and it seems to have differed from that of Kasmira in its opinion to some extent, for both were often cited side by side in some texts in use.

The geographical extent of this school was much greater than that of any other school as it was found in all India, its northern frontier, Persia, Central Asia, and also to the south in Sumatra, Java, Cochin-China and all of China.

The Sarvastivada School was closely related to the orthodox Theravada School, from which it was first separated probably before

---

[4] See my "On the Abhidharma Literature of the Sarvastivadins," *Journal of the Pali Text Society,* 1905.

[5] *Sutra*: Discourses of the Buddha; *Vinaya*: Disciplining rules enunciated by the Buddha.

[6] 上座部　　[7] 說一切有部　　[8] I-ching 義淨

[9] See my translation of *A Record of the Buddhist Religion as Practised in India and the Malay Archipelago* (A.D. 671-695) by I-Tsing, Oxford, 1896.

[10] See C. A. F. Rhys Davids and S. Z. Aung's translation, *Points of Controversy,* Pali Text Society Translation Series, Vol. V, Prefatory notes.

[11] 毘婆沙

the Council of Asoka. The idea that all things exist may go back even to the time of the Buddha himself, for the word *'sabban atthi'* (all things exist) is found already in the *Samyuttanikaya*.[12]

The principal *Abhidharma* text of this school was Katyayaniputra's *Jnana-prasthana* (Source of Knowledge),[13] otherwise called the *Asta-grantha* (Eight Books), probably compiled as early as 200 B.C. The subsequent works of the school seem to have been a special exegesis on the subject-matter contained in it. At least six *padas* ('Legs'),[14] as they are designated, have come down to us.

Then probably in the second century A.D.—whether before or after the Buddhist Council of King Kaniska's reign, we cannot tell—a great and minute commentary named *Vibhasa Sastra*[15] was compiled on Katyayaniputra's work. The word *'vibhasa'* means an extensive annotation or various opinions, and this title indicates that many opinions of the time were gathered and criticized in detail and that some optional ones were selected and recorded. The chief object of the *Vibhasa* commentary was to transmit the correct exposition of the Abhidharma School which has since then come to be called the Vaibhasika School.

Then there appeared a compendium of the Abhidharma doctrine called *Abhidharma-hridaya* ('heart of the Higher Dharmas,' translated into Chinese in 391 A.D.)[16] by Dharmottara who belonged to the Gandhara branch. A commentary on it called *Samyukta-abhidharma-hridaya* was written by Dharmatrata, a pupil of Dharmottara. This work became the fundamental text of the Gandhara branch and subsequently of the Chinese Abhidharma School.

The Abhidharma Literature

I

Katyayaniputra's *Jnana-prasthana* (Source of Knowledge)
alias *Asta-grantha* (Eight Books)
Six *Padas* (Legs)
on the above

---

[12] English translation by C. A. F. Rhys Davids and F. L. Woodward: *The Book of Kindred Sayings*, Pali Text Society Translation Series, Vols. VII, X, XIII, XV, XVI, 1918-30. See Rhys Davids' Index to the *Samyutta*, p. 107. 雜阿含經   [13] 發智論   [14] 六足論   [15] 毘婆沙論   [16] 阿毘曇心論

1	2	3
Vasumitra's	Devasarman's	Sariputra's
Prakarana-	*Vijnana-kaya*[18]	*Dharma-*
pada[17]	(Consciousness-	*skandha*[19]
(Category-leg)	body)	(Element-group)

4	5	6
Maudgalyayana's	Purna's	Mahakausthila's
Prajnapti[20]	*Dhatu-kaya*[21]	*Sangiti-paryaya*[22]
(World-	(Mental-	(Rehearsal-
system)	element-body)	reading)

Parsva's *Mahavibhasa* (Great Commentary)
200 Chinese volumes (*chüans* or parts)
Vibhasa (Abridged Commentary), 14 Chinese volumes

In Chinese we have thus two transmissions of the *Vibhasa*, Large (200 parts) and Small (14 parts). Whether one was an abridgement of the other we cannot tell for certain. But from several points of view we can imagine that the larger one belongs to the Kasmira School and the smaller to the Gandhara School.

II

Compendium of the Abhidharma School
Dharmottara's *Abhidharma-hridaya*
(Transl. A. D. 391)
|
Dharmatrata's *Samyukta-abhidharma-hridaya*
(Transl. A.D. 426.[23] From this the Chinese
Abhidharma School called P'i-t'an [24] was founded)
|
Vasubandhu's *Abhidharma-kosa*
|
Paramartha's [25] Chinese Translation
(A. D. 563-567)
From this the Chinese Kosa
School called Chü-shê[26] was founded

---

[17] 品類足論　[18] 識身足論　[19] 法薀足論　[20] 施設足論
[21] 界身足論　[22] 集異門足論　[23] 雜阿毘曇心論　[24] 毘曇
[25] 異諦　[26] 俱舍

Hiuen-tsang's [27] (Hsüan-tsang, A. D. 596-664) Chinese Translation
(A. D. 651-654)

After this translation the Kosa School was
completed as a philosophical system chiefly
by Ki,[28] (K'uei-chi, 632-682) pupil of Hiuen-tsang
|
Japanese Kosa School

The Realistic School

Sarvastivadins
|
```
  ┌──────────────────────┼──────────────────────┐
```
Gandhara-   Katyayaniputra's   Kasmira-
Abhidharmikas   Abhidharmikas

                       Jnana-prasthana
                              |
                       Six *Padas* on it
                              |
                       Vaibhasikas
                  Parsva's *Mahavibhasa* [29]

                     Neo-Vaibhasikas
                              |
```
        ┌─────────────────────┴─────────────────────┐
```
Vasubandhu (c. 420-500 A.D.)   Samghabhadra
         (Eclectic)   (Orthodox)
           Texts   Texts
Abhidharma-kosa-karika (Verses)   *Nyayanusara*
            and   and
Abhidharma-kosa Sastra (Commentary)   *Samaya-pradipika*

(2) Historical

The great philosopher Vasubandhu was born in Purusapura
(Peshwar) in Gandhara and received his ordination in the Sarvastivada School. He went to Kasmira *incognito* to learn the Abhidharma philosophy. On his return home he wrote the *Abhidharma-
kosa* which is preserved in sixty volumes (*chüans* or parts) of

---

[27] 玄奘   [28] 窺基   [29] 大毘婆沙論

61

Chinese translation. The Sanskrit text is lost, but fortunately we have a commentary written by Yasomitra called the *Abhidharma-kosa-vyakhya* which has facilitated the restoration of the lost text undertaken by the late Professor L. de la Vallée Poussin of Belgium and completed by Rahula Sankrityayana of Ceylon.

According to the published text and the Chinese version, the contents of the *Abhidharma-kosa* are as follows:

1. On Elements
2. On Organs
3. On Worlds
4. On Actions
5. On Drowsiness (Passion)
6. On the Noble Personality and the Path
7. On Knowledge
8. On Meditation

The Chinese text has a ninth chapter on Refutation of the Idea of the Self.

In writing the *Abhidharma-kosa,* Vasubandhu seems to have followed the work of his predecessor, Dharmatrata, called *Samyukta-Abhidharma-hridaya,* and this, again, is a commentary on Dharmottara's *Abhidharma-hridaya.* A careful comparison of the three works will indicate that Vasubandhu had before him his predecessors' works, or else such questions as discussed in these works must have been common topics of the school. The first eight chapters of the work explain special facts or elements of matter and mind, while the ninth and last chapter elucidates the general basic principle of selflessness that should be followed by all Buddhist schools. Especially the ninth chapter seems to originate from Vasubandhu's own idea, for there is no trace of this subject in the other books.

Though the *Kosa* thus resembles the *Hridaya* in subject matter, there is no indication that the former is indebted to the latter in forming opinions, for Vasubandhu was very free and thorough in his thinking, and he did not hesitate to take the tenets of any school other than his own when he found excellent reasoning in them.

When Vasubandhu's *Abhidharma-kosa* was made public in Gandhara, it met with rigorous opposition from within and from without his school. Yet the final victory seems to have been on his side, for his work enjoyed popularity in India; it was taught widely and several annotations of it were made in Nalanda, Valabhi and elsewhere. It was translated into Tibetan by Jinamitra and into Chinese first by Paramartha of Valabhi during 563-567 A.D. and later by Hiuen-tsang who studied at Nalanda University during 651-654 A.D. In China especially serious studies were made, and at least seven elaborate commentaries, each amounting to more than twenty or thirty Chinese volumes, were written on it.

Before the translation of the *Abhidharma-kosa* there was in China a school called P'i-t'an Tsung [30] which is the first one in the list of Chinese sects given above,[31] P'i-t'an being the Chinese abbreviation of *Abhidharma*. This Chinese school represents the Gandhara branch of Sarvastivadins. The principal texts of this school with the *Vibhasa* commentary were translated into Chinese as early as 383-434 A.D. The larger *Vibhasa* commentary belonging to the Kasmira branch was also translated, but there appeared no Chinese school or sect representing it. When the *Kosa* text of Vasubandhu was translated by Paramartha during 563-567 A.D. and again by Hiuen-tsang during 651-654 A.D., the Kosa School, or Chü-shê Tsung, came into existence, was seriously studied, and was made into an indispensable basis of all Buddhist studies. The P'i-t'an School came to be entirely replaced by the new Kosa School.

The Kosa School, or the Kusha School as it is called in Japan, is generally understood to have been brought into Japan by Chitsū [32] and Chitatsu,[33] in 658 A.D., two Japanese priests who studied some time under the famous Hiuen-tsang. It was brought in once again by Gembō [34] (in 735 A.D.) who was a pupil of Chih-chou,[35] the third generation pupil of Ki,[36] a direct disciple of Hiuen-tsang.

In an official document of 793 A.D. the realistic Kusha School was registered as a sect appended to the idealistic Hossō [37] School, no separate position being given to it, because it had no adherents belonging exclusively to it.

(3) Philosophical

The Sankhya philosophy (dualism), one of the oldest philosophies of India, which has several tenets in common with Buddhism,

---

[30] 毘曇宗　[31] See p. 14.　　[32] 智通　[33] 智達　[31] 玄昉
[35] 智周　[36] 窺基　[37] 法相

maintains that all things exist eternally though they are constantly changing; nothing new appears and nothing disappears.

Buddhism, however, holds that everything exists only instantaneously; there is no abiding substance at all.[38] Both Buddhism and the Sankhya philosophy deny the theory of inherence. Buddhism may be said to hold, therefore, the theory of momentariness or instantaneous being. All reality may be split into separate elements which are instantaneous. This form of pluralism stands in direct opposition to monism, especially that of the Upanishads.

This school further maintains the atomic theory and asserts the existence of three atoms: 1. The finest atom *(parama-anu)*; 2. The form atom *(anu)*; 3. The fine dust atom *(rajas)*. The finest atom is the finest divisible atom of all and cannot be further analyzed. It is conceived only by meditation.

Seven of these finest atoms constitute the form atom which is the finest substance. It is of cubic form. Seven of these form atoms constitute the fine dust atom which can be perceived by the eyes of a *Bodhisattva,* a future Buddha. Furthermore, the shortest of time measures is said to correspond to the transition of one atom to another, thus space and time being always correlative. Though the atomic theory is set forth very minutely by the realistic Kusha School and also by the nihilistic Jōjitsu School,[39] I shall not dwell on it anymore, as I do not think it essential to these schools which hold the doctrine of momentariness of being.

All elements or *dharmas* which constitute momentary sense-data and thought-data were enumerated by the Realistic School, perhaps for the first time in the history of Indian philosophy. The idea that a thing has no 'sub-stance' goes along with the theory of change or impermanence—everything having no duration. According to this theory only the present exists. The past does not exist, because it is no more, and the future is not real, because it has not yet come into existence.

This theory has been faithfully held by such other Buddhist schools as the Mahasanghika,[40] the Mahisasaka[41] and the Sautrantika.[42] The Sarvastivada School, however, because it has its origin

[38] Th. Stcherbatsky, *Buddhist Logic,* Vol. I, p. 109. Substance is *substance*, abiding essence.

[39] Satyasiddhi 成實宗　[40] 大衆部　[41] 法藏部　[42] 經量部

in the orthodox Theravada School,[43] raises a rigorous objection and asserts that the past and the future are real. because the present has its root in the past and its consequence in the future. Besides, it holds that the three periods of time ought to exist separately, because the notions of past and future would not occur in us without separate realities.

Judging from the discussions recorded in the *Mahavibhasa* literature, great importance seems to have been laid on the separateness of the three periods of time and the reality of each. The reality of the three periods of time, however, does not mean that the three periods themselves are eternally extant, nor does it mean that time is a real substance. It means that all things or elements are real in the past and in the future as they are in the present—but without enduring from one period to another.

In connection with this theory four arguments are quoted by Vasubandhu from the Exegetic Literature:

(1)   Dharmatrata's argument from the difference of kind or result—as a gold piece may be made into three different articles, yet each retains the real nature of gold.

(2)   Ghosa's argument from the difference of mark or factor as the same service can be obtained from three different employees.

(3)   Vasumitra's argument from the difference of function or position as in counting where the same numeral may be used to express' three different values, for instance, the numeral one may be 1 or the index of 10 or of 100.

(4)   Buddhadeva's argument from the difference of view or relation—as a woman can at once be daughter, wife and mother according to the relation she holds to her mother, her husband and her child.

Vasubandhu prefers Vasumitra's opinion (3) as the best of the four arguments though he was not entirely satisfied with it. According to this argument it is possible to give different values to each of the three periods of time—the future is the stage which has not come to function, the present is the actually functioning stage, and the past is the stage in which the function has come to an end. Owing to the differences in stage, the three periods are distinctly separate;

---

[43] 上座部

65

and all things or elements in them are real entities. Hence the formula: "The three periods (of time) are real and so is the entity of all elements at any instant."[44] The tenet "Void of abiding self (but) reality of elements *(dharmas)*" indicates that selflessness is still the basic principle of the Sarvastivada School.

Nevertheless, the theory of Sarvastivada, according to Vasubandhu, is not found in the genuine discourses of the Buddha, but it is an innovation of the *Vibhasa* (Exegetic) Literature of the Abhidharma School. The opinion of the Abhidharmikas is against the Sautrantic School[45] which clings solely to the discourses *(Sutranta)* of the Buddha and maintains that only the present exists.[46] Accordingly Vasubandhu in his *Abhidharma-kosa* adopts the opinion of the Sautrantic School, although professedly he follows the tenets of the Kasmiran Abhidharmikas in general.

Although a strong realistic tendency is a deviation from the original teaching of momentariness or instantaneous being, it is not so conspicuous as it seems at first sight as long as the deviating party does not forsake the original formula: "No substance *(anatma)*, no duration *(anitya)* and no bliss *(duhkha)* except Nirvana." Consequently the real entity of the Sarvastivada School would mean a momentary existence or the continuity of separate momentary existences.

In Buddhism there is no actor apart from action, no percipient apart from perception; therefore, no conscious subject behind consciousness. Mind is simply a transitory state of consciousness of an object. There is no permanent conscious subject, for no fabric of a body remains the same for two consecutive moments as the modern physicists say.[47] Buddhism contends that the same is true of the mind as well.

Seventy-five Elements or Dharmas of the Universe

All elements of the universe were minutely explained by Vasubandhu in his *Abhidharma-kosa*. The significant name of the School 'Sarva-asti-vada' (all-things-exist-doctrine) affirms all existences, both material and mental, as well as that which is neither matter nor mind. This, however, does not mean to admit the existence of Self *(Atman)*, an individual ego or soul or the universal principle or

[44] 三世實有法體恒有   [45] See next chapter.
[46] Th. Stcherbatsky, *Buddhist Logic*, Vol. I, p. 111.
[47] *Compendium of Philosophy*, p. 8.

First Cause. Whether or not he anticipated the danger of being involved in the admission of Self, Vasubandhu devoted the whole ninth chapter of his *Abhidharma-kcsa* to the refutation of the *Atman* theory.

The list of *dharmas* in the *Abhidharma-kosa* may well be compared with similar lists in the Pali *Compendium of Philosophy (Abhidhamma-sangaha)* by Anuruddha of the eighth century A.D.,[48] the *Essence of Metaphysics (Abhidharma-hridaya)* by Dharmottara (transl. 391 A.D.) and by Dharmatrata (transl. 426 A.D.) and possibly the *Completion of Truth (Satyasiddhi)*[49] by Harivarman (c.250-350).

In the *Compendium of Philosophy* all elements are divided into six classes and *dharmas,* whereas in the *Essence of Metaphysics* they are classified into five grades and *dharmas.* In the *Abhidharma-kosa* these are well arranged and systematized into five categories and *dharmas.* The *Completion of Truth* which is a Sautrantic and nihilistic text enumerates eighty-four *dharmas.*

All these schools hold that all *dharmas* are to be classified into two categories, created and uncreated. The created, or conditioned, elements are again divided into four classes:

I. Form (11 *dharmas*) consisting of the five sense-organs, five sense-objects, and form-with-no-manifestations.

II. Consciousness (1 *dharma*) sometimes subdivided into five *dharmas* corresponding to the sense-organs.

III. The Concomitant Mental Functions (46 *dharmas*) are subdivided into six grades, i.e., general, good, foul, evil, minor foul, and indeterminate functions.

IV. The Elements Independent of Consciousness: Neither Form nor Consciousness (14 *dharmas*).

These (I-IV) are all created things (72 in number) and with uncreated things (3 in number) constitute the five categories and the seventy-five *dharmas.* Among these what all schools and texts treat with the utmost care is the group called 'Concomitant Mental Functions.' There are 52 elements in three grades in the *Compendium of*

---

[48] Translated by S. Z. Aung, revised and edited by C. A. F. Rhys Davids, Pali Text Society Translations Series, Vol. II, 1910.
[49] 成實論

Philosophy, 58 elements in seven grades in the *Essence of Metaphysics,* and 46 elements in six grades in the *Abhidharma-kosa.*

Compared roughly, they are found to contain more than 'mentals' in common, but the *Abhidharma-kosa* and the *Essence of Metaphysics* possess much closer affinities than the rest, the former being a systematized version of the latter.

The *dharmas* comprise the whole world of both matter and mind—positive and negative becomings, presentative and representative psychological elements or sense-data and thought-data. Vasubandhu's enumeration was of elements. The last four elements of the Indeterminate Functions—covetousness, hatred, pride and doubt—are treated by him separately and not definitely as Indeterminate Functions. The addition of these seems to have been finally established by Chinese authors, especially P'u-kuang.[50]

The *dharmas* are generally arranged in a table, as in attached chart.

Some Explanations of the Table

The table enumerates all the elements of what might be called the objective world. In fact those with which the realistic school of Buddhism is concerned are objects only. It does not recognize any subject in the ordinary sense of the word. Even mind itself is not a subjective thing, for there is no actor apart from action and no conscious subject apart from consciousness. There is only a transitory state of consciousness. All reality can be assumed to have only momentary existence.

According to the original principle of Buddhism, all things (matter and mind) are considered to be separate, momentary elements, equal in value. The arrangement of all the elements into a co-ordinated system, dividing matter into subjective and objective groups or elements, and assuming the difference between the central elements of pure consciousness and the secondary elements of mental functions or moral forces, may seem, as Prof. Stcherbatsky says, to be a great deviation by this school from the original Buddhism (the doctrine of no substance). But as long as we do not lose sight of momentariness of being, we cannot regard it as an entire deviation.

The conditioned elements (*sarva-sanskara* or *sanskrita-dharmas*) constitute the first grand division in our table. Their specific character is impermanence.

---

[50] 普光

68

Sanskrita-dharmas: (I) Forms (*Rupa,* 11 *dharmas*). This group comprises practically all that we call matter. Of the eleven, the first five are sense-organs and the next five are sense-objects. The four gross elements—Earth, Water, Fire, Air—are represented by the sense-objects. In addition to these, there is a peculiar one. That is the 'form-element not manifested' outwardly (*avijnapti-rupa*). When we will to act, the mental function itself is called will (*cetana*). In Buddhism it is called will-action. This is usually expressed in words or in body, and is called word-action or body-action respectively. These two actions manifested outwardly, whether they are good or bad, present a corresponding and similar action in mind, and form an abiding impression or image. They are then called unmanifested action (*avijnapti-karma*). These actions being taken as form-elements are considered to be sense-objects though not manifested (*avijnapti-rupa*).

II. Consciousness or Mind (*Citta,* one *dharma*). This is consciousness itself. Though one, it naturally functions in five ways corresponding to the five sense-organs.

III. The Concomitant Mental Functions (*Citta-samprayukta-sanskara* or *Caitasika,* 46 *dharmas*). This category of mental faculties is the division given most attention by this school and on that account it seems quite reasonable to designate the school a psychological school of Buddhism. The mental elements, in all, are again grouped into six classes: (1) 'General functions' or 'universals' (*Mahabhumika,* 10 *dharmas*). *Mahabhumika* means 'of the universal ground,' the 'ground' meaning the mind. Whenever the mind functions, the universals such as perception, idea, will, etc., always appear concomitantly (*sarva-dharma-sadharana*). (2) 'General functions of good' or 'moral universals' (*Kusala-mahabhumika,* 10 *dharmas*) which accompany all good mental functions. (3) 'General Foul Functions' (*Klesa-mahabhumika,* 6 *dharmas*) are those tainted with earthly desire or passion (*klesa*). (4) 'General Functions of Evil' (*Akusala-mahabhumika,* 2 *dharmas*) which are concomitant with all evil thoughts. (5) 'Minor Foul Functions' (*Upaklesa-bhumika,* 10 *dharmas*) are those of ordinary passionate character. They always accompany evil mind and also the 'neutral mind which hinders the Noble Path' (*nivrita-avyakrita*), and they are to be eliminated gradually by the way of self-culture (*bhavana-marga*), not abruptly by the way of insight (*darsana-marga*). (6) 'Indeterminate Functions' (*Aniyata-*

bhumika, 8 dharmas) are those which cannot be classified as belonging to any of the five functions.

IV. Among the created, or conditioned, elements there are those which have no connection with form or mind *(Citta-viprayukta-sanskara, 14 dharmas)*. They are neither matter nor mind. (1) Acquisition *(prapti)* is the power that binds an acquired object to the one who acquires it. (2) Non-acquisition *(aprapti)* is the power that separates an object from the possessor. (3) Communionship *(sabhaga)* is the power that causes a species or a class to have similar forms of life. As to (4), (5) and (6), all of them are thoughtless and conditionless effects attained by meditation. (7) Life, or vital power, *(jivita-indriya)* is the power that gives longevity. The next four elements, (8), (9), (10) and (11), imply the life and death of being, i.e., the waves of becoming. The last three elements, (12), (13) and (14), are the groups *(kaya)* of names, sentences and letters, all related to speech *(vak)*.

Now we come to the second of the two grand divisions, i.e., the uncreated, or unconditioned, elements *(Asanskrita-dharma, 3 dharmas)*. (1) Space *(akasa)* is that which gives no hindrance and itself penetrates through any hindrance freely and manifests no change. The second element is an extinction attained by an intellectual power, *(pratisankhya-nirodha)* such as Nirvana, and (3) is an extinction caused by the absence of a productive cause *(apratisankhya-nirodha)*.

So much for the exposition of the elements of reality as enumerated in the seventy-five *dharmas*.

Some Peculiar Doctrines of the Kusha School

Several tenets peculiar to the Sarvastivada School which were finally established by Vasubandhu are to be noticed.

First of all, such distinctions as those between created *(sanskrita)* and uncreated *(asanskrita)*, manifested *(vijnapti)* and unmanifested *(avijnapti)*, determinate *(niyata)* and indeterminate *(aniyata)*, and concomitant with mind *(citta-samprayukta)* and non-concomitant with mind *(citta-viprayukta)*, ought to be carefully studied.

These seventy-five elements, though separate from one another, are found linked together in the actual world. This phenomenon is explained by the theory of causal relation or combination, sometimes called the Doctrine of the Ten Causes, in which six Chief Causes *(Hetu)* and four Sub-causes *(Pratyaya)* are assumed.

The six Chief Causes [51] are:

(1) The Active Cause *(Karana-hetu)*[52] as the leading factor in the production of an effect; (2) the Co-existent Cause *(Sahabhu-hetu)*[53]—more than two factors always working together; (3) the Similar-species Cause *(Sabhaga-hetu),*[54] a cause helping other causes of its kind; (4) the Concomitant Cause, *(Samprayukta-hetu),*[55] appearing at any time, from any motive, with regard to any fact, on any occasion and in any environment; (5) the Universally Prevalent Cause *(Sarvatraga-hetu),*[56] a cause always connected with wrong views, doubts or ignorance which produces all the errors of men; (6) the Cause Ripening in a Different Life *(Vipaka-hetu),*[57] a cause which produces its effect in a different life, as when retributions are obtained in the life after death.

The four Sub-causes [58] are as follows:

(1) The Cause-Sub-cause [59] which acts as Chief Cause *(Hetu-pratyaya),*[60] there being no distinction between the Chief Cause and the secondary cause; e.g., the water and the wind cause a wave; (2) the Immediate Sub-cause *(Samanantara-pratyaya),*[61] occurring in order, one after another—consequences coming immediately and equally after antecedents, as waves following one after another; (3) the Objective Sub-cause *(Alambana-pratyaya)*[62] which has an object or environment as a concurring cause; e.g., waves are conditioned by a basin, a pond, a river, the sea, or a boat; (4) the Upheaving Sub-cause *(Adhipati-pratyaya)*[63] which is the most powerful one to bring all the abiding causes to a culmination; e.g., the last wave that upsets a boat in a storm.

Of the above, the first, the Cause-Sub-cause which acts as chief cause, and the fourth, the Upheaving Sub-cause, are most important, and in order to elucidate these two, the six Chief Causes have been taught. To speak more plainly, the Active Cause is itself the Upheaving Sub-cause while the other five causes are identical with the Cause-Sub-cause. We must understand from this that the terms Cause and Sub-cause are not strictly defined ones. They concur either as chief or secondary cause as the occasion requires.

---

[51] 六因　　[52] 能作因　　[53] 俱有因　　[54] 同類因　　[55] 相應因
[56] 遍行因　　[57] 異熟因　　[58] 四緣　　[59] 因緣　　[60] 因緣　　[61] 次第緣
[62] 所緣緣　　[63] 增上緣

These four Causes roughly correspond to the Aristotelian four causes: (1) the Cause-Sub-cause as the 'efficient cause'; (2) the Immediate Sub-cause, the 'material cause'; (3) the Objective or Referent Sub-cause, the 'formal cause'; and (4) the Upheaving Sub-cause, the 'final cause.' A difference between the two groups of causes is that the Sub-cause in the Kusha School refers only to mental activities in which a similar function occurs immediately after another function has passed.

(4) Résumé

Buddhism assumes no substance, no abiding individual self, no soul, no Creator, no root principle of the universe. But this by no means implies that all beings and things do not exist. They do not exist with a substratum or a permanent essence in them, as people often think, but they do exist as causal relatives or combinations. All becomings, either personal or universal, originate from the principle of causation, and exist in causal combinations. The center of causation is one's own action, and the action will leave its latent energy which decides the ensuing existence. Accordingly, our past forms our present, and the present forms the future. This is the theory of self-creation.

We are, therefore, always creating and always changing. Men are ever floating on the waves of dynamic becoming called 'sansara,' the stream of life. Creating and changing ourselves as a whole, we go on. There should be no fear of the loss of identity, for our present self as a whole is an effect of the cause which we may call our past self; similarly in the future it is impossible that our self will be lost since we are necessarily self-creating beings. It is unreasonable to seek an unchanging essence in an all-changing being.

The seed-elements [64] are assumed to be four—Earth (hardness), Water (wetness), Fire (warmth) and Air (motion)—and all matters or forms are one or another combination of these four.

The formation of a personality and of the universe is similar, both consisting of matter and mind, the difference being that in a personality, mind is prevalent while in the universe matter is prevalent. Personality consists of five groups (skandha)[65]—Form (body), Perception, Conception, Volition and Consciousness (mind).[66] The Form or body, again, consists of earth, water, fire and air. Man is

---

[64] 四大種   [65] 蘊   [66] 色受想行識

72

therefore to be considered as one who has a form, perceives, conceives, wills and thinks. These are his actions *(karma)*[67] which altogether form his personal existence which has no other reality. A man is a temporary entity, and is only living in the contiguity of momentariness. In order to change his personality for better, the cultivation of his knowledge and wisdom is necessary, because the perfection of wisdom is the perfection of personality—Enlightenment.

The Kusha School, though it states that all things exist, is quite different from general naïve materialism, because, according to its theory, all things are *dharmas* (elements) which include mind as well as matter, all on an equal footing. It asserts the reality of all *dharmas* and yet it admits the theory of no substance, no duration and no bliss except Nirvana.

---

[67] 業

V. THE JŌJITSU SCHOOL
(THE SATYASIDDHI SCHOOL) [1]
(Sarvasunyavada, Sautrantika)

(Nihilism: *Non-ens* School)
[Hinayanistic]

(1) Preliminary

The Jōjitsu School is opposed to the Kusha School in that it asserts that nothing (matter or mind) exists at all. It is a Hinayanistic Negativism or Nihilism and is called Jōjitsu in Japanese (Satyasiddhi —Completion of Truth) after the title of the work by Harivarman [2] who lived in India (c. 250-350 A.D.) about a century before Vasubandhu.[3] The author says in his introductory note that he intended to elucidate the true purport of the sacred literature. From this we can infer that the title, 'Completion of Truth,' means the complete establishment of the truth propounded in the discourses of the Buddha himself.

Of the eighteen schools of Buddhism in India the Jōjitsu belongs to the Sautrantika [4] School which adheres to the original sacred scripture against the realistic Sarvastivada School,[5] some tenets of which are regarded by Vasubandhu as innovations of the Vaibhasikas [6] or those who adhere to the *Abhidharma* doctrine. If the realistic doctrine can be called a deviation from original Buddhism, this Nihilistic doctrine should be considered as a reversion to it. This Jōjitsu School, in a way, can be considered to be an orthodox school of Buddhism, especially because it is much nearer than the Realistic School to the original teaching of the Buddha: "No substance (*anatma*), no duration (*anitya*), and no bliss (*duhkha*) except Nirvana.

(2) Historical

We know little or nothing of the history of this school from the Indian side. Perhaps there never was a separate school called Satya-

---

[1] Ch'êng-shih 成實   [2] 訶梨跨摩, 師子鎧   [3] 世親 420-500 A.D.
[4] The word *Sautrantika* is derived from *Sutranta* (Scripture). 經量部
[5] 說一切有部   [6] 毘婆沙

siddhi in India. If there was a mother school to which Satyasiddhi belonged, it must have been one which adhered to the original discourse of the *sutras*. The Sutravadin, or Sautrantikavadin School, is mentioned as the latest offshoot among the eighteen schools of Buddhism.[7] Though Harivarman's connection with that school is not known, several points of the doctrine set forth by him can be traced to that school. It seems to have had an influential position in India, for it is referred to directly or indirectly by Vasubandhu, who adopted, in fact, the tenet of the school in some of the important points of contention, e.g., the problem of time.

The text, *Satyasiddhi*,[8] was translated into Chinese as early as 411-412 A.D. by Kumarajiva [9] who ordered some of his pupils to lecture on it. One of them, Sêng-jui [10] by name, while discoursing on it discovered that the author, Harivarman, had refuted the tenets of the Abhidharma School on several occasions—more than seven times. Hence we can assume that the two schools (Realistic and Nihilistic) used to hold antagonistic positions at or before the author's time.

Among the pupils of Kumarajiva there were two or three lines of transmission of this school between 411 and 498 A.D., and several important commentaries—twelve in all—were compiled. Many hundred lectures were delivered on the text all over China, each repeated twenty, thirty, forty, or even ninety times in one and the same place.

At first the text was taken by some authorities to be Mahayanistic, as by the three noted savants of the Liang dynasty (502-557), namely, Fa-yun,[11] Chih-tsang [12] and Sêng-min.[13] By other authorities such as Chih-i,[14] Chi-tsang [15] and Ching-ying [16] it was taken to be Hinayanistic. It was Tao-hsüan,[17] a famous pupil of Hiuen-tsang,[18] who finally settled the question by pronouncing that it was Hinayanistic and Sautrantic, because the Jōjitsu School had not gone beyond the level and influence of the Vaibhasika School.

---

[7] Rhys Davids, *Katha-vatthu*, pp. 3, 5. Vassilief, *History of Buddhism, Second Supplement*, p. 222.
[8] *Taishō*, No. 1464. 成實論   [9] 鳩摩羅什   [10] 僧叡   [11] 法雲 476-529
[12] 智藏 458-522   [13] 僧旻   [14] Chih-kai 智顗 531-597
[15] 吉藏 549-623   [16] 淨影   [17] 道宣 596-667   [18] Hsüan-tsang 玄奘 596-664

However, he recognized that it had a certain tendency toward the Mahayana doctrine.

The Jōjitsu School was introduced into Japan by Ekwan,[19] a learned priest of Kaoli, a state in Korea, who arrived at Hōryūji Temple in 625 A.D., and was appointed the first Buddhist prelate. Ever since that time the school has been studied in all Buddhist colleges and universities, but it was never recognized as an independent sect in Japan, always being treated as a subdivision of the Sanron School (The Three-Treatise School,[20] Mahayanistic Negativism) which will be explained in Chapter VII.

(3) Philosophical

The doctrine of the Satyasiddhi or Jōjitsu School is generally understood to be the void of self *(pudgala-sunyata)* and of elements *(sarva-dharma-sunyata)*.[21] It is, therefore, the twofold void [22] in contrast to the doctrine of the Realistic School (Kusha) which is the void of self *(pudgala-sunyata)* but the reality of elements *(dharma-ta)*. Personality which is made up of five groups (Form, Perception, Conception, Volition and Consciousness)[23] has no substratum and no individual self, just as an empty jar has no water or inner essence. Again, the universe consists of eighty-four elements, but all of them have no abiding reality at all, just as a jar itself has no permanent reality. Each of the five groups or the four great elements [24] (Earth, Water, Fire and Air) of which the universe is composed has no permanent, changeless substance. They are only temporary names.

According to Harivarman, all beings should ultimately come to the truth of extinction *(nirodha-satya)*, i.e., Nirvana, which is the final extinction. Thus voidness alone is the ultimate truth. This does not mean that this school denies the common-sense or phenomenal temporary existence of all beings, for it admits the five categories of all elements which are subdivided into eighty-four *dharmas* —instead of the seventy-five *dharmas* of the Kusha School. We see from the following table that its contents are not very different from those of the table of the Realists:

---

[19] 惠觀   [20] 三論   [21] 我法皆空   [22] 二空   [23] 色受想行識
[24] 四大種

The Eighty-four *Dharmas* [25]
of the Jōjitsu School

Created *Dharmas*

Non-created *Dharmas*
(3)
1-3 k

Forms (14)	Mind (1)	Mental Functions (49)	Elements Neither Substantial Nor Mental (17)
1-10 k		General, 1-10 k	
11 earth		Good, 1-10 k	1-2 k
12 water		Foul, 1-6 k	3 (k3, 7) life
13 fire		Evil, 1-2 k	4-6 k
14 wind		Minor Foul, 1-10 k	7 (k8) birth
		Indeterminate	8 old age
		1-8 k	9-11 k
		9 dislike	12 death
		10 pleasure	13-15 (k12-14)
		11 sleep	16 mediocrity
			17 things with no manifestation (k 1, 11)

The Satyasiddhi list of all the *dharmas* was certainly made after the model of the Realistic School. It is taught only in accordance with the worldly or common-sense or ordinary truth, for in the supreme truth [26] there will be no *dharmas* at all. Of these, the five objects of sense (form, sound, smell, taste and touch) are regarded relatively while the four elements (Earth, Water, Fire and Air) and the five sense organs are considered more transitory.

Analyzing those five objects the school reduces them to molecules, and further reduces them to even finer atoms, and by thus repeating the process the school finally attains the finest element which has an entirely different nature from the first objects. Going one step further, the school attains the Void. Thus the nihilism of this school is a 'destructed' or abstracted Void. In other words, the non-entity asserted in this school is simply an abstraction from entity, or merely an antithetic Void [27] as against existence. And this is not the synthetic Void or transcendental Void [28] advanced by the

---

[26] The letter 'k' indicates that the same items are also in the list of *Dharmas* given by the Sarvastivada or Realistic School in the previous chapter.

[26] 俗諦眞諦 [27] 偏空 [28] 不但空

Sanron School.[29] We may call it the doctrine of nothingness or *non-ens,* for it denies the existence of individual self and of all elements, matter and mind. To speak more clearly, mind (*citta*)[30] is not abiding and mental functions (*caitasika*)[31] have no independence; those *dharmas* or elements which are neither matter nor mind (*citta-viprayukta*)[32] are all temporary; the uncreated elements (*asanskrita*)[33] are also unreal. The doctrine of Void is here complete and it can be taken as total nihilism (*sarva-sunyata*)[34] if we follow the supreme truth. It is only from the point of view of worldly truth that they admit the existence of all things.

The doctrine of Void does not disavow the theory of the Chain of Causation, for our worldly existence is of causal combination, nor does it reject the principle of the stream of life (*sansara*), for it is necessary to explain the state of dynamic becoming.

We have seen already that the Realistic School assumes that the three worlds of time are real and so are all *dharmas* at any instant. Against this assertion, the nihilistic Jōjitsu School contends that the present only is real while the past and the future have no entity.[35] The school asserts, as all the other Mahayanistic schools do, the Void of all elements (*sarva-dharma-sunyata*)[36] as well as the void of self (*pudgala-sunyata*).[37] In addition, it recognizes the twofold truth —[38] the supreme truth and worldly truth. These are chiefly the reasons for which this school had long been treated as Mahayana in China.

To realize Total-Voidness, one must do away with the three attachments—attachment to the temporary[39] name, attachment to all elements[40] and attachment to the Void itself.[41] All beings and things, since they exist as the combination of causations, are given temporary names, because there is no way to designate their changing existence except by name. One must realize that it is useless to be attached to a self which is in truth only an appellation. One must first get rid of this attachment to one's temporary name. The elements are the basis on which the temporary name arises. To be rid of the attachment to the elements is to realize their voidness. When, as

---

[29] See Chapter VII.
[30] 心法 [31] 心所有法 [32] 心不相應法 [33] 無爲法 [34] 一切空
[35] 現在實有未來無體 [36] 法空 [37] 人空 [38] 二諦 [39] 假名心
[40] 法心 [41] 空心

78

above, we have realized the voidness of both the individual self and of the elements, we may seem to have attained Total-Voidness, but in truth there still remains the consciousness of the Void, and we are liable to be attached to the idea of the Void as much as if it were something existent. This Void-consciousness can be removed when one enters into the Meditation of Extinction (*nirodha-samapatti*)[42] or into Perfect Nirvana. The former is, as in an *arhat,* a state in which all passions have been done away with, and the latter is,[43] as in the case of the Buddha, the state in which all conditions of life, matter and mind, have been extinguished by the virtue of Enlightenment as darkness is extinguished by light, because the Buddha had attained the state of perfect Nirvana which is in itself devoid of any distinguishing qualities and he had transcended the 'four arguments.'

In India it is thought that there are only four arguments on any problem—'Yes', No,' 'Either Yes or No according to the circumstance' and 'Neither Yes nor No, meaning out of the question.' The state in which the Buddha is said to have transcended the four arguments is called the Buddha's True Body,[44] and the body of the Buddha which appeared in this world is called his Transformed Body.[45] This Transformed Body possessed all the attributes of a man in its forms, and followed all the ways of a human being, but he was a man of perfect knowledge and wisdom. In the elucidation of this point the Jōjitsu School relies upon the Mahayana *sutras* such as the *Prajna-paramita,*[46] the *Saddharma-pundarika,*[47] or the *Parinirvana.*[48] This was another reason why this school had long been thought to belong to Mahayana.

The way by which one attains the final state constitutes, as usual, the objects of learning—Precept (*sila*),[49] Meditation (*dhyana*),[50] and Wisdom (*prajna*).[51] The latter two are especially recommended to be seriously pursued.

---

[42] 滅盡定
[43] This is true especially in Mahayana.
[44] 眞身　[45] 化身　[46] 大般若波羅密多經　[47] 妙法蓮華經
[48] 大涅槃經　[49] 戒　[50] 定　[51] 慧

VI. THE HOSSŌ SCHOOL
(THE MERE-IDEATION SCHOOL)[1]
(Vijnaptimatrata, Yogacara)

(Idealism: Both *Ens* and *Non-ens* School)
[Quasi-Mahayanistic]

(1) Preliminary

Hossō *(Dharma-laksana)* means 'Characteristics of *Dharma*,' Dharma here denoting things substantial and mental (matter and minds), for the chief object of this school is to investigate the nature and qualities of all existences. The first founder of the school was Asanga[2]—an elder brother of Vasubandhu[3]—who was the author of the text *Yogacara-bhumi*.[4] In India the school was formerly called the Yogacara,[5] which means the practice of self-concentration.

Vasubandhu, when he was converted to Mahayana by his brother and succeeded in systematizing the philosophical views of the Yoga-cara School, designated the tenet of the school as Vijnaptimatra (Mere Ideation), attributing the existence of all the outer world to inner ideation—in short, holding that nothing but ideation exists. As to ontology this school stands between the realistic and nihilistic schools, given above. It adheres neither to the doctrine that all things exist, because it takes the view that nothing outside the mind (mental activity) exists, nor to the doctrine that nothing exists, because it asserts that ideations do exist. It firmly adheres to the doctrine of the mean, neither going to the extreme of the theory of existence *(ens)* nor to that of non-existence *(non-ens)*. This school can, therefore, be called the 'Ideal-realism' or 'Ideation Theory.' The academic name of this school is Yuishĭki (Wei-shih, Mere Ideation),[6] or Vijnap-timatra (Ideation only), Shōzō-gaku,[7] a Study of the Nature *(Sva-bhava)*[8] and Characteristics *(Laksana)*[9] of dharmas or elements.

The Middle Path which the Buddha himself taught against the two extremes of the hedonistic worldly life and the pessimistic ascetic life has now been promoted to the middle path between the two onto-logical views of the Hinayana schools.

---

[1] Fa-hsiang 法相   [2] 無著 c. 410-500 A.D.   [3] 世親 c. 420-500 A.D.
[4] 瑜伽師地論 *Taishō*, No. 1579.   [5] 瑜伽   [6] 唯識   [7] 性相學
[8] 性   [9] 相

For several reasons this school is considered to be still within the range of the formalistic, realistic Hinayana. It aims at an analysis of the phenomenal world, and is called a Quasi-Mahayana.[10] This we shall see later.

(2) Historical

The Shê-lun (Samparigraha) School,[11] the forerunner of Fa-hsiang (Dharma-Laksana or Hossō) School:

A representative work of Mahayana idealism named the *Mahayana-samparigraha* (Acceptance of the Great Vehicle) [12] was written by Asanga in the fifth century, annotated by Vasubandhu (420-500), and translated into Chinese in 531 by Buddhasanta, in 563 by Paramartha, and again by Hiuen-tsang during 648-649. Of these, the second, Paramartha's translation, laid the foundation of the Shê-lun School in China.

Paramartha,[13] a native of Ujjayini, probably connected with Valabhi University, a center of Buddhist learning, came to China in 548, and between that time and 557 translated thirty-two texts. He is also said to have written more than forty works—altogether amounting to two hundred Chinese volumes. His chief object was to propagate the doctrine of the *Abhidharma-kosa* [14] and the *Mahayana-samparigraha*. [15] His literary and religious activity seems to have greatly influenced the Chinese mind of the time as is testified by the fact that he had many able pupils under him.

Paramartha founded the realistic Kosa School, [16] as we have seen before, and the Samparigraha (Shê-lun) School. His activities can be compared only with Kumarajiva [17] who came before him and Hiuen-tsang [18] who came after him.

In studying the Shê-lun School we should know first the contents of the text, *Mahayana-samparigraha*. This text, with the commentary on it by Vasubandhu, is the first and the foremost comprehensive work which sets forth the doctrine of Mere Ideation and is a representative compendium of the Idealistic school. The text dwells chiefly on the ten special characteristics of Mahayana.

The contents are: 1. The store-consciousness *(Alaya-vijnana)*[19] from which all elements are manifested; 2. The theory of mere idea-

---

[10] 權大乘　　[11] 攝論宗　　[12] 攝大乘論 *Taishō*, Nos. 1592-1597
[13] 眞諦 499-569　　[14] 阿毗達磨俱舍論　　[15] 攝論　　[16] 俱舍宗
[17] 鳩摩羅什 344-413　　[18] Hsüan-tsang 玄奘 596-664　　[19] 阿賴耶識

81

tion—all elements have either the nature of interdependence, or that of imagination,[20] or that of real truth;[21] 3. The attainment of the insight of mere ideation; 4. The six perfections *(paramita)*;[22] 5. The ten stages *(bhumi)*[23] of the holy personages; 6. Moral precepts *(sila)*;[24] 7. Meditation *(samadhi)*;[25] 8. Perfect wisdom *(prajna)*;[26] 9. The higher knowledge without discrimination; 10. The threefold body[27] of the Buddha.

When all things are reflected on our mind, our discriminating or imaginating power is already at work. This is called our consciousness *(vijnana)*.[28] Since the consciousness co-ordinating all reflected elements stores them, it is called the store-consciousness or ideation-store—I prefer to use the word ideation-store. The ideation-store itself is an existence of causal combination, and in it the pure and the tainted elements are causally combined or intermingled. When the ideation-store begins to move and descend to the everyday world, then we have the manifold existence that is only an imagined world. The ideation-store, which is the seed-consciousness, is the conscious center and the world manifested by ideation is its environment. It is only from the Buddha's Perfect Enlightenment that pure ideation flashes out.

This pure ideation can purify the tainted portion of the ideation-store and further develop its power of understanding. The world of imagination and the world of interdependence will be brought to the real truth *(parinispanna)*. This having been attained, the seed-store, as consciousness, will disappear altogether and ultimately will reach the state where there is no distinction between subject and object. The knowledge so gained has no discrimination *(avikalpa-jnana)*.[29] This ultimate state is the Nirvana of No Abode *(apratisthita-nir-vana)*,[30] that is to say, the attainment of perfect freedom—not being bound to one place.

According to this text the Buddha has a threefold body:

1. The Dharma- or Ideal-body[31] whose nature is Principle and Wisdom; 2. The Sambhoga-, Enjoyment- or Reward-body[32] which appears only for the *Bodhisattva*; 3. The Nirvana- or Transformation-body[33] which manifests itself for ordinary persons for their worship.

---

[20] 分別性　[21] 眞實性　[22] 波羅密多　[23] 十地　[24] 戒　[25] 定
[26] 慧　[27] 三身　[28] 識　[29] 無分別智　[30] 無住涅槃　[31] 法身
[32] 報身　[33] 化身

The *Alaya* (store) is the consciousness in which the true and the false unite [34]—practically the same as in the theory set forth in the *Awakening of Faith* [35] of Asvaghosa.[36] The Shê-lun School regards the *Alaya*-store that has become pure and taintless as Thusness *(Tathata)* and gives it a special name *Amala-vijnana* (Taintless Consciousness). [37] It is designated as the Ninth Consciousness. Accordingly the conscious organs recognized in this school founded by Paramartha are as follows:

The Ninefold Consciousness:
  The First Five Consciousnesses:
    Visual consciousness [38]
    Auditory consciousness [39]
    Odor consciousness [40]
    Taste consciousness [41]
    Touch consciousness [42]
  The four Central Consciousnesses:
    Sixth, Sense-center Consciousness [43]
    Seventh, Thought-center Consciousness [44]
    Eighth, Ideation-store Consciousness [45]
    Ninth, Taintless Consciousness [46]

The Shê-lun School in this state was replaced by the new Fa-hsiang (Hossō) School which was taught by Hiuen-tsang and founded by his pupil Ki (Kuei-chi),[47] 632-682 A. D.

The Fa-hsiang (Dharmalaksana, Hossō)[48] School:

In India there seem to have been three lines of transmission of Yogacara Idealism after the death of Vasubandhu. The first was the line of Dignaga,[49] fifth century, Agotra,[50] and Dharmapala [51] whose center of transmission was Nalanda University. Silabhadra of Nalanda and his Chinese pupil Hiuen-tsang belong to this line. The second was the line of Gunamati [52] and Sthiramati [53] whose seat of trans-

---

[34] 真妄和合識
[35] 大乗起信論 *Taishō*, No. 1666. English translation by Timothy Richard and Yang Wen-hwui: *The Awakening of Faith in the Mahayana Doctrine*, 1894; and by D. T. Suzuki: *Asvaghosha's Discourse on the Awakening of Faith in the Mahayana*, Chicago, 1900.
[36] 馬鳴 [37] 無垢識 [38] 眼識 [39] 耳識 [40] 鼻識 [41] 舌識 [42] 身識
[43] 意識 [44] 末那識 [45] 阿頼耶識 [46] 無垢識 [47] 窺基 [48] 法相
[49] Diknaga 陳那 [50] 無性 [51] 法護 439-507 [52] 德慧 [53] 安慧

mission seems to have been Valabhi University; Paramartha the founder of the Shệ-lun School in China belongs to it. The third was the line of Nanda [54] whose tenet was followed by Paramartha, and Jayasena [55] who instructed Hiuen-tsang on certain questions. This last line of transmission did not flourish much in India and seems to have soon disappeared.

Hiuen-tsang, while still at home in China, heard lectures on the *Samparigraha* doctrine from more than seven different teachers. He was actually an earnest student of the Idealistic School. However, the opinions of his teachers varied greatly and, since he could not see which was the best to follow, he decided to go to India where he hoped to find an able instructor. In 629 he started from Ch'angan [56] for India. In 629 he was still in Karakobjo in Sinkiang. In 632 or later he arrived in Nalanda near Rajagriha, where Silabhadra, 106 years of age, was the head of the university.

Hiuen-tsang studied under Silabhadra the important doctrines of Buddhism—first the reformed idealism of Vasubandhu in his *Vijnaptimatrata* and then the realism of the same author in his *Abhidharma-kosa*. After seventeen years' sojourn in India, he came home in 645 and translated Dharmapala's *Vijnapti-matrata-siddhi* (Completion of Mere Ideation) [57] in addition to seventy-four other texts.

Hiuen-tsang's able pupil Ki seems to have monopolized the transmission of the idealistic doctrine. The Fa-hsiang (Hossō) School was actually systematized and founded chiefly by Ki. Ki's two important works *Fa-yüan-i-lin-chang* [58] and *Wei-shih-shu-chi* [59] are the fundamental texts of this school.

Dōshō, [60] 628-700, a Japanese priest, was sent to China in 653. He studied under Hiuen-tsang for more than ten years, living in the same room with Ki. The teacher specially instructed him in Meditation (Zen) and recommended that he propagate its practice to the East. On the eve of his departure he received from the teacher several sutras, treatises and commentaries on the works on Idealism. On his return home, Dōshō at once set out to transmit the Hossō doctrine

---

[54] 難陀　[55] 勝軍　[56] 長安
[57] 成唯識論 *Taishō*, No. 1585. French translation by L. de la Vallée Poussin: *La Siddhi de Hiuen-tsang*, 2 Vols., Paris, 1928.
[58] 大乗法苑義林章 *Taishō*, No. 1861.
[59] 成唯識論述記 *Taishō*, No. 1830.　[60] 道昭

in the monastery of Gwangōji. His first pupil was Gyōgi [61] (667-748).

This first transmission was called that of the Southern Monastery. The second transmission was by Chitsū [62] and Chitatsu [63] who were sent to China in 654 and who also received an earnest training from Hiuen-tsang and Ki. The third transmission was by Chihō,[64] a Korean priest from Simla, together with his friends Chiran [65] and Chio [66] who were in China for a while and studied under Hiuentsang. They arrived in Japan in 703 and transmitted the idealistic doctrine to Giyen,[67] a pupil of Gyōgi. The fourth transmission was by the learned Gembō [68] who was sent to China in 616 and was instructed by Chih-chou,[69] a pupil of Ki. He stayed abroad for nearly twenty years and in 735 came home and taught the doctrine in the monastery called Kōbukuji. He transmitted the teaching to Genju [70] who devoted himself to its propagation This is called the transmission of the Northern Monastery, and is generally accepted as the orthodox line.

Thus Japan has received the orthodox teaching sacrosanct from first hand authorities of the Indian and Chinese idealistic school, and with the Japanese even now it is the chief subject of Buddhist learning.

(3) Philosophical

The idealistic school of Vasubandhu is a reformed Yogacara system and its fundamental text is Vasubandhu's *Vijnapti-matratatrimsika*,[71] a versified text on the theory of mere ideation in thirty stanzas, of which the first twenty-four are devoted to the special character *(svalaksana)* of all *dharmas,* the next to the nature *(svabhava)* of all *dharmas,* and the last four to the stages of the noble personages.

The Hossō School, though idealistic, is different from the Shélun School which was representative idealism and was later replaced by the Fa-hsiang (Hossō) School in China. The Hossō idealists profess to have transmitted the orthodox system of Vasubandhu, but in reality this is rather uncertain. Vasubandhu's *Trimsika* was

---

[61] 行基 [62] 智通 [63] 智達 [64] 智鳳 [65] 智鸞 [66] 智雄
[67] 義淵 d. 724 [68] 玄昉 [69] 智周 688-723 [70] 玄宗 723-797
[71] 唯識三十論 French translation by S. Levi: *Matériaux pour L'étude du système Vijnaptimatra* Paris, 1932.

annotated by ten authorities of which Hiuen-tsang and his pupil Ki followed chiefly the opinions of Dharmapala of Nalanda. The result was summed up in thirty Chinese volumes *(chüans)* of the *Vijnapti-matrata-siddhi* which is the fundamental treatise of the school. Thus the Hossō idealists of China accepted Vasubandhu's opinions through Dharmapala's interpretation which may or may not be exactly in accordance with the original author's purports.

Dharmapala recognized the distinction between the specific character *(laksana)* of *dharma* and the nature *(svabhava)* of *dharma,* i.e., Thusness *(Tathata)*. His point of view was that of what is called the 'worldly truth' *(laukika-satya)*[72] and not the 'highest truth' *(paramartha-satya)*.[73] The worldly truth assumes that fact and principle always go 'parallel' and can never be synthetically identified. Such a view is not quite Mahayanistic but is half Hinayanistic, and on that account this school is generally classified as quasi-Mahayanistic.

The doctrine of the Hossō School chiefly concerns itself with the facts or specific characters *(laksana)* of all elements on which the theory of idealism was built in order to elucidate that no element is separate from ideation.[74] Although it is usually expressed by the saying that all *dharmas* are mere ideation or that there is nothing but ideation, the real sense is quite different. It is idealistic because all elements are in some way or other always connected with ideation.

As to the Ideation Theory of the school, an argument should be in accordance with the Sacred Word and also with the dialectic reason. The Ideation Theory that the three worlds exist only in ideation can be proved from the Word of the Buddha in the *Avatansaka Sutra*.[75]

But how can this be proved logically? The outer world does not exist but the internal ideation presents appearance as if it were an outer world. We know this from the fact that we can nowhere discover any self or element that is real. What we consider real is not real but only an outward manifestation of ideation. The whole world is therefore of either illusory or causal nature and no permanent reality can be found. But, one may ask, if everything is produced from ideation, how can anything be produced definitely in

---

[72] 世俗諦(理世論)　　[73] 第一義諦　　[74] 離識無別法
[75] 華嚴經 *Taishō*, Nos. 278 and 279.

one place and at one time and not everywhere and at any time according as one ideates? Why, again, can all beings perceive one and the same thing and their enjoyment of it have similar effect?

The customary answer brought forward by this school is very simple: even in a dream which has no actuality one sees a definite place at a certain time with all its surroundings. In it one may even have the bodily effect of sweating, crying or dancing. Various men, again, see similar definite objects, just as several departed spirits have before their eyes one and the same river which changes itself to filth the moment they attempt to drink from it. This is because they have had similar past actions (karma).[76]

In this way all sorts of arguments and refutations are given in the Idealistic treatises, but I do not think it necessary to go into detail here.[77]

From the table of all dharmas given below,[78] one will notice that they are divided into five categories: 1. Mind or Consciousness (Vijnana,[79] 8 dharmas); 2. Mental functions (Caitasika,[80] 51 dharmas); 3. Form (Rupa,[81] 11 dharmas); 4. Things not associated with mind (Citta-viprayukta,[82] 24 dharmas); 5. Non-created elements (Asanskrita,[83] 6 dharmas). Altogether they amount to one hundred dharmas.[84]

Among them, 'form' is an outward manifestation of consciousness; 'things not associated with mind' is a name given to a partial process of the conscious manifestation; and the 'non-created' is the static nature of consciousness. All of these have some relation to the mind. There is nothing separate from ideation.

The eight consciousnesses (mind) are all separate. The first five constitute sense-consciousness (Vijnana),[85] the sixth is the sense-center (Mano-vijnana),[86] the seventh is the thought-center or self-consciousness (Manas),[87] and the eighth is the store-consciousness (Citta).[88] By nature all of these consciousnesses are dependent

---

[76] 業
[77] See Vasubandhu's *Vimsatika* 唯識二十論 , *Taishō*, No. 1590. English translation by Clarence H. Hamilton, *Wei Shih Er Shih Lun or The Treatise in Twenty Stanzas on Representation-only*, New Haven, 1938.
[78] Before page 93.
[79] 心法　[80] 心所有法　[81] 色法　[82] 心不相應行法　[83] 無爲法
[84] 百法　[85] 前五識　[86] 意識　[87] 末那識　[88] 阿賴耶識

on something else, i.e., cause *(paratantra-laksana)*,[89] but they are not of mere imagination *(parikalpita-laksana)*.[90] The assumption of the separate reality of the eight consciousnesses is Dharmapala's special tenet and nowhere else in Buddhism can it be seen, not even in Hinayana.

Each of the consciousnesses has four functional divisions [91] of interdependent nature: 1. the objective or the seen portion *(laksana-bhaga)*,[92] 2. the subjective or the seeing portion *(darsana-bhaga)*,[93] 3. the self-witness or the self-assuring portion *(saksatkari-bhaga)*;[94] 4. the rewitnessing of self-witness or the reassuring portion.[95] The objective is a shadow image of an outer object reflected on the mind-face, and the subjective illumines, sees and experiences it. Now, who will know that the subject has seen the object or the shadow-image? It is the mind itself that will see and acknowledge the subjective function. This function of cognition is called the Self-witness, without which no knowledge can be obtained. The Rewitnessing of Self-witness completes the mental faculty. These are the four mental functions.

For instance, a sheet of paper presented in mind is the objective, i.e., the shadow-image of it. The subjective is a measuring instrument to see its length and width. The self-witnessing function cognizes how long and how wide it is, according to that measure. The rewitnessing function recognizes the accuracy of that measurement. Because there is this mutual recognition, no other function is needed.

Among the Indian Yogacarins, Dignaga and Agotra do not admit the fourth rewitnessing function in addition to the other three functions. Dharmapala and his successor, Silabhadra [96] of Nalanda, hold the theory of four functional divisions, yet they think that either the three or the four will do, because the fourfold analysis is only a more minute division of three. Sthiramati, though he allows the existence of three functions, admits in fact only the one function of self-witness which is the function of the consciousness itself.[97] According to him the subjective and the objective are by nature a false imagination arising from the consciousness itself, while the self-witness, i.e., the consciousness itself, is a causal existence and has reality. Nanda assumes the existence of only two functions, the

[89] 依他起相　[90] 遍計所執相　[91] 四分　[92] 相分　[93] 見分
[94] 自證分　[95] 證自證分　[96] 戒賢　[97] 自體分

subjective and the objective. The former is the main function and the latter originates from it, thus completing the theory of mere ideation.

The Hossō School regards both the three and the four functions as orthodox. The objective portion of mental faculty is simply a shadow-image of the outer world and belongs to the subjective domain in the ordinary sense of the word. The original substance [98] from which the shadow issues is quite separate from sense-data and thought-data.

The objects of the outer world (visaya) which throw shadows on the mind-face are of three species:[99] 1. The object-domain of nature[100] or immediate perception, i.e., the object that has the original substance and presents it as it is, just as the five objects of senses—form, sound, smell, taste and touch—are perceived as they are. The first five sense-consciousnesses and the eighth, the store-consciousness, perceive the object in this way. 2. The object-domain of mere shadow[101] or illusion. The shadow-image appears simply from one's own imagination and has no real existence. Of course, it has no original substance as a ghost which does not exist at all. Only the sixth, the sense-center, functions on it and imagines it to be. 3. The object-domain with the original substance.[102] The object has an original substance and yet is not perceived as it is. When the seventh, the thought-center, looks at the subjective function of the eighth, the store-center, it considers that it is self or ego. The subjective function of the eighth, the store-center, has its original substance (entity) but it is not seen as it is by the seventh consciousness and is regarded to be self or an abiding ego, which is in reality an illusion since it is not self at all.

The theory of three species of the object-domain may have originated from Nalanda but the four-line memorial verse current in the school is probably of Chinese origin. It runs as follows:

1. The object of nature does not follow the mind (=subjective) . . . The subject may be good or evil but the object is always neutral.

2. The mere shadow only follows the seeing (=subjective) . . . The object is as the subject imagines.

3. The object with the original substance.

---

[98] 本質   [99] 三類境   [100] 性境   [101] 獨影境   [102] 帶質境

4. The character, seed, etc. are various as occasions require . . .
The object has an original substance, but the subject does not see
it as it is.[103]

This four-line verse explains how the three species of the object-
domain are related to the subjective function and the outer original
substance. One may be puzzled in understanding how an idealism
can have the so-called original substance. We should not forget that
though it is an outer substance it is after all a thing manifested out
of ideation.

The eighth, the *Alaya*-consciousness itself, is not an unchangeable fixed substance *(dravya)* but is itself ever changing instantaneously *(ksanika)* and repeatedly; and, being 'perfumed' or having
impressions made upon it by cognition and action, it becomes habi-
tuated and efficient in manifestation. It is like a torrent of water
which never stops at one place for two consecutive moments. It is
only with reference to the continuity of the stream that we can
speak of a river.

That efficiency or energy to produce a result is called a 'seed'
as it is stored in a seed-bed and sprouts in time when a cause occasions
it. From the stored seeds come the object-world corresponding to
the manifestation of former cognition and action. Hence the stock
saying:

> A seed *(bija)* produces a manifestation *(samudacara)* ;
> A manifestation perfumes a seed;
> The three elements (seed, manifestation and perfume)
>   turning on and on;
> The cause and the effect at one and the same time.[104]

And another saying:

> A seed produces a seed;
> The cause and the effect differing in time.[105]

Thus the world of life and the world of 'vessel to live in' are
instantaneously issued from the *Alaya*-store and restored to it at
once; this constitutes our daily life of error and illusion.

The old seeds latent in the eighth store-consciousness exist from
time immemorial. These are called the original seeds.[106] The new
seeds are perfumed afresh from time to time. These are called the

---

[103] 心境不隨心　獨影唯隨見　帶質通情本　性種等隨應
[104] 種子生現行　現行薫種子　三法輾轉　因果同時
[105] 種子生種子　因果異時　[106] 本有種子

90

newly perfumed seeds.[107] The old and new seeds together produce all manifestations of an error-stricken existence of life. Therefore, the eighth, the store-consciousness may seem to be a false-natured or unreal one. However, it contains a taintless seed which is attached to it. As it grows up by self-culture, etc., it gradually subjugates the false nature of the eighth consciousness and as the result of this subjugation the life of error becomes a refined one until the highest stage of enlightenment is attained.

The Hossō School takes the nature *(svabhava)*[108] of *dharma* to be quite distinct from the specific character *(laksana)*[109] of *dharma*. Thus the principle is quite different from the fact, that is to say, the nature stands 'parallel' to the specific character, and so does the principle with facts. The parallel lines will never meet. The specific character or the fact, or in other words, the manifestations of all elements, are the chief concern of this school. Hence the name *Dharma-laksana (Hossō)*.[110] It is distinguished clearly from the schools which treat mainly the nature of *dharma* or the principle, i.e., the *Dharma-svabhava (Hosshō)*.[111]

The Hossō School, therefore, does not admit that all beings have the Buddha-nature. The five species of men are all separate and distinct.[112] There is a species of men who can never become a Buddha *(icchantika)*.[113] Therefore, according to this school, the three vehicles *(Sravaka-yana*[114]—Teaching for Buddha's direct disciple, *Pratyeka-Buddha-yana*[115]—Teaching for Buddha-for-himself, *Bodhisattva-yana*[116]—Teaching for the would-be Buddha) are real, because they belong to the actual world, i.e., they correspond to the conditions of the actual world of men. The *Ekayana* (One Vehicle leading to Buddhahood) is for 'convenience' and is temporary.[117] Exactly the opposite holds good in other schools. Further, they do not recognize the identification of the nature with the specific character of *dharmas*. So, Thusness *(Tathata)*[118] as the nature of all *dharmas* is in no way connected with the specific character of *dharmas*. The thing as in itself is separate forever from the thing for us. Thusness or Suchness will never be perfumed or influenced by the actual life. Noumenon has no relation at all with phenomenon. This school rejects the theory that Thusness receives any perfume or

---

[107] 新薫種子　[108] 法性　[109] 法相　[110] 法相　[111] 法性　[112] 五姓各別
[113] 一闡提　[114] 聲聞乘　[115] 緣覺乘　[116] 菩薩乘　[117] 三實一權
[118] 眞如

influence [119] and that it manifests itself as a causal consequence.[120] It firmly holds that Thusness lies ever in a static congelation and will never become dynamic in the sphere of *dharmas*.[121]

The schools which lay importance on the nature *(svabhava)* are attacked mercilessly by this Hossō School. Such a doctrine as set forth in the *Awakening of Faith* that Thusness manifests itself according to a cause either pure or tainted is the main object of their rigorous attack. But this is only the passive side of the argument as to the purport of Thusness. We will study the positive side of the argument toward the end of the chapter.

The Shê-lun School takes a somewhat different attitude on this point.[122] In the *Awakening of Faith* the author who is said to be Asvaghosa starts from Thusness which is somehow tainted by ignorance and takes the store-consciousness to be of a mixed nature, true and false, while the Hossō School starts from the world of phenomena that originates from the ideation-store, the eighth consciousness being of an unreal, false nature. The store-consciousness may in some way have a taintless seed attached to it and eventually develop it to enlightenment. The Shê-lun School, siding with the author of the *Awakening of Faith,* goes a step further and admits the existence of a ninth taintless consciousness *(amala-vijnana)*.[123] Thus all seem to assume the existence of two elements, true and false, in the store-consciousness. But still the Hossō School differs from the rest in treating Thusness as the nature and the store-consciousness as the characteristic of *dharmas*. Thusness is the ultimate entity *(parinispanna)*[124] while the store-consciousness is of the quality dependent on another, i.e., cause *(paratantra)*.[125]

Parinispanna, paratantra and *parikalpita*[126] are all called *laksana*[127] in Sanskrit, but in the case of *parinispanna* it is not *laksana* but is *alaksana*[128]—'Bereft of specific character,' i.e., *Svabhava*.[129]

THE ONE HUNDRED ELEMENTS IN FIVE CATEGORIES [130]

The Hossō School, though idealistic, takes the model of the analytical method used in the Realistic and Nihilistic Schools, and classifies the world of becoming into five categories which are subdivided

[119] 真如受薫　[120] 隨緣起動　[121] 真如凝然不作諸法　[122] See above—historical.　[123] 無垢識　[124] 圓成實　[125] 依他起　[126] 遍計所執　[127] 相　[128] 無相　[129] 自性　[130] 五位百法

into one hundred *dharmas*. The list is much more minute than the other tables. It is given on page 94a.

A special point in the table is that mind is divided into eight consciousnesses, each being a separate reality. No other school of Buddhism has such a doctrine. In addition to the first five mental faculties (eye-, ear-, nose-, tongue-, skin-senses or consciousnesses) there are the sixth, the sense-center, a general perceiving organ or conscious mind, the seventh, the thought-center or the self-conscious mind, and the eighth, the store-center or store-consciousness. The last two are called *Manas* (thought) [131] and *Alaya* (store-consciousness). [132]

Among these eight consciousnesses the former six constitute the sense-consciousness *(Vijnana)*, [133] the seventh is thought *(Manas)* [134] and the eighth is mind *(Citta)*. [135] To put it more plainly, the first five consciousnesses are simply the senses; the sixth, the sense-center, forms conceptions out of the perceptions obtained from the outside; the seventh, the thought-center, thinks, wills and reasons on a self-centered basis; the eighth, the store-center, stores seeds, i.e., keeps efficiency or energy for all manifestations. The sixth, the seventh and the eighth always act on one another, for the sixth is the general center of perception and cognition inwardly which acts outwardly on the basis of the thought-center which in turn acts on the basis of the all-storing center. The *Manas* is responsible for self-consciousness, self-interest or selfish motives. The subjective function of the eighth is seen and regarded by the seventh as self *(atman)* though in reality there is no such thing as self. This false idea pollutes all thoughts and gives rise to an idea of individual or personal ego or soul.

According to the Buddhist idea, all things are 'born from mind' *(manoja)* and 'consist of mind' *(manomaya),* and especially in the idealistic theory what we generally call existence proceeds from consciousness. Accordingly, everything that exists is classified as to the nature of its origin into three species:

First, those of false existence [136] which are at the same time bereft of an original substance *(adravya),* just as a ghost that exists merely in one's imagination but not in reality.

---

[131] 末那識　　[132] 阿賴耶識　　[133] 識　　[134] 意　　[135] 心　　[136] 妄有性

93

Second, those of temporary or transitory existence,[137] having no permanent character *(asvabhava),* as a house that is built by timbers, stones, tiles, etc. It exists only by a combination of causes, and is not self-existent. It has no permanent reality.

Third, those of true existence,[138] that is to say, non-existent in the highest sense of the word, bereft of all false and temporary nature *(alaksana).* This is, in truth, not non-existence but transcendental existence.

Technically these three [139] are called (1) character of sole imagination *(parikalpita-laksana);*[140] (2) character of dependence upon others *(paratantra-laksana);*[141] (3) character of ultimate reality *(parinispanna-laksana).*[142]

Of these the first exists in mere imagination, the second only in causal combination, and the third as the substratum (so to speak) of all and can only be known by a person of supreme knowledge. This third aspect of reality must not be interpreted too positively—it represents merely the remainder after the elimination of the first two.

This classification of all *dharmas* is in accordance with the viewpoint of *ens* (being), but when viewed from the point of view of *non-ens* (non-being), these three species will be the three of non-specific reality *(abhava).*[143] The first is non-existent as regards the characteristics *(laksana)*[144]—no substance, no quality at all. The second is non-existent as regards the origination *(jati)*[145]—no birth, no self-existent nature, no existence though it looks like an existence. The third is non-existent in the highest sense *(paramartha)*[146] —it is the true non-reality, far transcending all specific characters and conditions of life. This is Thusness, the true noumenon,[147] and the true nature of *dharmas.*

According to the Hossō School it is untainted knowledge to realize that all the phenomenal world with all beings is but a temporary and illusory existence [148] manifested by ideation [149] on the ultimate perfect 'reality' *(parinispanna).* The Middle Path, the Golden Mean *(Madhyama-pratipad)*[150] of the Buddha is now identified with Thusness which is the ultimate reality just mentioned. How

---

[137] 假有性　[138] 眞有性　[139] 三性　[140] 遍計所執性　[141] 依他起性
[142] 圓成實性　[143] 三無性　[144] 相無性　[145] 生無性　[146] 勝義無性
[147] 實相　[148] 假有　[149] 唯識所現　[150] 中道

the meaning of the Middle is established is explained by the mutual relation of the three species of elements. The first species of imagination does not exist, and therefore is void.[151] The second species of causal combination does exist, and therefore is temporarily real.[152] The Middle Path is, therefore, neither real nor void.[153] Thus the ultimate 'reality' of the third transcends voidness and reality.

Thusness transcends all the ideas of *ens* or *non-ens*. We can say 'It exists,' but it is not a phenomenal existence. Or we can say 'It does not exist,' but it is not a phenomenal non-existence. In contradistinction to phenomenal existence we call it *non-ens,* and to avoid a confusion with phenomenal nothingness we call it *ens.* Consequently we are obliged to designate it the '*true non-ens*'[154] and the '*true ens.*'[155] The true *non-ens* is *sunyata* (absence of speciality) in the highest sense and the true *ens* is *parinispannatva* (ultimate reality).[156] All this is beyond the reach of human knowledge.

When one's knowledge and wisdom have been perfected by self-culture, the eight consciousnesses will turn into perfect wisdom as follows:

The first five consciousnesses will become the wisdom that accomplishes all that should be performed.[157]

The sixth, the sense-center *(Mano-vijnana)*, will become the wisdom of good observation.[158]

The seventh, the thought-center *(Manas),* will become the wisdom of equanimity.[159]

The eighth, the ideation-store, will become the 'wisdom of magnificent mirror.'[160] These constitute the fourfold wisdom of the Buddha.

As we have seen before, the Kusha School had the theory of 'causation through action-influence.'[161] The Hossō School has replaced it with the theory of 'causation through mere ideation.'[162] This indicates a development of the causation theory, because action is nothing but a result of ideation and the causation of an idealistic school ought to be built on the assumption of mind-action as the origin of all *dharmas*.

Thus Hossō idealism is seen to be an elucidation of the causation theory of ideation.

---

[151] 空　　[152] 有　　[153] 非有非空　　[154] 眞空　　[155] 眞有　　[156] 妙有
[157] 成所作智　　[158] 妙觀察智　　[159] 平等性智　　[160] 大圓鏡智
[161] 業感緣起　　[162] 賴耶緣起唯識緣起

VII. THE SANRON SCHOOL
(THE THREE-TREATISE SCHOOL)[1]
(Sarvasunyavada, Madhyamika)

(Negativism: *Neither Ens nor Non-ens* School)
[Quasi-Mahayanistic]

(1) Preliminary

The Indian name of the Mahayanistic Negativism is Madhya-mika, the 'doctrine of the Middle Path,' or Sunyatavada, the 'Theory of Negativity'[2] or 'Relativity.' In China and Japan this school is known by the appellation of San-lun or Sanron, the 'Three Trea-tises.'[3] There are three fundamental texts which are devoted to the Doctrine of the Middle Path[4] by seriously refuting the wrong views of Brahmanism, Hinayana, and Mahayana schools other than the Sanron School. Of these, the first text is the *Madhyamika Sastra,*[5] by *Nagarjuna*.[6] Fortunately the Sanskrit text of it has been pre-served.[7] It was translated into Chinese by Kumarajiva.[8] In a trea-tise of 400 verses Nagarjuna refutes certain wrong views of Hina-yana or of general philosophers thereby rejecting all realistic and pluralistic ideas and indirectly establishing his monistic doctrine.

The second text is the *Dvadasa-dvara*, the 'Twelve Gates,'[9] of Nagarjuna, which is not known in Sanskrit but is preserved in a Chinese translation. It has twelve parts or chapters in all, and is chiefly devoted to correcting the errors of the Mahayanists them-selves. The third text is the *Sata Sastra*, the 'One Hundred Verse

---

[1] 三論 San-lun   [2] 空宗   [3] 三論   [4] 中道

[5] 中論 *Taishō*, No. 1564. German translation by Max Walleser: *Die Mitt-lere Lehre des Nagarjuna*, Heidelberg, 1912. English translation of chapters 1 and 25 with Candrakirti's commentary by Th. Stcherbatsky: *The Conception of Buddhist Nirvana*. See also Walleser's *Die Mittlere Lehre, nach der tibeti-schen version*, Heideberg, 1911.

[6] 龍樹 c. 100-200 A.D.

[7] See Th. Stcherbatsky, *The Conception of Buddhist Nirvana*, Leningrad, 1927, p. 65.

[8] 鳩摩羅什 409 A.D.   [9] 十二門論 *Taishō*, No. 1568.

Treatise' [10] of Aryadeva,[11] a pupil of Nagarjuna. This treatise of Aryadeva is mainly a refutation of the heretical views of Brahmanism.

As the Sanron School is much inclined to be negativistic idealism, there arose the more positive Shiron School (Shih-lun, Four-Treatise School)[12] which adds a fourth text by Nagarjuna, namely, the *Prajnaparamita Sastra*,[13] in which we see that he establishes his monistic view much more affirmatively than in any other text. But all being from Nagarjuna's hand, the general trend of metaphysical argument is much the same. As the Madhyamika system [14] in India had become a pure negative ontology, the Yogacara system [15] of Asanga [16] and Vasubandhu [17] came forward to restore Buddhism to the original more positive idealism. Yogacara idealism, however, ended in a causation theory of the ideation-store, and was ontologically very passive.

In China many renowned scholars appeared and made great strides in the idealistic philosophy; they were by no means inferior to their contemporary Indian authors. As the Sanron School carried the day, the Shiron School gave way to it and soon disappeared from the arena of *Sunyata* [18] controversy.

The efforts of the Sanron School are centered on the refutation of all positive and affirmative views of other schools which have no foundation of dialectical negation. The refutation is directed first against the wrong views of heretics, secondly against the one-sided views of Hinayana, and thirdly against the dogmatic views positively set forth by the Mahayanistic authors. The ideal of the Sanron School seems to have been *Nisprapanca,* the 'inexplicable in speech and unrealizable in thought.' [19] The basis of all arguments is what we call the 'Four Points of Argumentation':[20] 1. *ens (sat)*,[21] 2. *non-ens (asat)*,[22] 3. *either ens or non-ens*,[23] 4. *neither ens nor non-ens.*[24] If we are to answer a question put to us, we have no other way to answer than by one or more of these Four Points of Argumentation. If we express our answer it must be: 1. Yes; or 2. No;

---

[10] 百論 *Taishō*, No. 1569. English translation by Giuseppe Tucci: *Pre-Dinnaga Buddhist Texts on Logic from Chinese Sources*, Gaekwad's Oriental Series, No. XLIX, Baroda, Oriental Institute, 1929, pp. 1-89.

[11] 提婆   [12] 四論宗   [13] 智度論 *Taishō*, No. 1509.   [14] 中論
[15] 瑜伽   [16] 無著 c. 410-500 A.D.   [17] 世親 ‧ 420-500 A. D.
[18] 空   [19] 無戲論言亡慮絕   [20] 四句   [21] 有   [22] 空
[23] 亦有亦空   [24] 非有非空

or 3. Either yes or no according to circumstances; or 4. Neither yes nor no, i.e., having nothing to do with the question or no use answering.

Without understanding the above fundamental ideal underlying their arguments, it is by no means easy to follow the negativistic trend of this Sanron School.

(2) Historical

Prof. Stcherbatsky has indicated the following periods in the development of the Mahayana philosophy with special reference to Madhyamika:

1. First Century A.D. The rise of Mahayana *Alaya-vijnana* (Store-consciousness)[25] and *Tathata* (Thusness),[26] both admitted by Asvaghosa.[27]

2. Second Century A.D. The theory of universal relativity *(Sunyata)*[28] formulated by Nagarjuna and Aryadeva.

3. Third and Fourth Centuries. A gap.

4. Fifth Century. The idealistic interpretation of Asanga and Vasubandhu.

5. Sixth Century. A split between the idealistic and relativistic schools. Sthiramati[29] and Dignaga[30] representing the former, and Buddhapalita[31] and Bhavaviveka[32] the latter.

6. Seventh Century. Final establishment of the Madhyamika system in its extreme form by Candrakirti.[33]

The above is Prof. Stcherbatsky's list, but the gap of the third and the fourth centuries may be filled by bringing in Saramati[34] and Maitreya.[35] Maitreya is a direct or indirect teacher of Asanga and his historicity cannot be doubted, although, because of mysterious legends surrounding him, some scholars are inclined to regard him as an imaginary person. We must reserve this problem for future studies. In any case the Indian Sunyavada with its idealistic reaction, Vijnanavada, exhibited a great flourishing of Buddhist philosophy and the memory of its intellectual activity is forever preserved in the history of Indian philosophy.[36]

---

[25] 阿賴耶識 [26] 眞如 [27] 馬鳴 [28] 空 [29] 安慧 [30] 陳那
[31] 佛陀波利 [32] 毘吠加 [33] 清辨 [34] 堅慧 [35] 彌勒
[36] Madhyamikas, Yogacaras and Vaibhasikas are mentioned in the Vedanta work.

The history of the Sanron School begins in China with the advent of the famous Kumarajiva of Kucca ;[37] the line of transmission is said to have been as follows :

1. Fifth Century A.D. Nagarjuna's *Madhyamika Sastra* was translated and expounded by Kumarajiva and handed down to his pupils Tao-shêng,[38] T'an-chi[39] and Sêng-lang.[40] Sêng-lang, a distinguished successor, finally separated the Sanron School clearly from the Jōjitsu School,[41] the Hinayanistic Nihilism, which we have studied before. The Sanron School owes its real foundation to Sêng-lang's work.

2. Sixth Century. Fa-lang [42] was a great leader who had twenty-five pupils under him. Chi-tsang [43] was the outstanding member of this group. His father had entered the order and often took him to hear lectures by Paramartha.[44] the then flourishing Indian teacher in China. Chi-tsang himself joined the order under Fa-lang and received a special training from him. When nineteen years of age, he lectured and recapitulated his teacher's lectures without any mistakes, to the great astonishment of the listeners. He lived in the Chia-hsiang monastery and is known by the name Chia-hsiang Ta-shih (great master of Chia-hsiang).[45]

Chi-tsang wrote a commentary on the three Treatises,[46] a compendium of the Sanron system,[47] a work on Mahayana,[48] and a short treatise on the twofold truth.[49] Further, he compiled seven different works on the 'Lotus' text, two works each on the *Mahaprajna-paramita* [50] and the *Mahaparinirvana* [51] and altogether one hundred and twenty Chinese volumes (*chüans*) of commentaries on the *Avatansaka* [52] (Wreath), the *Srimala*,[53] the *Vimala-kirti*,[54] the larger *Sukhavati*,[55] the *Amitayur-dhyana*,[56] the 'Diamond Cutter',[57] the *Suvarnaprabhasa*,[58] the *Maitreya-Sutra*,[59] the *Book on Benevolent King*,[60] etc. His literary activity, indicating his wide reading and exhaustive references, is unparalleled in his age or before, and it is remarkable that all was done in a period of continuous warfare between the Ch'ên and the Sui dynasties.

---

[37] 鳩摩羅什 A.D. 409　[38] 道生　[39] 曇濟　[40] 僧朗
[41] Satyasiddhi 成實宗　[42] 法朗 507-581　[43] 吉藏 549-623　[44] 眞諦
[45] 嘉祥大師　[46] 三論疏　[47] 三論玄義　[48] 大乘玄論　[49] 二諦章
[50] 大般若波羅密多經　[51] 大涅槃經　[52] 華嚴經　[53] 勝鬘經
[54] 維摩詰經　[55] 大無量壽經　[56] 觀無量壽經　[57] 金剛經
[58] 金光明最勝王經　[59] 彌勒下生經　[60] 仁王經

3. Seventh Century. Chi-tsang's Korean pupil, Ekwan (Hui-kuan)[61] from Kauli, a state in Korea, came to Japan in 625 and taught the Sanron doctrine at the monastery Gwangōji [62] in Nara. This is the first transmission of the school to Japan. The second transmission was by Chizō,[63] a pupil of Ekwan. The third transmission was by Dōji,[64] a pupil of Yüan-k'ang,[65] the author of a commentary on the three *Treatises*.

In China the Sanron School did not flourish after the rise of the Hossō School of the famous Hiuen-tsang [66] and his pupil Ki.[67] However, an Indian teacher, Suryaprabhasa,[68] came to China in 679 and taught the Sanron to Hsien-shou,[69] the author of a work on the *Twelve Gates* of Nagarjuna. His line of transmission is called the New Sanron School to distinguish it from the Old Sanron School, a name given to that system from Kumarajiva to Chi-tsang during 409-623 A.D.

In Japan the school was never an independent institution, but the study of its doctrine has been ardently continued even to the present time because it is indispensable for a student of Buddhism as one of the chief objects of Buddhist learning and a strong weapon of dialectic argument, as well as the theoretical basis underlying many of the more positive and active schools of Buddhism in Japan today.

(3) Philosophical

The teaching of the Sanron School has three aspects: 1. the refutation of erroneous views and the elucidation of right views;[70] 2. the distinction between worldly truth and the higher truth;[71] 3. the Middle Path *(Madhyama-pratipad)* of the Eightfold Negation.[72]

What the school aims at is the absolute Sunyata,[73] i.e., nothing 'acquirable' *(apraptavya-sunyata)*,[74] i.e., the right view of 'non-acquisition' *(aprapti-tva)*.[75] Generally speaking, when one error is rejected by refutation, another view is grasped and held as right and as a natural outcome of it. In the case of this school, however, a selection is also an attachment to or an acquisition of one view and is therefore to be rejected. The refutation itself of a wrong view

---

[61] 慧灌 [62] 元興寺 [63] 智藏 [64] 道慈 [65] 元康 c. 649 A.D.
[66] Hsüan-tsang 玄奘 596-664 [67] K'uei-chi 窺基 632-682
[68] 日照 [69] 賢首 [70] 破邪顯正 [71] 眞俗二諦 [72] 八不中道
[73] 畢竟空 [74] 無所得空 不可得空 [75] 無得

ought to be, at the same time, the elucidation of a right view. That is to say, refutation is identical with elucidation, for there is to be nothing acquired. This is one of the peculiarities of the school.

However, the two terms are retained separately for practical purposes, since refutation is necessary to save all beings who are drowned in the sea of attachment while elucidation is also important in order to propagate the teaching of the Buddha.

Such refutation is to be complete. First, views based on acquisition are all refuted. Also, views such as the *atman* (self) theory of the Brahmanic philosophers, the pluralistic doctrines of the Buddhist Abhidharma schools (Vaibhasika, Kosa, etc.) and the dogmatic principles of Mahayana teachers are never passed without a detailed refutation. The Realistic ('All exists') and the Nihilistic ('Nothing exists') are equally condemned.

Among the Chinese Buddhistic views, Hui-kuan's [76] view that divides the teachings of the Buddha into two teachings and five periods, Chi-tsang's view of unity of the two truths, worldly and higher, and Sêng-chao's [77] as well as Fa-yün's [78] view of diversity of the two truths are all to be mercilessly attacked if they are too much adhered to. On the positive side, however, this school accepts the right man [79] and the right teaching.[80] Nagarjuna is regarded as the right personage because of the Buddha's prophesy concerning his appearance.[81] The right teaching is the Middle Path devoid of name and character [82] where no speech or thought can reach. It transcends all the points of dispute such as 'the four forms of argument and the hundred negations,' thus even going further than Yajnavalkya's famous theory of neti, neti (not! not!) in the Upanishads.[83]

The truth can be attained only by negation or refutation of wrong views within and without Buddhism and of errors of both the Great and Small Vehicles. When retaining wrong views or error, one will be blind to reason. How can a blind man get a right view without which the two extremes can never be avoided? The end of verbal refutation is the dawn of the Middle Path. Refutation—and refutation only—can lead to the ultimate truth.

The Middle Path, which is devoid of name and character, cannot be named and characterized, yet we are forced to designate it some-

[76] 慧灌   [77] 僧肇 384-414   [78] 法雲 467-529   [79] 人正   [80] 法正
[81] In the *Lankavatara Sutra* 楞伽經   [82] 無名相中道
[83] *Brihadaranyaka Upanishad,* II, 3, 6; III, 9, 26; IV, 4, 22; IV, 6, 15.

how for the sake of distinction. Therefore it is called 'the right (as) elucidated.'

Two aspects of right can be assumed: right in substance [84] and right in function.[85] The right in substance is the transcendental truth which is beyond both the higher and the worldly truths, while the right in function is the twofold truth, the higher and the worldly. In the *Madhyamika Sastra* [86] it is said that the Buddhas of the past proclaimed their teachings to the people by means of the twofold truth. It was by the worldly truth *(samvriti-satya)* [87] that the Buddha preached that all elements have come into being through causation; but it is by the higher truth *(paramartha-satya)*[88] that all elements are of universal relativity *(sarva-sunyata)* or Void. After all, the twofold truth is proclaimed in order to lead people to a right way.

For those who are attached to Nihilism the theory of existence is taught in the way of the worldly truth, and for those who are attached to Realism the doctrine of non-existence is proclaimed in the way of the higher truth in order to teach them the nameless and characterless state which is 'right in substance.'

Though we may speak of existence, it is temporary and not fixed. Even non-existence (Void) is temporary and not fixed. So there is neither a real existence nor a real Void. Being or non-being is only an outcome of causal relation and, therefore, unreal. Thus the ideal of the two extremes of being and non-being is removed. Therefore, when we deal with the worldly truth, the phenomenal world can be assumed without disturbing the noumenal state. When we deal with the higher truth, the noumenal state can be attained without stirring the world of mere name. Non-existence is at the same time existence, and existence in turn is non-existence. Form or matter is at the same time the Void, and the Void is at the same time form or matter.[89]

Thus the noumenon of all *dharmas* is without specific character.

It may be seen, therefore, that the twofold truth is taught only for the sake of convenience in instruction. The present Sanron School regards the theory of twofold truth to be word-teaching,[90] i.e., teaching for an explicatory purpose, while other Mahayanists take it to be the principle-teaching,[91] i.e., the twofold truth itself is the principle which the Buddha has taught. The question of differ-

---

[84] 體正　[85] 用正　[86] 中論　[87] 俗諦　[88] 眞諦　[89] 色即是空
[90] 言敎　[91] 理敎

102

ences is: whether the truth is the means or the object. The Sanron School takes it to be the means. This is another peculiarity of the school.

The theory of the eightfold negation is of similar purport. It is set forth by Nagarjuna in his dedicatory verse of the *Madhyamika Sastra,* which runs as follows:

"The perfect Buddha,
The foremost of all teachers I salute,
He has proclaimed
The principle of (universal) relativity.
'Tis like Blissful (Nirvana),
Quiescence of plurality.
There nothing disappears,[92]
Nor anything appears,[93]
Nothing has an end,[94]
Nor is there anything eternal,[95]
Nothing is identical (with itself),[96]
Nor is there anything differentiated,[97]
Nothing moves,
Neither hither nor thither." [98]

This eightfold negation is formulated in Chinese as follows:

No production
No extinction [99]
No annihilation
No permanence [100]
No unity
No diversity [101]
No coming
No departure [102]

Thus all specific features of becoming are denied. The fact that there are just eight negations has no special purport; this is meant to be a wholesale negation. It may be taken as a crosswise sweeping away of all eight errors attached to the world of becoming, or a reciprocal rejection of the four pairs of one-sided views, or a lengthwise general thrusting aside of the errors one after the other

---

[92] 不滅 [93] 不生 [94] 不斷 [95] 不常 [96] 不一 [97] 不異
[98] 不來不去 Th. Stcherbatsky, *The Conception of Buddhist Nirvana,* p. 69.
[99] 不生亦不滅 [100] 不常亦不斷 [101] 不一亦不異 [102] 不來亦不出

—for instance, refuting the idea of appearing (birth) by the idea of disappearance; the idea of disappearance by the idea of motion hither; this idea of motion hither by the idea of motion thither; this last idea by the idea of permanence; permanence by destruction (end); destruction by unity; unity by diversity; diversity by appearance; and so on.

In this way all discriminations of oneself and another or this and that are done away with. Therefore a refutation of a wrong or one-sided view is at the same time an elucidation of a right view. When right is opposed to wrong, it is an antithetic right,[103] i.e., right as opposed to wrong. When wrong is utterly refuted, there will be the right devoid of antithesis,[104] i.e., transcendental right. When the idea of right or wrong is altogether thrown aside, there will be the absolute right,[105] i.e., the truth.

Right is the middle. The middle versus two extremes is antithetic middle or relative middle.[106] The middle, after the two extremes have been totally refuted, is the middle devoid of extremes.[107] When the idea of two extremes is removed altogether, it is the absolute middle.[108] Thus the absolute right is the absolute middle.

When the absolute middle condescends to lead people at large, it becomes a temporary middle or truth.[109] We have thus the fourfold Middle Path.

Out of a practical necessity to guide people another gradation theory is adopted. This gradation theory will be explained in four stages below:

1. When the theory of being is opposed to the theory of nonbeing, the former is regarded as the worldly truth and the latter the higher truth.[110]

2. When the theories of being and non-being are opposed to those of neither being nor non-being, the former are regarded as the worldly truth and the latter the higher truth.[111]

3. If the four opposed theories just mentioned together become the worldly truth, the yet higher views denying them all will be regarded as the higher truth.[112]

---

[103] 對偏正　[104] 盡偏正　[105] 絕待正　[106] 對偏中　[107] 盡偏中
[108] 絕待中　[109] 成假中　[110] 有俗,眞空　[111] 有空俗,非有非空眞
[112] 有空非有空俗,非非有非非空眞

4. If the theories expressed in the last stage become the worldly truth, the denial of them all will be the higher truth.[113]

Thus, however high we proceed, if we adhere to one view or a group of views, we shall meet their denial again and again. Negation alone can lead us to the door of the absolute truth. In short, what we are driving at is the Principle of Non-acquisition *(apraptitva)* which is attained by the doctrine of universal negation expounded crosswise by the *eightfold negation* and lengthwise by the *four stages of the twofold truth*. It is in fact an infinite negation until the tinge of worldly truth is utterly washed off. Therefore, the ultimate truth thus arrived at by dialectical method is called either the Middle Path of the Eightfold Negation [114] or the Middle Path of the Twofold Truth.[115]

Further, the Middle Path of the Twofold Truth is expounded in several complicated ways. If one maintains the theory of the real production and the real extinction of the phenomenal world, it is called the one-sided worldly truth.[116] If, on the other hand, one adheres to the theory of the non-production and non-extinction of the phenomenal world, it is called the one-sided higher truth.[117] If one sees that there is a temporary production and a temporary extinction of phenomenon,[118] it is the middle path of worldly truth.[119] If one sees that there is neither temporary production nor temporary extinction,[120] it is the middle path of the higher truth.[121] If one considers that there is neither production-and-extinction nor non-production-and-non-extinction, it is the middle path elucidated by the union of both popular and higher truths.[122]

The above are called *the five terms and the three middle paths.* It is the 'true state of Middle Path.' [123]

The Sanron School divides the sacred teaching into two Pitakas —Sravaka and Bodhisattva, i.e., smaller and larger vehicles (Hinayana and Mahayana). The sacred teaching is also divided into three *dharma-cakra* (the wheels of the law): 1. the root wheel is the *Avatansaka* (Wreath); 2. the branch wheel is all Hinayana and Mahayana texts; 3. the wheel that contracts all the branches so as to bring them back to the root, i.e., the 'Lotus.'

---

[113] 非非有非非空俗,非非不有非非不空眞   [114] 八不中道
[115] 二諦中道   [116] 單俗   [117] 俗眞   [118] 假生假滅   [119] 俗諦中道
[120] 假不生假不滅   [121] 眞諦中道   [122] 二諦合明中道   [123] 中道實相

The root wheel was first preached for *Bodhisattvas* soon after the Buddha's Enlightenment. It was the truth gained by the Buddha in his Enlightenment, but this Buddha-yana [124] was too profound for people to understand. Then the Buddha began to propound the three *yanas* [125] (*sravaka*,[126] *pratyekabuddha* [127] and *bodhisattva*) [128] to lead up to the one Buddha-yana.

'Sunya' negatively means 'Void,' but positively 'relative,' i.e, 'devoid of independent reality' or 'devoid of specific character.' Thus *Sunyata* is non-entity and at the same time 'relativity,' i.e., the entity only as in causal relation. The idea of relativity seems to be strongly presented in the Indian Madhyamika School. In the Chinese San-lun School, too, we have the term 'causal union' [129] as a synonym of the Middle Path, absence of nature *(svabhava-abhava)*,[130] *Dharma* nature *(Dharma-svabhava)*[131] and Void. These words doubtless convey a similar idea, for it is well known that the causal origination is called *Sunyata*, but I cannot definitely state whether the Chinese San-lun teachers went so far as to treat causal relation *(pratitya-samutpada)* as an exact synonym of *Sunyata* or not. However, it is certain that the Chinese did not make much of the idea of relativity, because the Chinese equivalent of *Sunyata*, *K'ung*,[132] connotes all the necessary phases of meaning: first, Void in the sense of antithesis of being,[133] second, the state of being devoid of specific character *(svabhava-sunyata, svalaksana-abhava)*;[134] third, Void in the highest sense, or transcendental Void, i.e., all oppositions synthesized, *(paramartha-sunyata)*;[135] fourth, the absolute Void *(atyanta-sunyata)*;[136] and several others.

The word 'Void' is not entirely fitting and is often misleading, yet if we look for another word, there will be none better. It is, after all, an idea dialectically established. It is nameless *(akhyati)*[137] and characterless *(alaksana)*.[138] It is simply the negation of an independent reality or the negation of specific character. Besides the negation there is nothing else. The Sanron system is on that account a negativism, the theory of negation. All things are devoid of independent reality, that is, they are only of relative existence, or relativity in the sense of what is ultimately unreal but phenomenally real.

---

[124] 一佛乗   [125] 三乗   [126] 聲聞   [127] 緣覺   [128] 菩薩   [129] 緣會
[130] 無性   [131] 法自性   [132] 空   [133] 但空,偏空   [134] 自性
[135] 勝義空,第一義空   [136] 畢竟空 絕待空   [137] 無名   [138] 無相

(4) Résumé

The object of negativism is the realization of perfect wisdom. Wisdom here is opposed to all partial knowledge, or rather is inclusive of all partial knowledge. Thus, by not clinging to the knowledge of special things, one can attain perfect wisdom; and by not adhering to one thing or another, one can attain perfect freedom. Perfect emptiness or Void comprehends all things. Emptiness is different from space, for space is what anything can occupy. The doctrine of Void of this school is in reality Non-Void, i.e., not one-sided, abstracted Void, because it can comprehend anything whatever.

Denial or refutation is only the method of obtaining the white-paper state instead of the colored-paper state which we generally possess, cling to and cannot get rid of. Again, here is the principle of non-acquisition.

In fine, the training by negation means having no partial knowledge, dwelling in no special view, holding on to no abstracted Void, adhering to no special attainment, assuming no special characteristics and expecting no special interest or any special merit.

VIII. THE KEGON SCHOOL
(AVATANSAKA, THE 'WREATH' SCHOOL)[1]

(Totalism)
[Mahayanistic]

(1) Preliminary

Kegon means 'flower-ornament' and is considered a translation of the Sanskrit term 'Avatansaka' denoting a wreath or garland. It is the name of a *sutra* in which the mystic doctrine of the Buddha Mahavairocana[2] is minutely described. The scripture is said to have been preached by the Buddha soon after his Enlightenment, but none of those listening to him could understand a word of it as if they were deaf and dumb. Therefore he began anew to preach the easy four *Agamas* (discourses) and other doctrines.

What he preached first was what he had realized in his Enlightenment. The truth he had conceived was proclaimed exactly as it was. An advanced personage such as a *Bodhisattva* (saintly person) might have understood him, but an ordinary person could not grasp his ideas at all.

The *Avatansaka Sutra*[3] is represented in Chinese by three recensions, in eighty, sixty, and forty Chinese volumes. Of the first two we do not possess their Sanskrit original. For the last, the forty-volume text, we have its original which is called *Ganda-vyuha*,[4] now published in Japan.[5]

In the text, a pilgrimage undertaken by the youth Sudhana[6] to visit fifty-three worthies, religious and secular, is described. The object of the pilgrimage was to realize the principle of *Dharma-dhatu*[7] (Realm of Principle or Elements).

In India the Avatansaka School, as an independent school, is unknown. However, the story of Sudhana's pilgrimage is minutely told in the *Divya-avadana,* and his journey is depicted in detailed sculptures in Java.

---

[1] Hua-yen 華嚴   [2] 大日經 To be described in Chapter X.
[3] 華嚴經 *Taishō,* Nos. 278, 279 and 293.   [4] 入法界品
[5] By H. Izumi of the Ōtani University, Kyoto.
[6] 善財   [7] 法界

In the *Sutra* it is stated that the Bodhisattva Manjusri [8] is living on the Ch'ingliang Mountain [9] in China, and is proclaiming the law at all times. This Ch'ingliang Mountain is identified with the Wut'ai Mountain [10] of China. The name Wut'ai (five heights) itself seems to indicate Panca-sikha (five top-knots), a name of Manjusri. The great Avatansaka Monastery of that mountain is the shrine sacred to that Bodhisattva. Such a belief in India as well as in China seems to go back to the fifth century A.D. or still earlier.

In 477 A.D. an Imperial prince went up that mountain and burned himself to death as a sign of his ardent desire to meet the Bodhisattva. Later, in 735 A.D., an Indian priest, Bodhisena,[11] with a Malay-Indian musician named Fa-triet,[12] came to China and went up there to see Manjusri. They passed on to Japan in search of that saint when they were told that he was not on the mountain then but was sojourning in the Far East. At their arrival in Ōsaka they were received by Gyōgi [13] Bosatsu (=Bodhisattva), a learned Japanese priest who is generally called Bosatsu because Bodhisena and Fa-triet took him to be Manjusri himself. The two men were given some Imperial grants and were happily settled in Nara. Bodhisena, as the officiating priest, performed the dedication ceremony of the Grand Buddha of Nara and shared the honor of becoming one of the founders of the Tōdaiji Monastery.[14] He taught the 'Wreath' doctrine while in the Daianji Monastery, Nara.

The name 'Manch'u' of the last dynasty of China is said to have been an abbreviation of Manjusri. In the letters from Nepal to the Chinese court the Chinese emperors are addressed 'Sri, Sri, Sri Manjusri.' The official name of the dynasty was Ch'ing which itself is said to have been taken from the designation of Ch'ingliang Mountain. Even now Wut'ai Mountain is one of the most sacred spots of all the places connected with Buddhism in China.

(2) Historical

Prior to the Kegon School there was in China a school named Ti-lun [15] which was founded on Vasubandhu's commentary on the *Dasa-bhumi Sutra*.[16] The text was translated into Chinese in 508-

---

[8] 文殊　　[9] 清凉山　　[10] 五臺山　　[11] 菩提仙那　　[12] 佛徹　　[13] 行基
[14] There were four among the founders; see section 2.
[15] 地論宗　　[16] 十地經

512 A.D. by Bodhiruci,[17] Ratnamati [18] and Buddhasanta,[19] all from India.

There appeared in time a split in the Ti-lun School. Tao-ch'ung,[20] a pupil of Bodhiruci, lived in the north district of Lo-yang and exercised a great influence on the people, while Hui-kuang,[21] a pupil of Ratnamati, lived in the south district of the capital and was equally influential in his religious activities. The line of the former was called 'the Branch of the Northern Path,' [22] and that of the latter 'the Branch of the Southern Path.' [23]

As the *Dasa-bhumi Sutra* was annotated by Vasubandhu,[24] the *Alaya* (store) Consciousness [25] as well as the first six sense-consciousnesses were expounded in it. The relation between these consciousnesses and their connection with Thusness *(Tathata)*[26] or the so-called 'Matrix of Tathagata' (Thuscome)[27] were not expressly taught. On this account the two Indian teachers differed from each other in their opinions, and the two lines went so far as to take a separate way.

The Ti-lun (Dasa-bhumi) School

Northern Path	Southern Path
Tao-ch'ung, a pupil of Bodhiruci.	Hui-kuang, a pupil of Ratnamati.
Alaya-consciousness is unreal (false) and separate from Thusness.	*Alaya*-consciousness is real (true) and identical with Thusness.

Kegon School

At the outset the Northern Path seemed to have flourished, as the founder Tao-ch'ung is said to have had more than ten thousand pupils, he himself having been honored as one of the six Great Virtuous Men of the Ch'ên dynasty and later as one of the ten Great Virtuous Men of the Sui dynasty. But for some reason his successors did not succeed so well.

In the Southern Path, Hui-kuang seemed to have been more a scholar than a propagandist. He was well versed in Sanskrit, having studied under Buddhabhadra and Ratnamati, and understood the points of dispute as to the *Dasa-bhumi* text. He had ten able pupils

---

[17] 菩提流支 508-515 [18] 寶慧 508 [19] 佛陀扇多 520-539 [20] 道寵
[21] 慧光 468-537 [22] 北道派 [23] 南道派 [24] 世親 ∴ 420-500 A.D.
[25] 阿賴耶識 [26] 眞如 [27] 如來

among whom Fa-shang [28] (495-580) was the most prominent. The literary activity of his pupils also was worthy of admiration. However, when Tu-shun,[29] the nominal founder of the Kegon School, made his appearance on the scene, the best workers of this line were all attracted around him. Or, we can say at best the Ti-lun School was finally united with the new rising school of the Hua-yen (Kegon, Avatansaka, 'Wreath') philosophy.

The Kegon School, having absorbed the Ti-lun School, opened a flourishing period of Chinese Buddhism. The foundation-stone of the Kegon doctrine was laid once and for all by the famous Tu-shun His priestly name was Fa-shun,[30] but as his family name was Tu, people generally called him Tu-shun. He was famous as a miracle-worker, and Emperor T'ai-tsung [31] of T'ang invited him to his palace and gave him the title of 'the Venerable Imperial Heart.' [32] He was believed to be an incarnation of Manjusri.

His able pupil, Chih-yen [33] (602-668), the succeeding patriarch of the school, received from him all the culture of contemplation. He wrote several important works on the basis of his teacher's instructions. One of his pupils, I-hsiang [34] (625-702) from Simla, a state of Korea, returned home in 668 and founded the first Kegon School in Korea. But the third patriarch, Fa-tsang [35] (643-712), was the real founder of this school, for he was responsible for the final systematization of the philosophy. His activity was not only in literary work but also in translations and lectures. When in 680 Divakara [36] (613-687) brought the *Ganda-vyuha* (forty-volume text) to China, Fa-tsang went to him, made several inquiries about the doctrine and requested him to translate the section on the pilgrimage of the youth Sudhana which was wanting in the hitherto translated sixty-volume text. When Siksananda (652-670) of Khotan brought the eighty-volume text, Fa-tsang assisted him in his translation. He further helped I-ching [37] (635-713), that famous traveler in India, and Diva-prajna (who was in China during 689-691) in the work of translation. In 704 he lectured on the Kegon School for the Usurper Queen Wu-hou.[38] The subject matter of his lecture then was the 'tenfold profundity' and 'sixfold special nature,' [39] to which we shall return soon. His profound lectures were often accompanied by witty

---

[28] 法上   [29] 杜順   [30] 法順   [31] 太宗   [32] 帝心尊者   [33] 智儼
[34] 義湘   [35] 法藏   [36] 日照   [37] 義淨   [38] 則天武后   [39] 十玄門六相

examples. His works in commentaries and dictionaries are of eighteen kinds in more than one hundred Chinese volumes. His last commentary on the eighty-volume text is said to have been left in an unfinished state. His posthumous or honorary titles are Hsien-Shou [40] (Head of the Wise) and Kuo-i [41] (One in the State).

One of Fa-tsang's pupils, Shên-hsiang [42] of Simla, came to Japan in the twelfth year of the Tempyō Era (A.D. 740) and lectured on the school for the first time. Ch'êng-kuan[43] (760-820), another pupil, was honored as the fourth patriarch for his earnest effort in refuting the heresy of Hui-yüan,[44] also a pupil of Fa-tsang, and restoring their teacher's doctrine to its original purity.

Another pupil, Tao-hsüan,[45] came to Japan in 730 and taught the doctrine. Bodhisena from Central India arrived in Nara at the same time or earlier (probably 726) and taught the Avatansaka doctrine.

Emperor Shōmu (724-748) intended to govern Japan by the totalistic principle of the Kegon School. He built the Tōdaiji, or the Eastern Great Monastery, and in it he installed the gigantic bronze statue of Mahavairocana (the Great Sun Buddha).[46] This monastery was to be the Sanctuary for Permanently Preaching the Avatansaka Doctrine. Four founders of the monastery are recognized, namely, Shōmu the Emperor, Bodhisena the Brahman prelate. Gyōgi the Bodhisattva, and Rōben [47] the abbot.

In spite of these memorable monumental works of the Nara period, people of the time were soon aware of the fact that the religious institution and the political government should not be confounded. At present the Tōdaiji is the only prominent monastery which belongs to the Kegon School. In the Kamakura period Myōe,[48] a learned priest of Toganoo, Kyoto, endeavoured to establish a new school of the Avatansaka, and later in the Tokugawa period Hōtan,[49] a scholar of the Kegon doctrine, made an effort to have a special institute. But both of them did not succeed. However, the study of the Avatansaka doctrine is actively pursued in all the centers of Buddhist learning in Japan even today.

---

[40] 賢首　[41] 國一　[42] 審祥　[43] 澄觀　[44] 慧苑　[45] 道睿
[46] 大日如來　[47] 良辨　[48] 明惠　[49] 鳳潭

The Kegon School

China		Japan
Hua-yen School		Kegon School
1. Tu-shun (557-640)	==	Tojun
2. Chih-yen (602-668)	==	Chigen
3. Fa-tsang (643-712)	==	Hōzō
4. Ch'êng-kuan(C. 760-820)	==	Chōkwan

5. Shinshō (Chên-hsiang)
(to Japan in 736)
6. Rōben (689-772)

(3) Philosophical

The Totalistic principle of the Kegon School was developed chiefly in China. It is indeed a glory of the learned achievements of Chinese Buddhism. The Kegon School stands, as other schools do, on the basis of the theory of causation by mere ideation, but as held in the Kegon School the theory has a peculiarity. It is designated 'the theory of universal causation of *Dharma-dhatu*' (Realm of Principle or Element of the Elements).[50] The term 'Dharma-dhatu' is sometimes used as a synonym of the ultimate truth. Therefore, the translation 'the Element of the Elements' is quite fitting. But at other times it means the universe, 'the Realm of All Elements.' The double meaning, the universe and the universal principle, must always be borne in mind whenever we use the term. Either meaning will serve as the name of the causation theory.

The theory of causation by *Dharma-dhatu* is the climax of all the causation theories; it is actually the conclusion of the theory of causal origination, as it is the universal causation and is already within the theory of universal immanence, pansophism, cosmotheism, or whatever it may be called. The causation theory, as we have seen before, was explained first by action-influence,[51] but as action originates in ideation, we had secondly, the theory of causation by ideation-store.[52] Since the ideation-store as the repository of seed-energy must originate from something else, we had, thirdly, the causation theory explained by the expression 'Matrix of the Thus-come' (*Tathagata-garbha*)[53] or Thusness. This curious term means that which conceals the Buddha. Because of concealment it has an impure side, but because of Buddhahood it has a pure side as well It is a synonym

---

[50] 法界緣起　[51] 業感緣起　[52] 賴耶緣起　[53] 如來藏

113

of Thusness (*Tathatva* or *Tathata,* not Thisness or Thatness=*tattva*) which has in its broadest sense both pure and impure nature. Through the energy of pure and impure causes it manifests the specific character of becoming as birth and death, or as good and evil. Thusness pervades all beings, or better, all beings are in the state of Thusness. Here, as the fourth stage, the causation theory by *Dharmadhatu* (universe) is set forth. It is the causation by all beings themselves and is the creation of the universe itself, or we can call it the causation by the common action-influence of all beings. Intensively considered the universe will be a manifestation of Thusness or the Matrix of Tathagata (Thus-come). But extensively considered it is the causation of the universe by the universe itself and nothing more.

Dharma-dhatu—in its double meaning as Realm of Principle and Element of all Elements—is synonymous with Matrix of the Thuscome (*Tathagata-garbha*) and also with the universe or the actual world, i.e., the realm of all elements. This causation can be taken in the double sense accordingly. The causal origination *(Pratitya-samutpada)* [54] of *Dharma-dhatu* is thus the theory that the universe is universally co-relative, generally interdependent and mutually originating, having no single being existing independently. In the Twelve-Divisioned Cycle of Causation 'dependence on antecedent' was taught and, therefore, it was a dependence in time sequence. In this universal causation, on the other hand, it is a dependence of all upon one another and, therefore, it is meant in a spatial sense.

According to the critical classification of the Buddhist teaching set forth by this school, there are five aspects of teaching [55] subdivided further into ten doctrines.[56] During the early flourishing periods of Chinese Buddhism many critical divisions of Buddhism were proposed, but as they are confusing, I have not given any of them. Here for the first time we shall have a clear exhaustive classification, and I consider it worthwhile to review it in considerable detail.

Critical Classification of Buddhism

1. The Doctrine of the Small Vehicle (Hinayana).[57]

This refers to the teaching of the four *Agamas.*[58] Although they

---

[54] 緣生,緣起　　[55] 五敎　　[56] 十宗　　[57] 小乘敎
[58] 四阿含 In Pali there are 5 *Nikayas* or divisions: 1. *Digha*,長阿含.
2. *Majjhima*,中阿含 3. *Anguttara*,增一阿含 4. *Samyutta*,雜阿含
5. *Khuddaka.* Chinese *Agamas* (Discourses) have only the first four.

deny the existence of the personal self (*pudgala-sunyata*), they are realistic and admit the existence of all separate elements (*dharma*). They hold that Nirvana is total extinction, and yet they do not understand much of the unreality of all elements (*dharma-sunyata*), e.g., the Kusha [59] (Realistic) School. As to the causation theory, they attribute it to the action-influence. They can be designated the small vehicle for the foolish.[60]

2. The Elementary Doctrine of the Great Vehicle (Mahayana).[61]

Two grades are distinguished in it. First, the elementary doctrine based on the specific character of all elements (*dharma-laksana*),[62] e.g., Hossō [63] (Idealistic) School; second, the elementary doctrine based on negation of all elements (*dharma-sunyata*),[64] e.g., Sanron [65] (Negativistic) School. Since both do not admit the existence of the Buddha-nature (*Buddha-svabhava*) in all beings, both are considered to be elementary.

The former (Hossō) sets forth the theory of causation by ideation-store (*Alaya-vijnana*) [66] on the basis of phenomenal characteristics (*laksana*) [67] and does not recognize the unity of fact and principle. Also, since it maintains the basic distinction of five species of men, it does not admit that all men can attain Buddhahood. The latter (Sanron), on the other hand, holds the one-sided view of Void on the basis of 'own nature' (*svabhava-alaksana*) or no abiding nature. But admitting the unity of being and non-being, it affirms that men of the three vehicles (*yana*), and the five species (*gotra*), are all able to attain Buddhahood. In making this point the Sanron (Madhyamika) School is treading one step within the final doctrine of Mahayana which is as follows:

3. The Final Doctrine of the Great Vehicle (Mahayana).[68]

This is the teaching of Thusness of all elements (*dharma-tathata*), asserting that all living beings have Buddha-nature and can attain Buddhahood, according to the teaching found in the *Lankavatara* text, the *Mahaparinirvana* text and the *Awakening of Faith*.[69] (The Tendai School [70] adheres to this doctrine).

---

[59] 俱舍宗　　[60] 愚法乘　　[61] 大乘始教　　[62] 相始教　　[63] 法相宗
[64] 空始教　　[65] 三論宗　　[66] 阿頼耶識
[67] 相　　[68] 大乘終教
[69] *Taishō* No. 670. English translation by D. T. Suzuki: *Lankavatara Sutra*, London, 1932; 大涅槃經 *Taishō* No. 1527; 大乘起信論
See footnote on p. 83.　　[70] 天台宗

By this teaching the Ultimate Truth of Mahayana is expounded. Therefore, it is called the Doctrine of Maturity.[71] As it agrees with reality, it is also called the True Doctrine.[72] In the elementary doctrine fact and principle were always separate, while in this final doctrine fact is always identified with principle, nay, the two are one. The causation theory by Matrix of the Thuscome is special to this doctrine. It is also called the theory of causation by Thusness (*Tathata*).

4. The Abrupt Doctrine of the Great Vehicle.[73]

This means the training without word or order, directly appealing to one's own insight, by virtue of which one can attain perfect enlightenment all at once. All words and speech will stop at once. Reason will present itself in its purity and action will always comply with wisdom and knowledge—if thought ceases to arise in his mind, the man is a Buddha. Such an attainment may be gained through silence as shown by Vimalakirti, a saintly layman of Vaisali, or through meditation (Zen)[74] as in the case of Bodhidharma, an Indian priest and the founder of the Chinese Zen School. It teaches no special causation theory because it has no method of teaching of its own.

5. The Round Doctrine of the Great Vehicle.[75]

Two grades of the round or perfect doctrine are set forth.

A. One Vehicle (Ekayana)[76] of the 'Identical Doctrine'[77] in which the One Vehicle is taught in an identical or similar method with the other three Vehicles. The three Vehicles recognized by the Kegon School are different from the ordinary three. They are: 1. the Small (Hinayana). 2. the Gradual (a. the elementary; b. the final Mahayana). 3. the Abrupt (e.g., Zen practice of Mahayana).

The One Vehicle of the Kegon is inclusive of all Vehicles. For convenience the three Vehicles are taught to prepare the aspirants. The three flow out of the One Vehicle and are taught in the identical method as the one. In the Identical Doctrine the two aspects are distinguished; one within the meditation[78] and the other outside of meditation.[79] The meditation into which the Buddha entered before he preached the Avatansaka doctrine was the *Samadhi* of Sea-impression

---

[71] 熟教　　[72] 實教　　[73] 大乘頓教　　[74] 禪　　[75] 大乘圓教　　[76] 一乘　　[77] 同教　　[78] 定内　　[79] 定外

116

(*Sagaramudra*) in which all the doctrines that were to be preached during his lifetime and all beings that were to be converted during fifty years of his career were all at once reflected, just as all images are reflected in a quiet sea.[80] The other doctrines were preached when he was out of that meditation.

The Avatansaka doctrine is the representation of the Buddha's Enlightenment as it was conceived and experienced by him. The other discourses were preached to suit the occasion. The Kegon School is thus to be taken as the most fundamental of all.

B. One Vehicle of the 'Distinct Doctrine'[81] in which the One Vehicle is set forth entirely distinct or independent from the other Vehicles, as in the case of the teaching of the Kegon School in which the doctrine of the world of totalistic harmony mutually relating and penetrating is set forth. The One Vehicle is higher than the other three. The One Vehicle is real while the three are considered as temporary.[82]

Thus analyzing the whole teaching of the Buddha, the Kegon School was founded and systematized. The object of its teaching is the establishment of a harmonious whole of all beings having the perfectly enlightened Buddha at the center. The totalistic principle of the Avatansaka is further based on the theory of selflessness (*anatman*), on the causation theory by pure ideation, and on the belief in the existence of Buddha-nature dormant in every being.

Further, ten tenets are enumerated as the subdivisions of the five doctrines. They are :—

1. The existence of both *atman* (self) and *dharma* (element),[83] as admitted by the unusual—almost non-Buddhistic—Vatsiputriya School.[84]

2. The existence of *dharma* and the non-existence of *atman*,[85] the reality of the three time-periods (past, present and future), and the reality of all *dharmas*.[86] This tenet is admitted by the Sarvastivada School.[87]

---

[80] 海印三昧一時炳現　[81] 別教　[82] 三權一實　[83] 我法俱有宗
[84] 犢子部　[85] 法有我無宗　[86] 三世實有,法體恒有
[87] 說一切有部

3. All *dharmas* devoid of motion hither and thither,[88] the reality of present and unreality of past and future,[89] as admitted by the Mahasanghika School.[90]

4. The present possessed of both unreality and reality.[91] In the reality of the present the five *skandhas* (aggregates)[92]—form, perception, conception, volition and consciousness—are real, but the twelve *ayatanas* (six senses and six sense organs)[93] and the eighteen *dhatus* (six sense organs, six sense objects and six senses)[94] are temporary or unreal, as admitted by the Prajnaptivada School.[95]

5. The popular truth (*laukika* or *samvriti-satya*) as false but the higher truth (*lokottara* or *paramartha-satya*) as real [96] as admitted by the Lokottaravada School.[97]

6. All *dharmas* as nominal or mere names (*akhyati matra* or *nama matra*).[98] All elements are simply names and of no reality, as admitted by the Ekottiya School.[99]

7. All *dharmas* as void, or devoid of specific character (*sarva dharma sunyata* or *sarva sunyata*),[100] as taught by the *Prajnaparamita*[101] text or as admitted by the Sanron (Madhyamika) School.[102] This is the teaching of the Mahayana denying specific character [103] (*laksana abhava*) with the two elementary doctrines.

8. The attribute of Thusness not empty or 'void.'[104] Thusness, though it is without any determinate character, is possessed of innumerable potentialities from which all determinate or differentiated *dharmas* are manifested. This tenet is admitted in the final doctrine of Mahayana (the Tendai School) [105] and in the *Awakening of Faith*.[106]

9. The stage in which the distinction between subjective ideation and objective reality entirely removed,[107] the coalescence of subject and object, the state without specific character and without sense and thought. All the Abrupt Doctrines' belong to it, especially the Zen School.[108]

10. The 'round and bright doctrine' in which all attributes exist in a harmonious whole,[109] as in the Round Doctrine of the Kegon School.

---

[88] 法無去來宗　[89] 現在實有 過未無體　[90] 大衆部
[91] 現通假實宗　[92] 五蘊　[93] 十二處　[94] 十八界　[95] 假說部
[96] 俗妄眞實宗　[97] 說出世部　[98] 諸法但名宗　[99] 一說部
[100] 一切皆空宗　[101] 大波羅蜜經　[102] 三論宗　[103] 一切皆空宗
[104] 眞德不空宗　[105] 天台宗　[106] 大乘起信論　[107] 相想俱絕宗
[108] 禪宗　[109] 圓明具德宗

A critical division of the interpretation of the Buddha's teaching was proposed first by Ki (K'uei-chi,[110] 632-682), a pupil of Hiuen-tsang (Hsüan-tsang,[114] 596-664). It was a classification into eight doctrines. The present division into ten tenets is a modification of it. Of these ten, one to six are Hinayana, but five and six can be said to be semi-Mahayana, and seven to ten are the true Mahayana doctrines.

The fourfold universe peculiar to the Kegon School roughly corresponds to the five critical divisions of the Buddha's teaching. The universe is fourfold as follows:—

1. The world of reality,[112] the factual, practical world. It represents the Realistic Doctrine (Hinayana).

2. The world of principle or theoretical world.[113] It is represented by the Sanron and Hossō Schools which teach that principle is separate from facts.

3. The world of principle and reality united, or the ideal world realized.[114] It represents the doctine of the *Awakening of Faith* and the Tendai doctrine which teach the identity of fact and principle.

4. The world of all realities or practical facts interwoven or identified in perfect harmony [115] It is represented by the Kegon School which teaches that all distinct facts or realities will, and ought to, form a harmonious whole by mutual penetration and mutual identification [116] so as to realize the ideal world of One-true.

Generally speaking it should not be difficult to make practice adapted to theory, but such being the evil of men, some make too much of theory while others make too much of practice. So a rational solution becomes necessary. Moreover, in the world of realities (fact) practice often goes against practice, fact against fact, business against business, individual against individual, class against class, nation against nation. Such is the feature of the world of individualism and thus the whole world goes to pieces. Mere collectivism or solidarity will not prevent the evil of life. To harmonize such a state of being and to make all things go smoothly, the world of mutual reliance or interdependence ought to be created. Such an ideal world is called 'the fact and fact world perfectly harmonized.' [117]

---

[110] 窺基　　[111] 玄奘　　[112] 事法界　　[113] 理法界　　[114] 理事無礙法界
[115] 事事無礙法界　　[116] 相入相卽　　[117] 事事無礙法界

To elucidate the possibility of such an ideal world, the 'Ten Profound Theories'[118] are set forth:-

1. The theory of co-relation, in which all things have co-existence and simultaneous rise.[119] All are co-existent not only in relation to space but also in relation to time. There is no distinction of past, present and future, each of them being inclusive of the other. Distinct as they are and separated as they seem to be in time, all beings are united to make one entity—from the universal point of view.

2. The theory of perfect freedom in which all beings 'broad and narrow' commune with each other without any obstacle.[120] The power of all beings as to intension and extension is equally limitless. One action, however small, includes all actions. One and all are commutable freely and uninterruptedly.

3. The theory of mutual penetration of dissimilar things.[121] All dissimilar existences have something in common. Many in one, one in many, and all in unity.

4. The theory of freedom—i.e., freedom from ultimate distinctions—in which all elements are mutually identified.[122] It is a universal identification of all beings. Mutual identification is, in fact, self-negation. Identifying oneself with another, one can synthesize with another. Negating oneself and identifying oneself with another constitute synthetical identification. This is a peculiar theory or practice of Mahayana. It is applied to any theory or practice. Two opposed theories or incompatible facts are often identified. Often a happy solution of a question is arrived at by the use of this method. As the result of mutual penetration and mutual identification, we have the concept, One in All, All in One, One behind All, All behind One, the great and small, or the high and low, moving harmoniously together. Even the humblest partaking of the work in peace, no one stands separately or independently alone. It is the world of perfect harmony.

5. The theory of complementarity by which the hidden and the manifested will make the whole by mutual supply.[123] If one is inside, the other will be outside, or vice versa. Both complementing each other will complete one entity.

6. The theory of construction by mutual penetration of minute and abstruse matters.[124] Generally speaking, the more minute or

---

[118] 十玄門　[119] 同時具足相應門　[120] 廣狹自在無礙門
[121] 一多相容不同門　[122] 諸法相即自在門　[123] 隱密顯了俱成門
[124] 微細相容安立門

abstruse a thing is, the more difficult it is to be conceived. Things minute or abstruse beyond a man's comprehension must also be realizing the theory of one-in-many and many-in-one as in No. 3.

7.   The theory of inter-reflection, as in the region surrounded by the Indra net (a net decorated with a bright stone on each knot of the mesh) where the jewels reflect brilliance upon each other, so the real facts of the world are 'mutually permeating and reflecting.[125]

8.   The theory of elucidating the truth by factual illustrations.[126] Truth is manifested in fact and fact is the source of enlightening.

9.   The theory of 'variously completing ten time-periods creating one entity.' [127] Each of past, present and future contains three periods, thus making up nine periods which altogether form one period—nine and one, ten periods in all. The ten periods, all distinct yet mutually penetrating, will complete the one-in-all principle. All other theories are chiefly concerned with the mutual penetration in 'horizontal plane,' but this theory is concerned with the 'vertical connection,' or time, meaning that all beings separated along the nine periods, each complete in itself, are, after all, interconnected in one period—the one period formed by the nine.

10.   The theory of completion of virtues by which the chief and the retinue work together harmoniously and brightly.[128] If one is the chief, all others will work as his retinue, i.e., according to the one-in-all and all-in-one principle, they really form one complete whole, permeating one another.

The above are called the 'New Profound Theories.' The 'Old Theories' coming down from Tu-shun [129] to Chih-yen [130] were afterward reformed by Fa-tsang [131] (643-712), and this reformed version, called the New Profound Theories, is now used by the school as the authoritative theories. They are somewhat complicated, but the theories of co-relation (1), mutual penetration (3), mutual identification (4), and the completion of common virtue (10) are to be studied with special care as illustrating the one-in-all and all-in-one principle of this school.

Next we have the 'Sixfold Specific Nature of all *Dharmas*.' [132]

---

[125] 因陀羅網境界門   [126] 託事顯法生解門   [127] 十世隔法異成門
[128] 唯心迴轉善成門   [129] 杜順   [130] 智儼   [131] 法藏   [132] 六相

121

They are as follows :-

1. Universality ;[133] 2. Speciality [134] as to character itself; 3. Similarity ;[135] 4. Diversity [136] as to the relation of beings; 5. Integration ;[137] 6. Differentiation [138] as to the state of becoming.

For example, the human being. All human beings, in common, are entities.

(1) *Universality:* consisting of five aggregates.

(2) *Speciality:* (But) the organs of different human beings have 'speciality' in the sense of unique character or power.
All have eyes but not all eyes have the same power.

(3) *Similarity:* All organs are similar as organs, or in the sense of co-relation in one organism.

(4) *Diversity:* (But) each organ also possesses 'diversity' since it has a special relation to the whole.

(5) *Integration:* All organs working together to complete the whole unitary being.

(6) *Differentiation:* (But) each organ, being in its own special position, performs its own differentiating function.

Universality is the total of special parts, while Speciality is the special parts constituting the whole. Similarity means that all Specialities have the capacity of being equally harmonious in constituting the whole. Diversity means that Specialities, in spite of their being mutually harmonious, keep their special features. Integration means that Specialities, though they are special, make up Universality by uniting themselves. Differentiation means that Specialities, though they make up Universality, do not lose their own special features. For example, as to a building, Universality is the whole house; the one includes many special constituents. Speciality is the constituents themselves: the many are not one, but are not separate from one. Similarity means that all the constituents do not conflict with one another and all together constitute the whole house. Diversity means that all the constituents of the house keep their own Specialties. Integration is the perfect union of all parts, an interdependent causation of the one and the many. Differentiation means that all constituents, each staying in its proper position, keep their Specialties.

---

[133] 總相　[134] 別相　[135] 同相　[136] 異相　[137] 成相　[138] 壞相

The Sixfold Nature indicates that no elements *(dharma)* have single and independent existence, each possessing the Sixfold Nature immanent in itself. The theory of the Sixfold Nature is thus necessary for the proper understanding of the Ten Profound Theories.

Of the six characteristics 1, 3 and 5 are of the nature of equalization and unification while 2, 4 and 6 are of the nature of discrimination and distribution. Every *dharma* has a sixfold specific nature, and the one-in-all and all-in-one principles are expounded by the Ten Profound Theories.

The ground on which the Ten Theories are established is further explained. The ground is based on the general Buddhistic ideas. It is tenfold:

1. Because all beings as well as all things are manifested from ideation, the source is one.

2. Because all beings as well as all things have no determinate nature, all move freely, selflessness being the ultimate truth.

3. Because the causation theory means interdependence or interrelation, all are co-related.

4. Because the *dharma*-nature *(dharmata)* or the Buddha-nature *(Buddha svabhava)* is possessed in common by all, they have similar liability.

5. Because the phenomenal world is said to be as a dream or illusion, the world of One-Truth can be molded in any way without restraint.

6. Because the phenomenal world is said to be as shadow or image, the world of One-Truth can be molded in any way.

7. Since, in the Enlightenment of the Buddha, the causes of production are known to be boundless, the effects are manifold or limitless, but they do not hinder each other; rather they cooperate to form a harmonious whole.

8. Because the Buddha's Enlightenment is ultimate and absolute, the transformation of the world is at his will.

9. Because of the function of the Buddha's profound meditation the transformation of the world is at his will.

10. Because of the supernatural power originating from deliverance, the transformation of the world is free.

Of the above, 1 to 4 are most important and are easily realized.

The principle 'one-in-all and all-in-one' (mutual penetration) [139] is based on function, action, energy or efficiency, while the principle 'one-is-all and all-is-one' (mutual identification) [140] is expounded according to beings or things themselves or according to their own characteristics *(svalaksana)*.

The ten theories interdependently cause the manifestation of the ideal world, and such a causation theory is called the 'Causation by Ten Theories.' The theory of causation is otherwise called, as we have seen above, the Causation of *Dharma-dhatu* (Element of the Elements). These causations are, after all, the causation of mere mind,[141] that is, pure idealism. The causation theories peculiar to this school mean general interdependence, universal relativity, causes and effects being interwoven everywhere. Thus it makes from the beginning one perfect whole without any single independent thing— all comprehensive *mandala* (circle) and the Cycle of Permanent Wave illumined throughout by the great compassionate Sun-Buddha (Vairocana).

This is in fact the world of dynamic becoming on the basis of selflessness *(anatmata)*. The ideal world in perfection is called the 'Lotus-store'[142] or the Universe of One-Truth,[143] or the World of Illumination by the Buddha, the Perfectly Enlightened.

The Ten Stages of the *Bodhisattva*,[144] originally found in the *Dasabhumi Sutra* of this school, are simply namesakes for ordinary persons who have no experience in the Path of No Learning *(asaiksamarga)*. These Mahayanistic Stages are said to have been propounded in order to distinguish the position of the *bodhisattva* from those of the Hinayanistic *sravaka* (direct disciple) and *pratyeka-buddha* (Buddha for himself).

The first is the Stage of Joy *(pramudita)* [145] in which one attains the holy nature for the first time and reaches the highest pleasure, having been removed from all errors of Life-View *(darsana-marga)* and having fully realized the twofold *sunyata (pudgala* and *dharma)*.

The second is the Stage of Purity *(vimala)* [146] in which one reaches the perfection of discipline *(sila)* and becomes utterly taintless with regard to morality.

The third is the Stage of Illumination *(prabha-kari)*[147] in which

---

[139] 相入,相容　　[140] 相即,即切　　[141] 唯心緣起　　[142] 蓮華藏世界
[143] 一眞法界　　[144] 菩薩十地　　[145] 歡喜地　　[146] 離垢地
[147] 發光地

one gets the perfection of forbearance *(ksanti)* and becomes free from the errors of Life-Culture *(bhavana-marga)*, having attained the deepest introspective insight.

The fourth is the Stage of Flaming Insight [148] in which one attains the perfection of bravery or effort *(virya)*, thereby increasing the power of insight more and more.

The fifth is the Stage of Utmost Invincibility *(sudurjaya)* [149] in which one gets the perfection of meditative concentration *(samadhi)*, thereby completing, in the mental activity, the correspondence of the twofold truth (worldly truth and higher truth).

The sixth is the Stage of Mental Presence *(abhimukhi)*[150] in which one attains the perfection of wisdom or insight *(prajna)* and ever retains equanimity as to purity and impurity.

The seventh is the Stage of Far-Going *(duran-gama)* [151] which is the position farthest removed from the selfish state of the two Vehicles. Here one completes the perfection of expediency *(upaya)*[152] and begins to exercise the great mercy to all beings.

The eighth is the Stage of Immovability *(acala)* [153] in which one completes the perfection of vow *(pranidhana)* and, abiding in the View of No Characteristic *(alaksana)*, wanders freely according to any opportunity.

The ninth is the Stage of Good Wisdom *(sadhumati)* [154] in which one attains the ten holy powers, having completed the perfection of power *(bala)*, and preaches everywhere discriminating between those who are to be saved and those who are not.

The last is the Stage of Ideal Cloud *(dharma-megha)* [155] in which one is able to preach the Ideal to all the world equally, just as the rainclouds pour down heavy rains during drought. This is practically the Stage of the Buddha who is represented by such a *Bodhisattva*.

These Ten Stages are given in the 'Wreath' text *(Dasabhumi Sutra)* and are special to the Mahayana. Although they are an enumeration of the ascending Stages of *Bodhisattva*, they can be used for practical purposes by any aspirant who is studying or practising meditation in order to proceed to the holy stages in the future.

Besides these there are other different enumerations in the Hinayana as well as in the Mahayana, but the above is representative of the Ten *Bodhisattva* Stages.

---

[148] 焔慧地   [149] 極難勝地   [150] 現前地   [151] 遠行地   [152] 方便
[153] 不動地   [154] 善慧地   [155] 法雲地

125

IX. THE TENDAI SCHOOL[1]
(THE LOTUS SCHOOL)
(Saddharma-Pundarika)

(Phenomenology)
[Mahayanistic]

(1)   Preliminary

'Tendai' (T'ien-t'ai) is the name of a mountain in T'aichou, South China. A great philosopher, Chih-i[2] (Chih-kai, 531-597) lived on the mountain and taught his disciples during the Ch'ên and Sui dynasties. The school founded by him was generally called the T'ien-t'ai after the mountain but was properly named the 'Fa-hua'[3] (Japanese, Hokke) after the title of the text *Saddharma-pundarika*[4] from which the doctrine of the school is derived—'Fa-hua' being a translation of this title. We often designate it the 'Lotus' text or school as the *Lotus of the Good Law* is the full translation of the title.

Prior to the establishment of the school a study of the *Lotus* text was commenced as early as 300 A.D. and lectures were delivered everywhere. A commentary (in 4 vols.) was completed by Chu Fa-tsung [5] but research into the subject matter of the *Lotus* was started after Kumarajiva's [6] translation of the text in 406 A.D.

By noticing the many commentaries compiled in the fifth century by his pupils and successors, we can well understand and appreciate to what an extent and how seriously the study of the *Lotus* was undertaken. During this time eight complete commentaries were written and many special studies of particular aspects of the doctrine were made.

Although the study was commenced in the North and the work on the *Lotus*, i.e., the translations and commentaries, was begun in the North, the school of learning flourished particularly in the South,

---

[1] 天台   [2] 智顗   [3] 法華   [4] 妙法蓮華經 English translation by H. Kern: *The Saddharma-Pundarika, or the Lotus of the True Law*, Sacred Books of the East, Vol. XXI, London, 1884 and by W. E. Soothill: *The Lotus of the Wonderful Law*, London, 1930.
[5] 竺法汰   [6] 鳩摩羅什

a fact which eventually gave rise to the foundation of the Tendai School.

The *Lotus* text, we should bear in mind, was originally translated by Kumarajiva into seven volumes of twenty-seven chapters. Fa-hsien,[7] in the quest of another chapter (28th), started for India in 475 A.D. When he reached Khotan, he found the chapter on Devadatta, a cousin and a traitor of the Buddha. He returned and requested Fa-i,[8] an Indian, to translate it. This translation was later added to the earlier text. Thus, there are twenty-eight chapters in the present *Lotus.*

The doctrine of the *Nirvana* text was another fascinating subject of learning at that period. Tao-sheng,[9] already conspicuous in the study of the *Lotus,* was also a leader in the exposition of the ideal of Nirvana. On reading the old *Nirvana* text, whch was in six Chinese volumes, he set forth the theory that the *icchantika* [10] (a class of men who were bereft of Buddha-nature and destined to be unable to evolve to the Buddha stage) could attain Buddhahood. Soon afterwards, a Sanskrit text of the *Mahaparinirvana Sutra* [11] was introduced and translated. The theory that the *icchantika* could attain Buddhahood was found in the text. People marveled at his deep insight, and he himself was satisfied. He compiled a commentary on the *Nirvana* soon thereafter. His other theory of an abrupt attainment of Buddhahood [12] is equally famous.

Although the study of the *Nirvana* text continued in the South and in the North, the Nirvana School was founded in the South where most of the able scholars lived. When the T'ien-t'ai School appeared, the southern branch of the Nirvana School was absorbed into it.

Nirvana is not a natural death according to both Hinayana and Mahayana. Even in Pali Buddhism, Nirvana is held to have happened at the free will of the Buddha. Mahayana goes one step further and asserts that the birth and death of his physical body were simply manifestations but his 'spiritual' body exists permanently. The term 'spiritual body' is 'dharma-kaya' in Sanskrit. The Buddha said, "Grieve you not, O Brethren, saying 'Our master has past!' What I have taught, (*Dharma,* ideal and *Vinaya,* disciplinary rules) will

---

[7] 法獻　　[8] 法意　　[9] 道生　　[10] 一闡提　　[11] *Taishō.* No. 1527. 大涅槃經
[12] 頓悟

be your masters after my death. If you keep to my teachings and practice them, is it not the same as if my *Dharma*-body [13] remained here forever?" [14] The *Dharma-kaya* here means that his body remains as 'dharma' (scripture) after the death of his physical body. According to the development of the idea of *Dharma,* the intensive meaning of *Dharma-kaya* will also be changed. The body is conceived as scripture, element, principle, cosmical, spiritual and ideal. The Mahayana takes it to be a spiritual body or a cosmic body that remains forever. This is the fundamental idea of the Nirvana School.

The pansophistic idea developed out of the cosmical body of the Buddha does not admit the existence of the *icchantika* who are destined never to attain Buddhahood. Further study disclosed the theory that all beings without exception have the Buddha-nature. Even the attribute of the cosmical body which is bereft of attribute is described as permanence, bliss, self and purity,[15] the first three being contrary to the fundamental ideas of Buddhism; i.e., impermanence, suffering, and selflessness *(anitya, duhkha, anatman)*. Nirvana for the school is liberation (from human desire, *moksa*), perfect wisdom *(prajna)* and the *Dharma-kaya* (cosmical body). On the whole, the Nirvana School of the South held the doctrine of permanency of Nirvana while the Nirvana scholars of the North regarded the Nirvana doctrine as subordinate to the Avatansaka (Wreath) doctrine. Although the Nirvana School was not very influential, its tenets of *Dharma-kaya* (cosmical body) and *Buddha-svabhava* (Buddha-nature) have had immense influence over all Mahayanistic schools of China.

In the end, this school lost its independence and was absorbed into the T'ien-t'ai School, just as the Ti-lun School [16] was united with the Avatansaka School,[17] as we have seen before.

(2) Historical

The founder of the T'ien-t'ai School is Hui-wen (550-577) [18] who seems to have been a great scholar and a leader of many hundreds of students. When he discovered a verse on the Middle Path in the *Madhyamika Sastra* [19] and an annotation concerning the word

---

[13] Cf. p. 50.
[14] *The Nirvana Sutra*
[15] 常樂我淨   [16] 地論宗   [17] 華嚴宗   [18] 慧文   [19] 中論

128

'insight' in the *Mahaprajnaparamita S'āstra*[20] both by Nagarjuna,[21] he at once awoke to the truth.

The verse runs as follows:

"What is produced by causes,
That, I say, is identical with Void.
It is also identical with mere name.
It is again the purport of the Middle Path."[22]

This would make the causal origination *(pratitya-samutpada)* a synonym of 'Void' *(Sunyata)* and the temporary name of the Middle Path. The triple truth of the T'ien-t'ai School originates here.

Hui-wen further found in the *Mahaprajnaparamita* a sentence concerning the knowledge of the species of the path or teaching,[23] the knowledge of all that exists,[24] and the knowledge of the species of all that exists.[25] By the knowledge of the species of the path, the knowledge of all that exists is obtained. By this, the knowledge of the species of all that exists is attained. By this last, the inertia of human desire is cut off.

In annotating the above passage, Nagarjuna says: "All the aspects of knowledge now in question are obtained at the same time. But in order to promote the understanding of the perfection of wisdom *(prajnaparamita)*, they are propounded distinctly one after another." Reading this annotation, Hui-wen at once understood the meaning. The knowledge of the species of the path is the knowledge of the path or teaching that illumines the world of distinction and mere name. The knowledge of all that exists is that of non-existence *(sunyata)* and reveals the world of non-distinction and equality, while the knowledge of the species of all that exists is the knowledge of the middle view that illumines the Middle Path which inclines neither to existence nor to non-existence and neither to distinction nor to non-distinction. Thus the threefold knowledge of this school is obtained.

Therefore, objectively, we have the triple truth, and, subjectively, we have the triple knowledge. Of the triple truth the Void[26] is at the same time the temporary,[27] the temporary is at the same time the middle,[28] which is at the same time the Void.

[20] 大般若波羅蜜多經 [21] 龍樹 [22] Ch. XXIV, verse 18 衆因緣生法 我說卽是無, 亦爲是假名, 亦是中道義 [23] 道種智 [24] 一切智 [25] 一切種智 [26] 空 [27] 假 [28] 中

The triple identity is the fundamental theory of this school.

The second patriarch, Hui-ssu [29] (514-577), received careful training from his teacher Hui-wen. When he became ill, he realized that illness originates from action which, in turn, originates from the mind and has no objective reality. If we trace it to its source in the mind, action cannot be seized and our body is like the shadow of cloud which has specific character but no reality. He thus acquired purity of his mind. In 554, he retired to Tasu Mountain [30] in Kuang-chou,[31] where he taught many hundred pupils.

The third patriarch, Chih-i [32] (Chih-kai 531-597), came to him at this time and received special instruction in the meditation of the *Lotus*. Later Chih-i, at the age of thirty-eight, went to T'ien-t'ai with his pupil Hui-pien [33] and some twenty others. Here he found an old scholar, Ting-kuang, [34] who had come there forty years ago. He welcomed Chih-i and gave instructions in all branches of Buddhist learning.

Chih-i lived on the mountain for nine years and built the great monastery called Kuo-ch'ing.[35] He was generally honored by the name 'Great Master of T'ien-t'ai.' [36] The Emperor Yang-ti of Sui, who was then the Governor General of Yangchou, gave him the title of 'Chih-chê,' [37] a Man of Great Wisdom. As regards the superiority of his personal character and the depth of his learning, he stands high above all the rest of the Buddhist scholars of China. In his power of organization of Buddhist doctrine and of training of Buddhist students, no one will ever measure up to him. The final completion of the T'ien-t'ai School is due to him, and, therefore, he is honored as the first patriarch of the school, though he was actually the third patriarch in the lineage of learning of the T'ien-t'ai doctrine.

The second patriarch of the school was his able pupil Kuan-ting [38] (561-632). The three great works of Chih-i are all compilations of Kuan-ting.

The sixth patriarch, Chan-jan[39] (717-782), was a great scholar and the reviver of the school which was somewhat declining in later years. One of his pupils, Tao-sui,[40] was the next patriarch and the teacher of Saichō, or Dengyō Daishi,[41] founder of the school in Japan. Saichō, when twenty years old, went to Nara and studied the T'ien-

---

[29] 慧思 [30] 大蘇 [31] 光州 [32] 智顗 [33] 慧辯 [34] 定光 [35] 國清寺
[36] 天台大師 [37] 智者 [38] 灌頂 [39] 湛然 [40] 道邃 [41] 最澄·傳改大師

130

t'ai doctrine under some scholars, who came to Japan with the *vinaya* master Kanjin,[42] and read the three great works of Chih-i. When he was half-way through in his second perusal of those works, he received an Imperial order to go to China for Buddhist study. He received the T'ien-t'ai doctrine and the *bodhisattva* ordination from Tao-sui, the mystic doctrines *(mantra)* from Shun-chiao [43] and the Zen meditation from Hsiu-jan.[44] On his return after one year's sojourn in China, he founded the Tendai School and taught the *'Lotus'* doctrine, the Shingon [45] mysticism, the Zen [46] meditation and Vinaya [47] practices. The educational headquarters on the Hiei Mountain was established by Saichō and became the greatest center of Buddhist learning in Japan. Once there were some 3,000 monasteries to house the students thronging there from all branches of Buddhism, exoteric and esoteric. At present there are three branches of the Tendai School; namely, Sammon,[48] Jimon [49] and Shinsei,[50] the last being an Amita-pietism.[51] The monasteries belonging to the three branches number more than 4,000 at the present time.

(3) Philosophical

The critical classification of the Buddha's teaching by the Tendai School is 'Five Periods and Eight Doctrines.'[52] The first period was the Time of Wreath (Kegon).[53] The doctrine taught in this period was what the Buddha had conceived in his Enlightenment, i.e., the elucidation of his Enlightenment itself. His disciples could not understand him at all and they stood as if they were 'deaf and dumb.'

The second period was the Time of the 'Deer Park'[54] where he preached the early *Agamas* [55] to suit the people of inferior capacity. His disciples were now able to follow his teaching and practiced accordingly in order to attain the fruition of *arhat* (saintly position). This period is also called the Time of Inducement,[56] or a period in which. the people were attracted to the higher doctrine.

The third period was the Time of Development.[57] It was the time when the Hinayanistic people were converted to the Mahayana doctrine and for that purpose the Buddha preached what we call *Vaipulya* (developed) texts. As the Buddha often rebuked the *arhats*

---

[42] 鑑眞　[43] 順教　[44] 修然　[45] 眞言　[46] 禪　[47] 律　[48] 山門
[49] 寺門　[50] 眞盛　[51] See Chapter XII.　[52] 五時八教　[53] 華嚴
[54] 鹿苑時　[55] 阿含　[56] 誘引時　[57] 方等時

for their wrong or short-sighted views, this period is called the Time of Rebuke.[58] The Hinayanists, after the Buddha's reasoning, became aware of their short-sightedness and learned to appreciate Mahayana.

The fourth period was the Time of Wisdom (*prajna*),[59] when the *Prajnaparamita* was preached and all the ideas of distinction and acquisition were mercilessly rejected. It is, therefore, called the Time of Selection.[60] During this period, the doctrine of 'Void' was taught but the Void itself was again negated. In the end everything reverts to the ultimate Void. So the time of *prajna* was also called the Time of Exploring and Uniting of the *Dharmas*,[61] denying all analysis and unifying them all in one.

The fifth period was the Time of the *Lotus* and *Nirvana Sutras*.[62] Here the exploring or analyzing and the uniting of the doctrines are taught. The view that the three Vehicles (those of disciples, self-enlightened ones and would-be Buddhas) can obtain saintly fruition was only a temporary teaching (exploring), but the three finally were united into one Vehicle (uniting). Thus the fifth period is specially called the Time of Opening and Meeting.[63] The object of the Buddha's advent on earth was to save all beings and that object can only be accomplished by the *Lotus*. Therefore, the *Lotus* is the ultimate doctrine among all the Buddha's teachings and is the king of all the *sutras*. The *Nirvana* text was taught at the same time, but it is a résumé of all that he had expounded before.

The division into five periods shows that the Buddha's teaching is here arranged chronologically. But the Buddha, while teaching, would utilize all five at once when occasions required. Therefore, in order to know the nature of the Buddha's teachings we must arrange them properly. This division into eight doctrines is proposed to meet this purpose. First the four doctrines as to the method of teaching:[64]

1. *Abrupt Doctrine*.[65] In it the Buddha preaches what he had conceived without using any expediency; this is the time of the *Wreath*.

2. *Gradual Doctrine*.[66] In it the Buddha induces people gradually into deeper thinking, using all sorts of measures; this is the time of the Deer Park, of Development and of Wisdom.

---

[58] 彈呵時   [59] 般若   [60] 淘汰時   [61] 會一切法   [62] 法華涅槃時
[63] 開會時   [64] 化儀四教   [65] 頓教   [66] 漸教

132

3. *Mystic Doctrine*.[67] It is in reality a mystical indeterminate doctrine. It is indeterminate and varied because many a listener is concealed from another by the Buddha's supernatural power and each thinks that the Buddha is teaching him alone. Thus, all hear separately and variously. Such indeterminacy exists from the time of the *Wreath* to the time of Wisdom.

4. *Indeterminate Doctrine*.[68] It is a non-mystical indeterminate doctrine. All listeners know that all are hearing together and yet they hear differently and understand variously.

These four methodological doctrines are to cultivate the learners' capacity, and are, therefore, applied only prior to the preaching of the *Lotus*. Such methodology is useless in the *Lotus* because the teaching of the *Lotus* is neither abrupt, nor gradual, nor mystical, nor indeterminate. That is, the time of the *Wreath* will include the abrupt, mystic, and indeterminate doctrines while the times of the Deer Park, Development and Wisdom include the gradual, mystic and indeterminate.

Next, the four doctrines as to the nature of the teaching itself :[69]

1. *The Doctrine of Pitakas* (Scripture).[70] *Agamas* (traditions or discourses) and all Hinayana doctrines, such as those found in the *Vaibhasika* literature.

2. *The Doctrine Common to All*.[71] It is common to the three Vehicles and is the elementary doctrine of Mahayana. While an inferior *bodhisattva* follows the same practices as the people of the three Vehicles, a superior *bodhisattva* will penetrate into the state of the following two steps or doctrines.

3. *Distinct Doctrine*.[72] It is purely Mahayana and is special to *bodhisattvas*. The first and second doctrines teach the simple one-sided Void [73] while this doctrine teaches the Middle Path,[74] and, therefore, is distinct and separate.

4. *Round Doctrine*.[75] 'Round' means perfection, all-pervading, all-fulfilling, all-permeating. The Distinct Doctrine teaches an independent and separate Middle Path and is a simple-separate mean, while the Round Doctrine teaches the Middle Path of perfect permeation and mutual identification. Therefore, it is not a separate, one-sided Middle Path, but

---

[67] 秘密敎　　[68] 不定敎　　[69] 化法四敎　　[70] 三藏敎　　[71] 通敎　　[72] 別敎
[73] 偏空　　[74] 中道　　[75] 圓敎

the Middle Path as noumenon, perfectly harmonious, theoretically and practically. Thus, 'round' means that one element contains all elements, i.e., the principle of "One is all and all is one."

Now if we examine these five periods of teaching in relation to the four doctrines as to the nature of the teaching, we have the following result:

1. The Time of the *Wreath* is not yet pure 'round' because it includes the Distinct Doctrine.

2. The Time of the Deer Park is only one-sided as it teaches only Hinayanistic views.

3. The Time of Development teaches all four doctrines together and therefore is still relative.

4. The Time of Wisdom mainly teaches the Round Doctrine and yet is linked with the Common and Distinct Doctrines. Therefore, it is not quite perfect or complete.

5. The Time of the *Lotus* alone is purely 'round' and superlatively excellent, wherein the purpose of the Buddha's advent on earth is fully and completely expressed.

The supplementary *Nirvana* summarizes what the Buddha had preached during his whole life, i.e., the three Vehicles and the four doctrines were dismissed by converting the three Vehicles to the One Vehicle and combining the four doctrines with the one ultimate Round Doctrine. Thus, all teachings of the Buddha are absorbed finally into the *Lotus* which is considered by Tendai to be the Supreme Doctrine of all Buddhism.

The school admits the existence of only One Vehicle (Ekayana) to convey all beings across the ocean of life, though it also admits the temporary existence of the three Vehicles (Triyana), i.e., *sravaka* (hearers, disciples),[76] *pratyeka-buddha* (self-enlightened, enlightened for himself),[77] and *bodhisattva* (would-be Buddha).[78]

For expediency, these three Vehicles are taught, but ultimately they are all brought back to the one true *Buddha-yana*.[79]

In Nagarjuna's commentary on the *Mahaprajnaparamita* there is an annotation of the fundamental principles: All conditioned things are impermanent *(sarva-sanskara-anityam)*;[80] all elements are self-

---

[76] 聲聞乘   [77] 緣覺乘   [78] 菩薩乘   [79] 佛乘   [80] 諸行無常

less [81] *(sarva-dharma-anatman);* and Nirvana is quiescence *(nirvana-santam),*[82] in which it is said that these 'three law-seals' (signs of Buddhism) [83] can be extended to four by adding another, all is suffering *(sarva-duhkham),* or can be abridged to one 'true state' seal. The 'true state' [84] may be translated as 'noumenon.' [85] This school interprets the 'true state' as 'no state' or 'no truth,' but it does not mean that it is false; 'no truth' or 'no state' here means that it is not a truth or a state established by argument or conceived by thought but that it transcends all speech and thought. Again, Tendai interprets it as 'one truth' *(eka-satya),*[86] but 'one' here is not a numerical 'one'; it means 'absolute.' The principle of the Tendai doctrine centers on this true state of all elements.

The true state or noumenon can only be realized through phenomena. In the second chapter of the *Lotus* it is said: "What the Buddha has accomplished is the *dharma* foremost, rare and inconceivable. Only the Buddhas can realize the true state of all *dharmas;* that is to say, all *dharmas* are thus-formed,[87] thus-natured,[88] thus-substantiated,[89] thus-caused,[90] thus-forced,[91] thus-activated,[92] thus-circumstanced,[93] thus-effected,[94] thus-remunerated [95] and thus-beginning-ending-completing." [96]

Through these manifestations of Thusness or phenomena we can see the true state. Nay, these manifestations *are* the true state. There is no noumenon besides phenomenon; phenomenon itself is noumenon.

One should not think, as is ordinarily done, that there exists an abiding motionless substance at the center, around which its qualities exist, moving and changing. If you suppose noumenon to be such an abiding substance, you will be misled altogether. Even the Mahayanistic people who maintain the doctrine of two truths—the worldly or popular truth and the higher truth—are often mistaken by a dichotomic idea of argument. The Tendai School, therefore, sets forth the threefold truth; i.e., the truth of void,[97] the

---

[81] 諸法無我　　[82] 涅槃靜寂　　[83] 三法印　　[84] 實相
[85] This 'true state' or noumenon must not be interpreted as separate from, or above, or beyond phenomena. The word 'noumenon' is only a partially accurate term.

[86] 一諦　　[87] 如是相　　[88] 如是性　　[89] 如是體　　[90] 如是因　　[91] 如是力
[92] 如是作　　[93] 如是緣　　[94] 如是果　　[95] 如是報　　[96] 如是本末究竟
[97] 空諦

135

truth of temporariness [98] and the truth of mean.[99] All things have no reality and, therefore, are void. But they have temporary existence. They are at the same time mean or middle, that is, true state, Thusness.[100]

According to the school the three truths are three in one, one in three. The principle is one but the method of explanation is threefold. Each one of the three has the value of all. Therefore, when our argument is based on the void, we deny the existence of both the temporary and the middle, since we consider the void as transcending all. Thus, the three will all be void. The same will be the case when we argue by means of the temporary truth or the middle truth. Therefore, when one is void, all will be void; when one is temporary, all will be temporary; when one is middle, all will be middle.[101] They are otherwise called the identical void, identical temporary and identical middle.[102] It is also said to be the perfectly harmonious triple truth [103] or the absolute triple truth.[104]

We should not consider the three truths as separate because the three penetrate one another and are found perfectly harmonized and united together. A thing is void but is also temporarily existent. It is temporary because it is void, and the fact that everything is void and at the same time temporary is the middle truth.

Non-existence and temporary existence may be regarded as contrasts. The middle does not mean that it is between the two. It is over and above the two; nay, it is identical with the two, because the true state means that the middle is the very state of being void and temporary. The three truths are found ever united and harmonious. In fact, they are mutually inclusive. The Middle Path *(madhyama pratipad)*,[105] the True State *(svalaksana)*[106] and Thusness *(tathata)*[107] are here synonymous and identical in every way. Here one must bear in mind that though the word 'void' is used, it does not mean 'nothingness' but 'devoid of any thinking or feeling' or 'free from attachment.' [108] Even the idea of void is negated; it is altogether a negation. Then any existence ought to be temporary

---

[98] 假諦   [99] 中諦
[100] These names are derived from the verse of the *Madhyamika* 中論 which we quoted above. See Section 2, *Historical.*
[101] 一空一切空 一假一切假,一中一切中   [102] 卽空, 卽假, 卽中
[103] 圓融三諦   [104] 絕待三諦   [105] 中道   [106] 實相   [107] 如如   [108] 離情空

because all *dharmas* are 'established' in mind or exist by causal combinations. They exist only in name, not in reality; that is, they have 'nominal existence.'[109] Any permanent existence should be negated, but temporary existence should be admitted. That all things are void and temporary is the middle truth, i.e., the absolute.[110]

The ultimate truth taught in the Tendai School is Thusness *(Tathata)*, not thisness *(tattva)*. Thusness means the true state of things in themselves, the phenomenal world being the state of things manifested before us. The true state of things cannot be seen directly or immediately. We must see it in the phenomena which are ever changing and becoming. Thus the true state is dynamic. The phenomena themselves *are identical with* the true state of things. The true state of things is Thusness, i.e., things as they are manifested, just as moving waves are not different from the still water. We generally contrast the still water with the moving waves, but moving or staying they are only the manifestation of one and the same water. What is being manifested or shown outwardly is nothing but the thing itself. There is no difference between the two.

This is the theory of the true state of all *dharmas;* that is, all elements manifested are the elements in their own state *(sarva-dharma-svalaksana-ta)*.[111] Or, to use another expression, the 'worldly state (phenomenal) is permanent' *(lokalaksana-nityata)*.[112]

According to the Tendai doctrine any *dharma* expresses itself in all three truths. All existences are thus mutually permeating in all three truths.

The whole universe is said to have the constituency of 'three thousands,' but the theory is quite different from other pluralistic systems. It is not an enumeration of all *dharmas;* nor is it the world system of three Chiliocosms. What is it then? We must explain these 'three thousands.' The expression 'three thousands' does not indicate a numerical or substantial immensity, but is intended to show the inter-permeation of all *dharmas* and the ultimate unity of the whole universe.

As the basis of 'three thousands' the school sets forth a world-system of ten realms.[113] That is to say, the world of living beings is divided into ten realms, of which the higher four are saintly[114] and the lower six are ordinary:[115]

---

[109] 立法假   [110] 絕待中   [111] 諸法實相   [112] 世間相即常住   [113] 十界
[114] 四聖   [115] 六凡

137

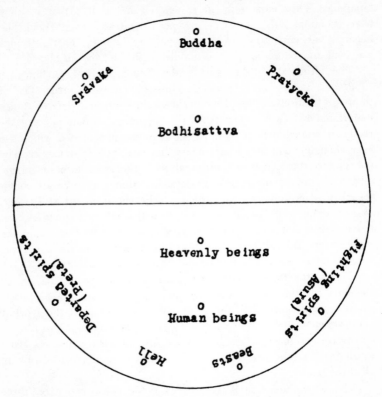

1. The realm of Buddhas.[116] A Buddha is not inside the circle of ten, but as he advents among men to preach his doctrine he is now partially included in it.

2. A *bodhisattva*:[117] a would-be-Buddha.

3. *Pratyeka-buddha*:[118] a Buddha for himself, not teaching others.

4. *Sravaka*:[119] a direct disciple of the Buddha.

The above four are classed as the saintly stages.

5. *Heavenly Beings:* [120] superhuman as they are, they cannot get perfectly enlightened without the teaching of the Buddha.

---

[116] 佛   [117] 菩薩   [118] 緣覺   [119] 聲聞   [120] 天

6. *Asura:*[121] fighting spirits. Though partially heavenly, they are placed in the lower half of the realm.

7. *Men:*[122] neutral in nature.

8. *Preta:*[123] departed beings, otherwise called 'hungry spirits.'

9. Beasts:[124] innocent in nature, including the whole animal kingdom.

10. Depraved men:[125] 'hellish beings' who are in the lowest stage.

These ten realms are mutually immanent and mutually inclusive, each one having in it the remaining nine realms. For example, the realm of men will include the other nine from Buddha to Hell, and so will any of the ten realms. Even the realm of Buddhas includes the nature of hell and all the rest, because a Buddha, though not hellish himself, intends to save the depraved or hellish beings, and therefore also has hell in his mind. In this sense, the realm of the Buddhas, too, includes the other nine realms.

This immanence of each of the ten worlds in all of them accounts for 100 worlds. Further, each of these realms has ten different features as we have seen above, i.e., form, nature, substance, force, action, cause, circumstance, effect, remuneration and the ultimate state. These are the ten features of Thusness.[126] By discovering these ten features in the 100 worlds, this school arrives at the doctrine of 1,000 realms.

Moreover, each realm consists of three divisions: the species of living beings, the species of space-region or vessel to live in and the species of five aggregates *(skandhas)* taken separately from living beings—form (=matter), perception, conception (idea), volition (will) and consciousness.[127] Thus there are three thousand realms, constituting the whole of manifested reality.

In Buddhism, 'three thousands' usually refers to the great Chiliocosm consisting of 1,000 small, 1,000 middle, and 1,000 large worlds.[128] With the Tendai School, however, it is not such a world-system, but is the universe of all beings and things, i.e., the whole world of dynamic becoming.

---

[121] 阿修羅　[122] 人　[123] 餓鬼　[124] 畜生　[125] 地獄　[126] 如是十相　[127] 色受想行識

[128] For example, in the Realistic (Kusha) School where an extensive world-system is elaborated along these lines.

It is not Buddhistic to seek the original principle or to consider the absolute as separate or independent. Here the Tendai School at once comes back to the ideation theory but expresses it somewhat differently. It is set forth that a conscious-instant or a moment of thought has 3,000 worlds immanent in it.[129] This is a theory special to this school and is called 'three thousand originally immanent,'[130] or 'three thousand immanent in principle,'[131] or 'three thousand immanent in nature'[132] or sometimes 'three thousand perfectly immanent.'[133] The immanency, either original, theoretical, natural or perfect, conveys one and the same idea; namely, that the one moment of thought is itself 3,000 worlds. Some consider this to be the nearest approach to the idea of the Absolute, but if you consider the Absolute to be the source of all creation it is not exactly the Absolute. Or, it may be considered to be a form of ideation theory, but if one thinks that ideation manifests the outer world by the process of dichotomy it is quite different, for it does not mean that one instant of thought produces the 3,000 worlds, because a production is the beginning of a lengthwise motion, i.e., timely production. Nor does it mean that the 3,000 worlds are included in one instant of thought because an inclusion is a crosswise existence, i.e., spacely coexistence.

Although here the 3,000-world doctrine is expounded on the basis of ideation, it is not mere ideation, for all the *dharmas* of the universe are immanent in one thought-instant but are not reduced to thought or ideation.

That the world is immanent in one moment of thought is the philosophy of immanence, phenomena being identical with conscious action. It may be called 'phenomenology,' each phenomenon, matter or mind, expressing its own principle or nature.

The principle each phenomenon expresses is the triple truth of harmony [134] (as void, as temporary and as mean), i.e., noumenon originally immanent, perfectly immanent, immanency in principle and immanency in nature. This means simply that a thing or being itself is the true state. Hence the phrase: "Everything, even the color or fragrance, is identical with the Middle Path, the Truth."[135]

---

[129] 一念三千　　[130] 本具三千　　[131] 理具三千　　[132] 性具三千
[133] 圓具三千　　[134] 圓融三諦　　[135] 一色一香，無非中道

140

The Threefold Body (*Trikaya*) of the Buddha is mentioned as Buddhahood; its representative theory is held by the Tendai School. Every Buddha of Perfect Enlightenment is supposed to possess three bodies. Although the original names of *Dharma-kaya, Sambhoga-kaya,* and *Nirmana-kaya* mean literally 'Principle-body,'[136] 'Enjoyment-body'[137] and 'Transformation-body,'[138] the term 'body' in the ordinary sense is rather misleading because it conveys the idea of a bodily existence. The Principle-body or Truth-body is the Ideal or the Principle or Truth itself without any personal existence. It is identical with the Middle Path Truth. The Enjoyment- or Reward-body is the person embodied with real insight, i.e., the body attained as the value of a long causal action. It is twofold: (a). The body for self-enjoyment, i.e., the person when he is enjoying his own enlightenment. (b). The body manifested for the enjoyment of others, i.e., *bodhisattvas* above the primary stage of saintly perfection. The Transformation-body is a body variously appearing to save people. It is also twofold: (a). The body exclusively for *bodhisattvas* of the primary stage that is a superior body of Transformation. (b). The body for those who are prior to the primary stage.

Every Buddha has these three aspects. While a Buddha represents the Principle or Truth which he himself has realized, he is, on the one hand, the realizer of the ideal or the enjoyer of his Enlightenment and, on the other hand, is the giver of the ideal or the deliverer of all who are suffering or perplexed. Thus the Buddha is viewed as the ideal (Enlightenment) itself, the enjoyer of it (the Enlightened), the giver of it to others (the Enlightener). The Enjoyment-body is obtained by the Buddha as a reward for long effort, while the Transformation-body is freely assumed by him in order to meet the needs of others and the world.

The Three Bodies of the Buddha are further divided into four, five, six or ten, but the above stated Threefold Body of the Tendai School may be regarded as the fundamental theory of Buddhahood.

---

[136] 法身　　[137] 應身　　[138] 化身

X. THE SHINGON SCHOOL
(THE TRUE WORD SCHOOL)[1]
(Mantra)

(Mysticism)
[Mahayanistic]

(1) Preliminary

Shingon or 'true word' is a translation of the Sanskrit 'mantra
which means a 'mystic doctrine' that cannot be expressed in ordinary
words. The doctrine which has been expressed in the Buddha's
words should be distinguished from the ideal which was conceived
in the Buddha's mind but not expressed in words. The Shingon
School aims at the Buddha's own ideal not expressed in any way.
An organization of Buddhists something like a Mantrayana seems
to have existed at Nalanda at the time of I-ching[2] in the 7th century,
for he mentions the existence of a bulk of Mantra literature there
and he himself is said to have been trained in the esoteric doctrine
though he could not master it satisfactorily. The center of learning
of mysticism, however, seems to have moved to the Vikramasilas
University farther down the Ganges, for Tibetan Buddhism had
special connections with the University.

It is a well known fact that in India as early as the Vedic period
there existed the Atharva practice of sorcery, which had four kinds
of the Homa cult (burnt sacrifice) in an exact coincidence with
those of the Buddhist practice. Such a cult might have been the
practice of Indian aborigines or at any rate of earlier immigrants.
Through a prolonged practice it eventually amalgamated into what
we call 'Tantrism,' which is often erroneously confused with the
Buddhist Diamond Vehicle Vajrayana.[3] If it is in any way connected
with obnoxious practices, it cannot be called Diamond Vehicle, for
that is a name given to a higher mystic doctrine, transcending all
Hinayana and Mahayana doctrines. Such Diamond Vehicle is only
represented by Kōbō Daishi[4] to whom the completion of the Mantra
doctrine is due.

---

[1] Chên-yen 眞言　　[2] 義淨　　[3] 金剛乘　　[4] 弘法大師 Kūkai, 774-835

The critical classification of the Buddha's teaching proposed by Kōbō Daishi is in reality the Ten Stages of spiritual development: [5] (1) Various paths of blind life driven by the instinctive impulse (the stage of common people). (2) The Vehicle of human beings striving to have a moral life (the stage of Confucianism). (3) The Vehicle of heavenly beings striving to have a supernatural power (the stage of Taoism and Brahmanism). These three are the worldly Vehicles. (4) The Vehicle of the direct pupils of the Buddha (Sravaka)[6] striving for a higher spiritual life as in Hinayana schools, Kusha,[7] and Jōjitsu [8] (stage of direct disciples). (5) The Vehicle of the self-enlightened ones (Pratyeka-buddha) [9] enjoying self-enlightenment yet falling into egoism. (6-7) The doctrine of Three Vehicles, holding the three Vehicles as real (the stages of the Sanron [10] and Hossō [11] Schools). (8-9) The doctrine of One Vehicle holding the one Vehicle as real (the stages of the Kegon [12] and Tendai [13] Schools). (10) The Diamond Vehicle as held by the Shingon School. These stages, coming one above the other, show the timely progress of the human mind, while those which stand co-ordinated at one time show the state of the progressive world.

Of these ten, the first is not to be classed as a Vehicle, but since the group of beings is on the way to a Vehicle it is included in the classification of Vehicles. According to the Shingon idea the Diamond Vehicle stands above all others; it is the supreme Vehicle of mysticism.

One must not forget that there exist two forms of the mystic doctrine; namely, the Taimitsu [14] and Tōmitsu.[15] The former is the mysticism handed down by the Tendai School and the latter transmitted in the Tōji Monastery of the Shingon School. They are not altogether different, but in practice the Tōmitsu is a special school for it seems to be much more thorough-going than the Taimitsu, while in theory neither side seems to concede in any way. For example, they agree in their treatment of the Buddhas, Sakyamuni and Mahavairocana, and further in the application of it to the Shinto, 'the Way of Gods,' of Japan. Those who would study the relation of Buddhism with

---

[5] 十住心 Not to be confused with the Ten Stages (dasa-bhumi 十地) of Mahayana. 異生羝羊心, 愚童持齋心, 嬰童無畏心, 唯蘊無我心, 拔業因種心 他緣大乘心, 覺心不生心, 一道無爲心, 極無自性心, 秘密莊嚴心
[6] 聲聞 [7] 俱舍 [8] 成實 [9] 緣覺 [10] 三論 [11] 法相 [12] 華嚴
[13] 天台 [14] 台密 [15] 東密

Shinto should clear up this point, for the Shinto names of Ryōbu ('Double Aspect') [16] and Ichijitsu ('One True') [17] originate from the difference of ideas in these two mystic schools.

(2) Historical

What we generally call the 'Miscellaneous Mystic' [10] was translated early in the 4th century A.D. Srimitra of Pai (Kucha, a state inhabited by a white race) translated some texts into Chinese. These were charms, cures and other sorts of sorcery, often containing some Mantra prayers and praises of gods or saints of higher grades, but generally speaking they could not be regarded as expressing a high aspiration.

What we can designate as 'Pure Mystics' [19] begins with the three able Indian teachers who arrived in China during the August T'ang period (713-765). The first arrival was Subhakarasinha [20] (637-735) who had been king of Orissa. He joined the priesthood and went to the Nalanda University over which Dharmagupta presided. Well versed in Buddhist concentration *(yoga)*, mystical verses *(dharani)* and fingers inter-twining *(mudra)*, he started for Kasmir and Tibet, and at last came to Ch'angan in 716, where he was well received by the Emperor Hsüan-tsung [21] (685-762).

Wu-hsing, [22] a learned Chinese, who traveled in India, met I-ching [23] at Nalanda and collected all sorts of Sanskrit texts. He died on his way home, but his collection reached Hua-yen Monastery in Ch'angan. On hearing this Subhakarasinha together with I-ching selected some of the important texts and in 725 translated the 'Great Sun' text *(Mahavairocana)* [24] and others. He wanted to return to India, but was not allowed to depart and died in 735

The second arrival was Vajrabodhi [25] (663-723) who, coming from South India, became a novice at Nalanda. At the age of fifteen, he went to West India and studied logic for four years under Dharmakirti, but came again to Nalanda where he received full ordination at twenty. For six years he devoted himself to the study of the *Vinaya* (Discipline) text and the Middle (Madhyamika) Doctrine under Santabodhi; for three years he studied the *Yogacara* by Asan-

---

16 兩部   17 一實
18 'Miscellaneous Mystics' texts are Nanjio Nos. 167, 309, 310. 雜密
19 純密   20 善無畏   21 立宗   22 無行   23 義淨
24 *Taishō,* Nos. 848 大日經   25 金剛智

ga, the *Vijnaptimatra* by Vasubandhu and the *Madhyanta-vibhanga* by Sthiramati under Jinabhadra, at Kapilavastu, North India; and for seven years he studied the *Vajra-sekhara* (Diamond Head) and other mystical texts under Nagabodhi, in South India. At last, he sailed to the southern sea and reached Loyang, China, in 720. He translated several important mystical texts, such as the *Vajra-sekhara*.[26] In 741, while in Ch'angan, he obtained permission to return to India, but on his way died in Loyang.

Amoghavajra [27] (705-774), an able pupil of Vajrabodhi, was from North India. He became a novice at the age of fifteen and arrived in Kuangtung together with his teacher whom he followed as far as Loyang, and received ordination at twenty. In twelve years he master-ed all the mystical doctrines and practices. When his teacher died he went to Ceylon together with his fellow pupils, thirty-seven in all, and visited a teacher, Samantabhadra,[28] from whom he learned the doc-trines of the *Vajra-sekhara-yoga* and *Maha-vairocana-garbhakosa*. With his rich collections he returned to Ch'angan in 746.

Amoghavajra was an instructor of Hsüan-tsung, Su-tsung [29] and Tai-tsung,[30] the three successive Emperors. He translated 110 differ-ent texts, in 143 Chinese volumes *(chüans)*. Among them was the most important text *Rita-sangraha* or *Tattva-sangraha (i.e., Vajra-sekhara)*,[31] 'Diamond Head' which, it is interesting to note, was incidentally discovered at the same time by Professor Tucci of Italy and Professor Ono of Japan. The former found in Tibet the Sanskrit text and the latter discovered in Japan the pictorial annotation of the text, which was brought back from China by Enchin (Chishō Daishi) [32] in 853. The happy coincidence of discovery of the two dis-tinguished professors will contribute much to the history of the mys-tical school of India, Tibet, China and Japan.

Ichigyō (I-hsing,[33] 683-727), a pupil of Subhakarasinha, who was well versed in the Sanron, the Zen, the Tendai, and the calendar, assisted Subharakarasinha in his translation of the 'Great Sun' text. On hearing the lecture from his teacher, Ichigyō compiled a com-mentary on the 'Sun' text called *Ta-jih Ching Su*.[34] Since he was a savant of the Tendai doctrine, his commentary is said to contain

---

[26] *Taishō*, No. 932
[27] 不空 [28] 普賢 [29] 肅宗 [30] 代宗 [31] *Taishō*, No. 865. 金剛頂經
[32] 圓珍, 智證大師 [33] 一行 [34] 大日經疏

some of the Tendai tenets. The commentary, as it was left in an unrevised manuscript, was afterward revised by Chih-yen,[35] a pupil of Subhakarasinha, and Wên-ku,[36] a pupil of Vajrabodhi, and was called by a new name *Ta-jih Ching I-shih*.[37] The Tōmitsu follows the former revision while the Taimitsu adopts the latter. Ichigyō studied under the two Indian teachers, Subhakara and Vajrabodhi, and received the cults of both the Realm of 'Matrix Repository,' *(Vajra-dhatu)* [38] and the Realm of Diamond Elements *(Garbha-kosa* [39] or *Garbha-kuksi)*, but he is said to have held the latter as the more important of the two.[40] To show the line of transmission we will give here a table of succession:

1. Subhakarasinha,[41] 637-735

I-hsing (Ichigyō),[42] 683-727

(Taimitsu)   Tōmitsu

2. Subhakarasinha, 637-735

I-lin (Girin) [43]

Shun-hsiao (Jungyō) [44]

Saichō,[45] Taimitsu, First transmission

3. Subhakarasinha, 637-735

Hsüan-ch'ao [46]

Hui-kuo [47] (Keikwa), 746-805

Kūkai,[48] Tōmitsu, Matrix Repository transmission.

4. Amoghavajra,[49] 705-774

Hui-kuo (Keikwa),[50] 746-805

---

[35] 智儼   [36] 温古   [37] 大日經義釋   [38] 金剛界   [39] 胎藏界
[40] For explanation of the two Realms, see below.
[41] 善無畏   [42] 一行   [43] 義林   [44] 順曉   [45] 最澄.傳敎大師   [46] 玄超
[47] 惠果   [48] 空海.弘法大師   [49] 不空   [50] 惠果

Kūkai, Tōmitsu, Diamond Element transmission.
|

1. Amoghavajra, 705-774   6. Amoghavajra, 705-774
    I-ts'ao (Gisō)[51] Gishin [52]   Hui-tsê (Esoku) [53]
                                       Genshō [54]

|_____|
                    |
Ennin (Jikaku Daishi)[55] , Taimitsu, Second transmission.

During the Hui-ch'ang [56] period (845) in China when there was destruction of Buddhism, Ennin (Jikaku Daishi) of the Tendai School was in China. He encountered troubles in this period but because of the disorder was able to collect valuable materials of mystic Buddhism.

Fortunately the mystical doctrine and practices were brought home by the four Daishis (Great Masters) and others, and were once and for all organized and systematized by the able hand of Kōbō Daishi [57] (Kūkai). The Kōyasan,[58] the center of learning of mystic doctrine, is said to have had 990 monasteries during its flourishing period.

Kōbō Daishi, the founder of the Shingon School in Japan, was the first and foremost artist in sculpture and in calligraphy. His literary style was admired in China as well as in Japan. He founded a private school of arts as an educational center of common people in Kyoto. Although it was dropped soon after his demise, his influence in primary education remained forever in Japan. It is but reasonable that the verse *Iroha* (alphabet) attributed to him was popularized and perpetuated in Japan.

At present the Shingon School has two branches, old and new; the monasteries under it number 10,000 in all.

(3) Philosophical

The Shingon School claims to be the only esoteric doctrine whereas all other schools are considered exoteric. The distinction of the two doctrines is found in the treatment of the spiritual body *(Dharmakaya)* of the Buddha. The spiritual body is the body of principle and therefore is colorless, formless and speechless, according to the exoteric doctrine; whereas according to the esoteric doctrine of the

---

[51] 義操   [52] 義眞   [53] 慧則   [54] 元政   [55] 圓仁.慈覺大師   [56] 會昌
[57] 空海.弘法大師   [58] 高野山

mystic school the preaching Buddha himself is of spiritual body and is with form, color and speech. His speech is found in the *Great Sun* text and the *Diamond Head (Vajra-sekhara)*. Again, the exoteric schools recognize that the state of cause of Buddhahood is explicable in parts, but the state of effect of it can in no way be explained. This state of the inexplicable Buddhahood has been explained in the above mystic texts. As to the time occupied before the attainment of Buddhahood the exoteric schools hold it to be three long periods *(kalpas)*, while the esoteric school regards it as merely one thought-moment or at any rate the one life, and asserts that this body of ours becomes Buddha. In the one school the Tripitaka literature is depended upon, but in the other schools the rituals *(kalpa* or *vidhi)* [59] are regarded as authoritative.

A mystic hymn *(mantra)* is the source of obtaining the enfolding power of Buddha. If we speak of the preaching of the spiritual body and the explicability of the state of effect, we can speak so because we presume that all speeches are the real speeches issuing from the Buddha's own will, or we should say, a voiceless speech for his own enjoyment of the taste of *Dharma*.

According to the exoteric schools the Buddha's preachings are all for others' enjoyment, and the spiritual body itself is unknowable and the state of Buddhahood is altogether inexplicable. Thus no preaching of the spiritual body will be recognized. The Shingon School, on the other hand, asserts that the Buddha had no 'secret fist,' which he demonstrated by his own hand, and was preaching the truth perpetually, but the listeners had no ear to hear and no mind to understand.

The three mysteries [60] of the body, speech and thought of the Buddha will remain mysteries forever if there is no means of communion. Such a means of communion should come from the mystic power *(adhisthana,* enfolding power) of the Buddha but not from the limited effort of an aspirant. The means itself is nothing but the manifestation of the mystic power, which can be expressed through the three activities [61] of men, i.e., our body, speech and thought. According to the ritualistic prescription *(vidhi* or *kalpa)*,[62] the means of communion has three aspects: 'finger-intertwining' [63] *(mudra)* and other attitudes of one's body, 'mystical verse' [64] *(dharani)* and other

---

[59] 儀軌 [60] 三密 [61] 三業 [62] 儀軌 [63] 手結印契 [64] 口誦眞言

words of prayer, and *yoga* concentration,[65] corresponding to our three activities. So through the prescribed ritual we can realize the perfect communion between the Buddha and the aspirant, thus attaining the result of the 'Buddha-in-me, I-in-Buddha';[66] hence, the theory of the Buddhahood attainable in this corporeal life.

The Mahavairocana, as the Great Sun Buddha is called in Sanskrit, is apparently different from the Buddha Sakyamuni, but if mystically considered, the latter himself will be the former, and the Bodhisattva Samantabhadra who is attending Sakyamuni will be Vajrapani under the mystical Buddha. Even the mystical Buddha is of two aspects, generally represented as two separate Buddhas.

In Buddhism, a Buddha, however remote in age or however great in origin, will be individual, for the perfection of knowledge and wisdom is the perfection of personality and that is a Buddha. A personal perfection embellished by the three mysteries is the spiritual body of knowledge and wisdom.[67] The static nature of the Buddha is potentially perfected like the great luminary (Diamond Element), and is the Mahavairocana (Great Sun) of the Diamond Element. To us it is not yet clear that the all-illumining dynamic force, like warmth or mercy, is to enfold all beings which are in the realm of natural principle (Matrix Repository). Therefore, the spiritual body of principle [68] is depicted as if the world of nature, i.e., universe itself, should become illumined and assume a splendor of perfect wisdom. This Buddha is possessed of the perfect harmony of the sixfold greatness; i.e., earth, water, fire, air, space and consciousness [69] and is the Buddha Mahavairocana of the Matrix Repository. These curious names of the worlds of 'Diamond Element' and 'Matrix Repository' indicate the indestructible character of personal wisdom, otherwise called the realm of effect and the natural source of beings (sometimes called the realm of cause).

These two aspects of the Buddha are strictly distinguished. I used the word 'static' or 'dynamic' with regard to the person of the Buddha on the basis of the manifestation of his enfolding power. Seen from the attainment of his perfect wisdom, the Buddha of the realm of nature is static and therefore has the sign *(mudra)* of 'meditation,' while the Buddha of the realm of wisdom is dynamic owing to the vivid realization of his ideals and has the sign of 'wisdom-fist.'

---

[65] 心入本尊三摩地   [66] 入我我入   [67] 智法身三密莊嚴   [68] 理法身
[69] 六大無礙

149

Suppose an individual develops himself and attains enlightenment and advances so far as to conform to the universal principle; he will then be the Buddha Mahavairocana of the individual realm (Diamond Element). In sculpture he is represented with the left hand grasping the index finger of the right hand, the sign of 'wisdom-fist.'

On the other hand, when the universe itself becomes illumined and assumes a splendor of wisdom, he then will be the Buddha Mahavairocana of the natural realm (Matrix Repository). In sculpture he is represented as having the sign of meditation on the universe, with the right hand on the left, the thumbs touching each other.

Thus there are two Buddhas with one and the same name, different in manifestation but identical in quality. "They are two and yet not two."[70] When the six great elements (earth, water, fire, air, space and consciousness) are coordinated crosswise (according to space) we get the universe, i.e., the universal body of the Buddha of the Matrix Realm. When the six elements are arranged lengthwise or vertically (according to time), we get the individual of five aggregates, i.e., the personal body of the Buddha of the Diamond Realm. Mystically speaking, the two persons of ultimate perfection would be of one and the same width and height.

To illustrate the sphere of activity of the two Buddhas a diagram-like circle *(Mandala)* was invented for each, having the whole show of saintly beings with the Buddha at the center.

The Realm of Diamond Element [71]

This has the central party of nine representing the Diamond Realm. Figures represented here amount to 414.

414.

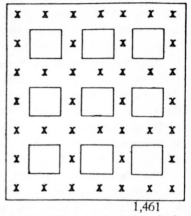

Each of the four quarters has a Buddha, and each of the four corners has a Bodhisattva, thus making up the party of nine with the central one. Saintly beings represented are 1,461 in all.

1,461

The circle is of four kinds:[73]

1.   The Great Circle *(Maha-mandala)* [74] is the circle of the Buddha and his companions represented by pictures or painted figures, i.e., a plane representation.

2.   The Symbol Circle *(Samaya-mandala)* [75] is the circle of the same assembly represented by symbols or an article possessed by each. *Samaya* in Sanskrit means the 'original vow' but here it is represented by an article borne by each.

3.   The Law Circle *(Dharma-mandala)* [76] is the circle of letters *(bija-aksara)* representing all the saintly beings.

4.   The Artcraft Circle *(Karma-mandala)* [77] is the circle of sculptured figures.

In Japan we have no circle of sculptural representation. The multitude of Buddhistic images of Java is said to be of this kind. *Karma* in Sanskrit means 'action' or 'work'; here it especially means the artistic work of solid representation.

The fourfold circle indicates the efficacious power of the three mysteries. The figures, painted or sculptured, show the mystery of the body of the Buddha; the letters show the mystery of speech of the Buddha; and the symbol indicates the 'original vow,' the thought of the Buddha.

The Shingon School has the ritual of anointment *(abhiseka)* as well as the ordination ceremony. The area of anointment must be

---

[72] 胎藏界十三大院　　[73] 四曼　　[74] 大曼多羅　　[75] 三昧耶曼多羅
[76] 法曼多羅　　[77] 羯摩曼多羅

decked with the Circles of the two realms; all ritual requirements must be fulfilled. Sometimes the Circles are spread out and thereby the ritual area is formed. So the area is called Circle.' Only the adequate performance of the ritual can make the evoking of any enfolding power of Buddha effective.

According to tradition, Subhakarasinha and his pupil, I-hsing, transmitted the Matrix doctrine, while Vajrabodhi and his pupil, Amoghavajra, taught the Diamond doctrine. Thus we must presume that there were two traditions of transmission, both being only partial or one-sided.

However, the recent discovery of the *Tattva-sangraha* in Tibet by Professor Tucci and the *Vajra-sekhara (Rita-sangraha)* in Japan by Professor Ono make the old traditions entirely untenable, because the *Vajra-sekhara* represented in the *Five Assemblies* [78] was kept in secret in the Mii Monastery in Ōmi and Shōrenin in Kyoto. The 'Five Assemblies' are *Buddha, Padma, Ratna, Vajra,* and *Karma.* These being originally the divisions of the Diamond Realm, it is clear that we had from the beginning the text of the 'Diamond' doctrine brought by Subhakarasinha. They were actually the transmission by Subhakarasinha. From this it will be seen that at the time of Subhakarasinha both the 'Diamond' and 'Matrix' doctrines were existing in China. Tucci's text is Sanskrit and Ono's is a pictorial explanation without which often a perusal of the Sanskrit original becomes impossible. Students of mysticism may expect a real contribution from the study of these texts.

---

[78] 五部心觀

XI. THE ZEN SCHOOL
(THE MEDITATION SCHOOL)[1]
(Dhyana)

(Pure Intuitionism)
[Mahayanistic]

(1) Buddhist Schools of the Kamakura Period (1185-1335 A. D.)

Buddhism in the Nara period (710-794 A. D.) was a philosophy of investigation and speculation, while that of the Heian period (794-1185 A. D.) was externally an eclecticism or syncretism of Shintoistic and Buddhistic ideas and internally a unification of the theory of universal immanence (exoteric). Buddhism in this later period greatly influenced the social life and culture on all sides by its doctrine of enfolding power (esoteric). In the Kamakura period (1185-1335 A. D.) the specific character of Buddhism was pre-eminently practical, national and markedly enthusiastic in preaching, exclusive in doctrine, more simplified and specific than ever, but extensive in the application or the realization of the ideal, since all Buddhist schools in the period preached salvation—i.e., the way of enlightenment—for all, that is, pansophism.

The religious activity of this period was, in a way, a strong protest against the previous orthodox schools which seemed to end in an exhibition of either speculative achievement or ritualistic efficacy, betraying in their aristocratic pomp and ceremonial display the fast degenerating tendency of philosophical-religious life in general. The importance of a reversion to the monistic and practical religion of Prince Shōtoku[2] was strongly felt. The consensus of the leading ideas and the necessity of spiritual reform among the populace brought about the uniformity of the religious type of the time. Certainly the memory of Prince Shōtoku was greatly awakened and a considerable increase in his images, sanctuaries, memorial services and even guilds of artisans connected with him was conspicuous during the period. One of the Buddhist schools founded at the time enshrined him as the patriarch of Japan.

---

[1] Ch'an 禪   [2] 聖德太子 574-622 A.D.

Kamakura Buddhism, the Buddhism of 'All-Enlightenment,' may be summarized into seven schools:

1. The Zen School [3] of meditative intuitionism
   a. Rinzai Sect [4] founded by Eisai [5] (1141-1215)
   b. Sōtō Sect [6] founded by Dōgen [7] (1200-1253)

2. The Fuke School [8] of introspective asceticism, founded by Kakushin [9] in 1255

3. The Jōdo School [10] of Amita-pietism, founded by Hōnen [11] (1133-1212)

4. The Shin School [12] of Amita-pietism, founded by Shinran [13] (1173-1262)

5. The Ji School [14] of Amita-pietism, founded by Ippen [15] (1239-1289)

6. The Nichiren School [16] of Lotus-pietism, founded by Nichiren [17] (1222-1282)

7. The Shin-Ritsu Sect,[18] the reformed school of self-vow discipline, founded by Eison [19] (1201-1290), the restorer of the disciplinary school

(2) Preliminary

As an inheritance from the ancient Aryan race, India has had the habit of meditation practiced in all schools of philosophy as well as in religion. There are six systems of Indian philosophy *(darsana,* 'view'), one of which, called Yoga, is especially devoted to meditation or concentration.

The Yoga system is the practical side of the Sankhya philosophy, which is dualistic. In Sankhya, Self *(Atman)* and Nature *(Prakriti),* one blind as it were, and the other lame, cannot function without being united. Self has the intellectual function, but cannot move without the physical function of Nature. When the two combine together, they see the way and move at will. Self, like the promoter of a theatrical play, simply looks on his mate's acting and

---

[3] 禪宗　[4] 臨濟宗　[5] 榮西　[6] 曹洞宗　[7] 道元　[8] 普化宗
[9] 覺心　[10] 淨土宗　[11] 法然　[12] 眞宗　[13] 親鸞　[14] 時宗　[15] 一遍
[16] 日蓮宗　[17] 日蓮　[18] 新律宗　[19] 叡尊

moving but curiously thinks that he himself is acting in the moving, though in reality only Nature is moving and achieving. Only self-culture brings about freedom, that is, independence of Self. The method of self-culture is practically the Yoga system of Patanjali (second century B.C.). The Sankhya system, originally heterodox since it was atheistic, asserted only the existence of the individual *Atman* (Self) and not of *Mahatman* (Universal Self, Brahman). But in the practice of abstract meditation an object of self-concentration was necessary and so the doctrine assumes the form of deism (but not theism). At the end of meditation, when the absolute separation of Self from Nature has been effected, the object of meditation, Brahman, *Parama-atman* or God, whatever it is, is no longer used.

The constituents of Yoga abstraction (concentration) are generally eight: 1. restraint *(yama)*; 2. minor restraint *(niyama)*; 3. sitting *(asana)*; 4. restraint of breaths *(pranayama)*; 5. withdrawal of senses *(pratyahara)*; 6. retention of mind *(dharana)*; 7. concentration of mind *(dhyana)*; 8. concentration of thought *(samadhi)*. These practices of the Yogin are actually similar to those of the Yogacara School of Buddhism.[20] Yogacara means 'practice of self-concentration' and has several things in common with the Yoga philosophy. The Yogacara School is Buddhist idealism taught by Asanga,[21] systematized by his brother Vasubandhu[22] as the Theory of Mere Ideation (Vijnaptimatrata), and introduced to China by Hiuen-tsang[23] as the Fa-hsiang (Hossō) School.[24] According to I-tsing,[25] famous traveler in India, it was one of the only two Mahayana schools in India (Madhyamika and Yogacara).[26] This fact is fully confirmed by Sayana's commentary on the *Vedanta Sutra*, in which these two are treated as the only existing Buddhist systems.

The meditation *(dhyana)* practiced in the Zen School consisted of twelve ways of meditation, three grades and four kinds in each; namely, four form-realm-meditations *(rupa-dhatu)*, four formless-realm-meditations *(arupya-dhatu)* and four measureless-meditations *(apramana-dhyana)*. The last, the measureless-meditations, are

---

[20] See Ch. VI.
[21] 無著 c. 410-500 A.D.   [22] 世親 c. 420-500 A.D.
[23] Hsüan-tsang 玄奘, 596-664   [24] 法相   [25] I-ching 義淨, 635-713
[26] See my translation, *A Record of the Buddhist Religion as Practised in India and the Malay Archipelago by I-tsing* (A.D. 671-695), Oxford, 1896, p. 15.

155

exactly identical with those of the Yoga system. Which one is indebted to the other we cannot say, though they look quite Buddhistic. They are: 1. benevolence (*maitri,* to give joy to others) ; 2. cheerfulness (*mudita,* to keep oneself happy) ; 3. mercy (*karuna,* to remove the suffering of others) ; 4. indifference (*upeksa,* to transcend the above three). These, though subjective, have all beings as their objective, whereas the four form-realm-meditations and four formless-realm-meditations have the form-heaven and the formless-heaven as their objectives. It is a well-known fact that in the Buddha's career he practiced the formless *dhyana* with Arada Kalama, an ascetic who attained the mental state of boundless consciousness, and Udraka Ramaputra, another ascetic who reached the highest stage of being neither conscious nor unconscious. Finally, the would-be Buddha surpassed his teachers and, having found no more to learn from them, went his own way in spite of their eager requests to stay and train their respective pupils.

The importance of the abstract meditation of the Yoga system is laid upon the evolution and reversion of the dual principles and upon the final liberation of self from nature, while that of the idealistic Yogacara School of Buddhism is centered on the unification of the world within and without, on the synthesizing of our causal and illusory existences, and thus negatively discovering the state of Thusness *(Tathata).*

Buddhism has, of course, a special doctrine of meditation. Although the depth and width of contemplation depend upon one's personal character, the methods or contents of meditation taught by the Buddha are similar in Hinayana and Mahayana. This special meditation is generally called 'Tathagata meditation,' [27] as it forms one part of the sacred teaching. The highest development of it is seen in the perfect 'calmness and insight' *(samatha-vipasyana)*[28] of the Tendai School and in the mystical *yogacara* of the Shingon School.

(3) Historical

To understand Tathagata meditation, one must study the history of the meditative teaching of the Buddha. When we speak of the Tathagata meditation, we presuppose the rise of patriarchal meditation[29] by the advent of Bodhidharma[30] in China in 520 A. D.

` [27] 如來禪　　[28] 止觀　　[29] 祖師禪　　[30] 菩提達摩

The Buddha first taught the Threefold Basis of Learning *(tri-siksa):* Higher Discipline *(adhi-sila),* Higher Meditation *(adhi-citta)* and Higher Wisdom *(adhi-prajna.)* In the sixfold perfection of wisdom, concentration *(samadhi)* is one of the most important factors. He further taught meditation as the 'basis of action' *(kar-ma-sthana),* such as meditation on the ten universal objects, on impurity, on impermanence, on breaths, etc. The object of meditation with the Buddha seems to have been to attain first, tranquillity of mind, and then activity of insight. This idea is common to both Hinayana and Mahayana. To intensify the original idea and to apply it extensively, each school seems to have introduced detailed items of contemplation.

Generally speaking, the mental cultivation of Buddhism is divided into three: 1. 'effort' stage; 2. 'view-path' stage; 3. 'practice-path' stage. The adjustment of one's self so as to proceed to the path, that is, the beginner's undertaking, comes first. The first path one treads is the 'effort' stage in which there is the practice of calmness and insight. One must practice:

Calmness

A. Fivefold restraint of mind

1. Meditation on impurity of the worldly life to adjust the mind with regard to passion and avarice. (individual)
2. Meditation on mercy to cultivate the idea of sympathy to others and to stop the tendency of anger. (universal)
3. Meditation on causation to get rid of ignorance. (individual)
4. Meditation on diversity of realms to see the difference of standpoints and to get rid of selfish views. (universal)
5. Meditation on breathing leading to concentration so as to correct the tendency of mental dispersion. (individual)

When one's faulty mind has been adjusted and calmness has been obtained, one proceeds to the next.

Insight

B. Fourfold retention of mind

1. The impurity of body is meditated upon and fully realized.
2. The evils of sensations are meditated upon and fully realized.

3. The evanescence or impermanence of mind and thoughts is meditated upon and fully realized.

4. The transiency of all elements or selflessness is meditated upon and fully realized.

Hinayana Buddhism calls these practices 'basis of action' (kammatthana) which is one of the modes of analytical meditation. Some forty of such meditations are given in the *Visuddhi Magga*: four 'measureless meditations'; ten 'impurities'; four 'formless states'; ten 'universals'; ten 'remembrances'; one 'sign'; and one 'mental reflex.' We need not go into the detail of all these meditations.

The ordinary way of meditation is as follows:

> Arrange your seat properly, sit erect, cross-legged, and have your eyes neither quite closed nor quite open, looking ten or twenty feet ahead. You should sit properly but your body will move on account of your breaths. To correct such movement, count your in-breath and out-breath as one and slowly count as far as ten, never beyond.

> Although your body may become upright and calm, your thought will move about. You must therefore meditate upon the impurity of human beings in illness, death, and after death.

> When you are well prepared to contemplate, you will begin to train yourself by concentration on the ten universals. This is a meditative unification of diverse phenomena into one of the ten universals, that is, blue, yellow, red, white, earth, water, fire, air, space, consciousness. In this you must meditate on the universe until it becomes to your eyes one wash of a color or one aspect of an element. If you meditate on water, the world around you will become only running water.

Such a process of meditation is common to all Buddhist schools, Hinayana as well as Mahayana, and is the feature of the Tathagata meditation.

Patriarchal Meditation

The history of Zen is mythical. It is said that one day Brahma came to the Buddha who was living at the Vulture peak, offered a Kumbhala flower, and requested him to preach the Law. The Buddha ascended the Lion seat and taking that flower touched it with his fingers without saying a word. No one in the assembly could understand the meaning. The venerable Mahakasyapa alone smiled with joy. The World-Honored One said: "The doctrine of the Eye of the True Law is hereby entrusted to you, Oh Mahakasyapa! Accept and hand it down to posterity." Once when Ananda asked him what the Buddha's transmission was, Mahakasyapa said: "Go and take the banner-stick down!"[31] Ananda understood him at once. Thus the mind-sign[32] was handed down successively. The teaching was called the 'school of the Buddha-mind.'[33]

The 28th patriarch was Bodhidharma.[34] He was the third son of the King of Kancipura, South India. Obeying the instruction of Prajnatara, his teacher, Bodhidharma started for the East and arrived in China in 520 A. D. The Emperor Wu-ti[35] invited him to Nanking for an audience. The Emperor said: "Since my enthronement, I have built many monasteries, copied many holy writings and invested many priests and nuns. How great is the merit due to me?" "No merit at all," was the answer. "What is the Noble Truth in its highest sense?" "It is empty, no nobility whatever." "Who is it then that is facing me?" "I do not know, Sire." The Emperor could not understand him. Bodhidharma went away, crossed the Yangtze River and reached the capital, Loyang, of Northern Wei. After a sojourn there he went to Mount Wu-t'ai[36] and resided in the Shao-lin Temple[37] where he remained and for nine years, facing a cliff behind the edifice, meditated in silence.

A strong-minded Confucian scholar, Hui-k'o,[38] came to Bodhidharma and asked for instruction. He obtained no reply. Thereupon he stood in the snow and cut off his left arm, thereby showing his sincerity and eagerness. Bodhidharma then made him a pupil and gave him a robe and a bowl as a sign of transmission. This is the line of the patriarchal meditation. The fifth patriarch, Hung-jên,[39] had two able pupils. The regular succession fell on one of them, Hui-nêng,[40] who became the founder of the Southern Meditation School.[41] His aim was an abrupt attainment of enlightenment[42] and his school is called the Southern School of Abrupt Enlightenment.[43] He is the sixth patriarch of Zen. The other able pupil was Shèn-

---

[31] The presence of the banner outside the temple was indicative of preaching of the Law. To take the banner down means to do away with word-preaching.

[32] 心印　　[33] 佛心宗　　[34] 菩提達摩 c. 470-534　　[35] 武帝　　[36] 五台
[37] 少林寺　　[38] Eka 慧可　　[39] Gunin 弘忍　　[40] Enō 慧能 638-713
[41] 南宗禪　　[42] 頓悟禪　　[43] 南頓

hsiu [44] who remained in the north and propagated the Zen of patriarchal meditation earnestly. His school was called the Northern School of Zen.[45] His teaching was a gradual attainment of enlightenment and named the Northern School of Gradual Enlightenment.[46] Since the Northern School taught the Tathagata meditation as well, Dengyō Daishi [47] is said to have belonged to it. All of the Japanese sects belong to the Southern School.

Japanese Zen

Zen was introduced to Japan several times. Hiuen-tsang's pupil, Dōshō,[48] who went to China in 654 A. D., introduced and taught it for the first time in the Zen Hall of Gangōji, Nara. Next, Tao-hsüan,[49] a Chinese *vinaya* (discipline) master, came to Nara in 710 A. D. and taught the Zen of the Northern School. He transmitted it to Gyōhyō [50] in 733 A. D., who in turn taught it to Saichō (Dengyō Daishi).

A special Zen instructor of the Southern School, Gikū,[51] a pupil of Ch'i-an,[52] came to Kyoto and taught Zen from 851 to 858 A. D. in the Danrinji Temple built by the Empress Danrin. He was successful in the teaching. In all the above cases the propagation was assisted by the Court but did not continue long. The last-mentioned teacher went home disappointed in 858 A. D., leaving a monument at the Rashōmon, Kyoto, inscribed: a record of the propagation of Zen in Japan.

The watchword of Zen in China was "not to pay respect even to king or prince." [53] Such an attitude did not appeal to the nationalistic mind of Japan. In the Kamakura period several Chinese teachers were invited or welcomed by the Shogunate government. Tao-lung Lan-hsi (Dōryū Rankei,[54] founder of the Kenchōji Temple in 1249),Tsu-yüan W'u-hsüeh (Sogen Mugaku,[55] founder of the Engakuji Temple in 1273) and I-ning I-shan (Ichinei Issan,[56] who though not invited, came to the Shuzenji Temple in 1299) came to Kamakura and busied themselves in the instruction of Zen. We must remember, however, that it was only after the able founders of Japanese Zen, Eisai [57] and Dōgen,[58] had opened and brilliantly

---

[44] Jinshū 神秀, 605-706 [45] 北宗禪 [46] 北漸 [47] 最澄, 傳敎大師
[48] 道昭 629-700 [49] Dōsen 道睿(王旁) [50] 行表 [51] 義空
[52] Enkwan Saian 監官齊安 [53] 沙門不敬王者 [54] 道隆蘭溪 [55] 祖元
無學 [56] 一寧一山 [57] 榮西 [58] 道元

160

led the way, that these Chinese teachers made their appearance on the scene. Eisai, who built the Kenninji Temple in Kyoto, wrote a treatise, "Kōzen Gokoku-ron" [59] (Propagation of Zen as the Protection of the Nation), in which he asserted that the propagation of the Zen practice would serve to protect the prosperity of the Empire. He was right in his view, as the new religion greatly helped to pacify and strengthen the hearts of the warriors. Zen taught that even fighters must introspect and think of morality and responsibility. Dōgen wanted to rectify the abnormal system of government and went so far as to advise Tokiyori, then the *de facto* ruler, to restore the regime to the Throne. As the proposal was not complied with, he left at once and retired to the Eiheiji Monastery which he built in the province of Echizen. This deepened the ruler's respect for him and one of Dōgen's pupils in Kamakura was persuaded to take the document of a generous grant of land to his teacher. The priest gladly did so. Upon receiving it, Dōgen was so enraged that he at once drove his pupil away. He ordered the chair the priest sat on destroyed, the ground under the chair dug three feet deep and the earth thrown away. After this incident he was admired more than ever, and the Zen practice became popular among the people.

The second Zen school, Fuke,[60] was founded by Kakushin [61] who, like Dōgen and Eisai, went to China in 1249 and received the Zen training under Fu-yen (Butsugen),[62] a great teacher of the school. On his return home in 1255 he founded the school of homeless mendicancy, commonly called 'community of nothingness,' [63] in which the members were said to be 'lying on dew and feeding on air.' The school eventually became a community of *rōnin* ('lordless warriors') and as such helped the government and the people in various respects. This was abolished after the Great Restoration in 1868.

In the Zen School we have at present three principal sects: 1. Rinzai Sect,[64] first introduced from China by Eisai in 1191 and then by Benen [65] in 1235; 2. Sōtō Sect,[66] introduced by Dōgen in 1127; 3. Ōbaku Sect,[67] introduced by Ingen [68] in 1654. This last sect, though of late introduction, has 640 monasteries.

---

[59] 興禪護國論　[60] 普化　[61] 覺心, 法燈國師　[62] 佛眼　[63] 虛無僧
[64] 臨濟宗　[65] 辨圓　[66] 曹洞宗　[67] 黃檗宗　[68] 隱元

(4) Philosophical and Religious

Zen has much philosophy but is not a philosophy in the strict sense of the term. It is the most religious school of all and yet not a religion in the ordinary sense of the word. It has no scripture of the Buddha, nor does it hold any discipline set forth by the Buddha.

Without a *sutra* (discourse) or a *vinaya* (discipline) text no school or sect would seem to be Buddhistic. However, according to the ideas of Zen, those who cling to words, letters or rules can never fully comprehend the speaker's true idea. The ideal or truth conceived by the Buddha should be different from those taught by him because the teaching was necessarily conditioned by the language he used, by the hearers whom he was addressing, and by the environment in which the speaker and hearers were placed. What Zen aims at is the Buddha's ideal, pure and unconditioned. The school is otherwise called 'the School of the Buddha's Mind.' [69] The Buddha's mind is after all a human mind. An introspection of the human mind alone can bring an aspirant to a perfect enlightenment. But how?

The general purport of Buddhism is to let one see rightly and walk rightly. The way of viewing *(darsana-marga)* is different from the way of walking *(bhavana-marga)*. People walk often without seeing the way. Religions generally lay importance on practice, that is, how to walk, but neglect teaching the intellectual activity with which to determine the right way, that is, how to see. To judge whether the path we are going to take is right or not, first of all, science is important, but as we go on, we discover that philosophy is much more important than anything else. In case science and philosophy do not give a satisfactory result, we must resort to the meditative method of Zen in order to get insight into any given problem.

First, find out your way and begin to walk on it. The foot acquired by meditation can carry you across the wave-flux of human life, and over and above the air region of the heavenly world and finally make you perfect and enlightened like the Buddha. Contemplation is the eye which gives insight, and at the same time, the foot which procures a proper walk. Zen (meditation and concentra-

---

[69] 佛心宗

162

tion) is the lens on which diverse objects outside will be concentrated and again dispersed and impressed on the surface of the negative plates inside. The concentration on the lens itself is concentration *(samadhi)* [70] and the deeper the concentration is, the quicker the awakening of intuitive intellect. The further impression on the negative film is wisdom *(prajna)* [71] and this is the basis of intellectual activity. Through the light of reflection *(prajna)* outwardly, i.e., insight, we see and review the outer world of diversity once again so as to function or act appropriately toward actual life.

The meditation of the patriarchal Zen, therefore, was not an analytical method like science nor was it a synthetical method like philosophy. It was a method of thinking without ordinary thinking, transcending all methods of logical argument. To think without any method of thinking is to give opportunity for the awakening of an intuitional knowledge or wisdom. All methods of meditation as taught by Hinayana, by Yogacara (quasi-Mahayana), by the abrupt method of calmness and insight *(samathavipasyana)* of Tendai, or by the mystical *yoga* of Shingon can be used if the aspirant likes, but are in no way necessary.

The ideas peculiar to Zen may be summarized as follows: "From mind to mind it was transmitted," [72] "not expressed in words or written in letters"; [73] "it was a special transmission apart from the sacred teaching." [74] "Directly point to the human mind, see one's real nature and become an enlightened Buddha." [75] Or, "the very body or the very mind is the Buddha." [76] The idea was very well expressed in Hakuin's hymn on sitting and meditating: [77] "All beings are fundamentally Buddhas; it is like ice (which represents our actual condition) and water (which represents an underlying Buddha-nature); without water there will be no ice. . . . This very earth is the lotus-land and this body is Buddha."

The basic idea of Zen is the identity of *ens* and *non-ens*. "The true state is no (special) state;" [78] "the gate of *Dharma* is no gate;" [79] "holy knowledge is no knowledge." [80] The mutual identification of two opposed ideas, such as black and white, good and evil, pure and impure, or the like, results from deep meditation. "The

---

[70] 定　[71] 慧　[72] 以心傳心　[73] 不立文字　[74] 教外別傳　[75] 直指人心
見性成佛　[76] 此心即佛　[77] 坐禪　[78] 實相無相　[79] 法門無門
[80] 聖智無智

ideal body has no form, yet any form may come out of it." "The golden mouth has no word, yet any word may come out of it." Ideas of a similar nature are often encountered.

There is, however, a peculiar process in Zen. To concentrate one's mind in silent meditation, a *kōan* ('public theme') [81] is given to an aspirant to test his qualification for progress towards enlightenment. On receiving a theme, one sits in silence in the Zen hall. One must sit at ease, cross-legged and well-posed with upright body, with his hands in the meditating sign, and with his eyes neither quite open nor quite closed. This is called sitting and meditating,[82] which may go on for several days and nights. So the daily life, lodging, eating, sleeping, swimming or bathing should be regulated properly. Silence is strictly required and kept; that is, while meditating, dining or bathing, no word should be uttered and no noise should be made. Sometimes a public dialogue called 'question and answer' takes place where the 'cloud or water'[83]—the name used for traveling students —ask questions of the teacher who gives answers, hints or scoldings. When a student or any aspirant thinks that he is prepared on the problem, he pays a private visit to the teacher's retreat, explains what he understands and proposes to resolve the question. When the teacher is satisfied, he will give sanction; if not, the candidate must continue meditation.

The Zen which is generally practiced in a forest retreat seems to be far away from the real world, but the general trend of mind of the Zen people is always towards a strict observance of rules and a minute accomplishment of discipline. Their ideals are immediately expressed in their daily life and in personal experiences. They are generally very practical. The famous words of the Zen patriarchs, such as "no work, no food" ("one day without work, one day without food"), "every day, good day (to work)," "daily mind the way," "the living, the teaching" ("going, staying, sitting, or lying are the sacred teaching"), exemplify their practical application of ideals. We can say without hesitation that it requires training to hear a voice in silence, to find action in inaction, motion in absence of motion or to have preparedness in peace and fearlessness in death. Such a tendency must have appealed to the warrior class, thus eventually producing the way of knightly behavior *(bushidō)*.[84]

---

[81] 公案　　[82] 坐禪　　[83] 雲水　　[84] 武士道

164

Besides, when we see the Zen influence so conspicuously discernible in literature, (poetry, short poems, etc.), drama, *(Nō, ballad-drama)*, painting (monochrome, portraiture), architecture (temple-building, paper windows, tea houses), industrial arts (lacquer, etc.), and the social life (tea ceremony, vegetable cookery, flower arrangement, interior decoration), and at present, in the educational training of Japan, the Zen ideas can be regarded as almost inseparable from the Japanese national life. Probably the national ideal of simplicity, purity and sincerity can find its expression most appropriately in the Zen practice of Buddhism.

XII. THE JŌDO SCHOOL
(THE PURE LAND SCHOOL)[1]
(Sukhavati)

(Amita-pietism)
[Mahayanistic]

(1) Preliminary

The general Japanese name for Amita-pietism is Jōdo meaning
'Pure Land,' which is a translation of *Sukhavati* ('Land of Bliss').
Those who believe in Amita Buddha will be born in the 'Pure Land'
to become a Buddha.

The idea of being 'saved' is generally considered new in Buddhism. But King Milinda (Menandros, a Greek ruler in Sagara,
about 115 B.C.) questioned a learned priest Nagasena, saying that
it was unreasonable that a man of bad conduct could be saved if
he believed in a Buddha on the eve of his death. Nagasena replied:
"A stone, however small, will sink into the water, but even a stone
weighing hundreds of tons if put on a ship will float." Nagarjuna[2]
again asserted that there were two ways for entering Buddhahood,
one difficult and one easy. One was traveling on foot and the other
was passage by boat. The idea of boat or vehicle expressed here
at least suggested the appellations 'Hinayana' and 'Mahayana,' the
Great and Small Vehicles, even though the terms were not actually
designated by Nagarjuna himself. Amita-pietism will be the greatest
of all vehicles to convey those who are in need of such means.

There are two original texts in Sanskrit, a large[3] and a small[4]
Sukhavati-vyuha ('Sutra of the Land of Bliss'), both of which were
translated into Chinese. Chinese translations from 147 to 713 A.D.
were twelve in number, but at present only five are in existence.

---

[1] Ching-t'u 淨土   [2] 龍樹 c. 100-200 A.D.
[3] *Taishō* No. 360 大無量壽經   English translation by F. Max Müller:
The Land of Bliss, in Sacred Books of the East, Vol. XLIX, The Clarendon
Press, 1894.
[4] *Taishō* No. 362 阿彌陀經   English translation by F. Max Müller:
The Smaller Sukhavati-vyuha, in Sacred Books of the East, Vol. XLIX,
The Clarendon Press, 1894.

From the facts just stated one can scarcely doubt the origin of this doctrine of salvation by Amita. Since the faith seemed so strange to some people, various ideas and hypotheses have been proposed regarding this faith. Some have asserted that it was borrowed from Christianity, chiefly from the legend of Thomas' mission in India (Dahlmann). Others have pointed out certain resemblances in the *Avesta* or in Manichaeism (Eliot). Some have gone so far as to say that it might have been acquired on the way from Central Asia to the East (Reischauer).

These authorities generally formed their opinions from outward resemblances without entering into the internal development of Mahayanistic ideas. The faith in Amita was simply the outcome of a far-reaching contemplation of the Buddha-nature. If you strip away all the external features of Sakyamuni and all the conditions of his Indian life, you will find an ideal Buddha to suit his perfect Enlightenment. To be more definite, if we depict a Buddha on the basis of perfect Enlightenment we come to the ideal of Buddhahood, i.e., Buddha of Infinite Light and Infinite Life. When the ideal of Nirvana which is spaceless and timeless, birthless and deathless, changeless or waveless is realized, it will be nothing but the Infinite (Amita or Amitabha). The description of the Land of Bliss, the name of Unbounded Light and Life, and the illumined person of limitless wisdom and benevolence, are simply interpretations given to the Infinite.

(2) Historical

Nagarjuna's *Dasabhumi Sutra*[5] and Vasubandhu's[6] commentary on it are the Indian authorities recognized by the Jōdo School. The easy way and the 'power of another' are already indicated and elucidated by them. In China the authorities of the faith are many, but the following four lines of transmission are generally recognized:

(1)	(2)
Fu-t'u-ch'êng,[7] an Indian in China between 310 and 348 A.D.	Bodhiruci,[9] an Indian in China between 503 and 535 A.D.
:	:
Tao-an (Dōan, 584-708)[8]	Hui-ch'ung (Eryū)[10]

---

[5] 十地經   [6] 世親 c. 420-500   [7] 佛圖澄   [8] 道安   [9] 菩提流支
[10] 慧寵

167

Hui-yüan (Eon)[11]

Tao-ch'ang (Dōjō) [12]
:
T'an-luan (Donran, 476-542) [13]
:
Ta-hai (Daikai) [14]
:
Fa-shang (Hōjō, 495-580 A.D.)[15]

(3)

Bodhiruci
:
T'an-luan (Donran)
:
Tao-ch'o (Dōshaku, c. 645) [16]
:
Shan-tao (Zendō, d. 681) [17]
:
Huai-kan (Ekan) [18]
:
Shao-k'ang (Shōkō) [19]

(4)

Tz'u-min (Jimin),[20] who went to India during the T'ang period (618-709 A.D.) and received the Amita-pietism in Gandhara

The decisive authorities chosen by Shinran (1173-1262) [21] are T'an-luan, Tao-ch'o and Shan-tao, by whom the details of the easy way and the perfect reliance on the Buddha's power are minutely annotated. In Japan there are many authorities (the history of the faith is very long), though Genshin (942-1017) [22] and Hōnen (1133-1212) [23] are the pre-eminent promoters of the doctrine. Prince Shō-toku,[24] in the reign of the Empress Suiko (593-628 A.D.), is said to have believed in Amita. At any rate, a reference to the Western Land of Bliss is found in one of his commentaries. Ein,[25] a Korean priest, lectured in 640 A.D. on the *Sutra of the Land of Bliss* before the Throne. In the Nara period (710-793 A.D.) Gyōgi [26] is said to have traveled about and propagated the faith among the people. Kanjin,[27] a Chinese *vinaya* (discipline) master who came to Nara in 754 A.D., imparted the worship of Amita to his Japanese pupil, Eiei,[28] on the eve of the latter's death near Kuangtung.

---

[11] 慧遠　[12] 道塲　[13] 曇鸞　[14] 大海　[15] 法上　[16] 道綽　[17] 善導
[18] 懷感　[19] 少康　[20] 慈愍　[21] 親鸞 1173-1262　[22] 源信 1133-1212
[23] 法然 1133-1212　[24] 聖德太子　[25] 慧印　[26] 行基　[27] 鑑眞
[28] 榮叡

But in the Nara period the Amita-pietism was not systematically taught, though there must have been some followers who privately adhered to it. In the Tendai School the Amita worship was taken up and promoted as an all-inclusive faith. It was Jikaku Daishi (Ennin),[29] the third patriarch, who instituted the two forms of repeating the Amita formula, standing and sitting, and introduced a music relating to the Land of Bliss. Even now adherents read the smaller *Sukhavati* text in the daily service. On that account their protest against Hōnen's founding a new exclusive school of Amita-pietism was exceptionally strong. Prohibition of the Jōdo School did not satisfy them and they attempted to insult Hōnen's corpse although it was already buried. On Mount Hiei[30] there were earnest followers of Amita-pietism who devoted themselves to the study and practice of the school. A brilliant representative was Genshin, otherwise known as Eshin,[31] who wrote, among others, an important treatise for the faith and invented a special pictorial art of paradise and Amita welcoming the pious believers. A learned follower of his line, Ryōnin,[32] founded an eclectic sect of the Tendai and Jōdo Schools called Yūzūnembutsu Sect ('All Permeating Faith of the Buddha Amita')[33] which, in reality, is a compromise between the Lotus doctrine and Amita-pietism. He is said to have been inspired by Amita himself about the truth, "One in all, all in one; one acts for all, all act for one." It is the idea of salvation by another's power, mutual help being the basic idea. Accordingly, an act of adoration to the Buddha done by one will be of help to another. Their practice will be not only for one another but also for the salvation of society at large. This faith became extinct soon after Ryōnin's death but was revived by Hōmyō,[34] one of the believers, in 1321. Although it belongs to Amita-pietism, it uses the *Lotus* text and the *Wreath* text as well. Thus we can regard it as belonging to the doctrine of the 'Holy Path' rather than to that of the 'Pure Land.'[35] The headquarters of this school are at the Dainembutsuji Temple, Hirano, near Ōsaka, where it governs some 357 monasteries.

In this respect, we must remember that there is in the Tendai School itself a sub-sect called Shinsei Branch,[36] founded in the To-

---

[29] 圓仁 794-864 A.D.   [30] 比叡   [31] 慧心   [32] 良忍 1071-1132
[33] 融通念佛   [34] 法明
[35] See p. 171 for the distinction of the two doctrines.
[36] 眞盛

169

kugawa period (about 1780), which devotes itself to the worship of Amita and rules over more than 400 monasteries, while the two branches, Sammon [37] and Jimon,[38] govern more than 3,000 and 800 monasteries, respectively. The worship of Amita has prevailed considerably in the Shingon center, Kōyasan, as it has in the Tendai center, Mount Hiei, but we cannot determine how far the school was studied or practiced in the Shingon School at an early period. However, among some sixty-six existing monasteries at Kōyasan, the older edifices have the Buddha Amitabha as the chief object of worship. At the end of the Heian period, Kakuban (Kōkyō Daishi, 1095-1145),[39] a distinguished priest of the Daidenpōin at Kōya and afterwards the founder of the new sect of Shingon, earnestly devoted himself to the faith of Amita and aspired for a birth in the Land of Bliss in the ensuing life. Thus we can presume that the school must have been taken up by influential circles.

Ryōhen,[40] a learned priest of Kongōsammaiin, who was a professed believer of Amita, traveled to Tanabe, Kii, and converted a chief of the fishing village there. According to his teacher's instruction, the new convert went to Kōyasan and built the Karukaya Hall ('Grass-thatched Hall') which became the headquarters of the Amita faith. Almost all of the Hijiri class (sage) at Kōyasan were Amita-pietists who traveled throughout the district and worked for Kōyasan as propagandists. "Wherever we go the voice of the Amita-formula is heard," is recorded in one of the memorials presented to the Government. "In front of and behind the monasteries, under the roofs, and by the waysides the sacred place is getting so noisy that no one can quietly meditate and concentrate one's mind." Iyeyasu [41] finally ordered that the Amita formula should be repeated only in the Karukaya Hall.

Kūya [42] was the earliest Amita-pietist who publicly worked for the propagation of the faith. He is said to have been a son of Emperor Daigo, or at any rate a scion of the Imperial family. He traveled to the country places, built bridges and dug wells for the people whenever needed. In 938 A.D. he came to the capital (Kyoto) and strolled through the streets loudly reciting the Amita hymns specially composed by himself, modulating the voice to music, beating

---

[37] 山門　[38] 寺門　[39] 興教大師 1095-1145　[40] 良遍 about 1200
[41] 家康　[42] 空也 903-972 A.D.

a bowl and dancing as he went on. The people called him 'sage of the streets.' He built the Rokuhara Monastery in which he enshrined a large statue of the Eleven-faced Kwannon (Avalokitesvara) [43] and a copy of the Tripitaka literature. Taira no Sadamori [44] followed him from a deep admiration of his personality. He traveled farther to the Ainu district and the Buddhist teaching was for the time accepted by the aborigines. The Amita formula recited according to his style was called *Kūyanembutsu* [45] and the dance was called *hachi-tataki* ('beating a bowl').[46] His school was famed as the School of Kūya.[47] The Kōshō Monastery (one of Kūya's priestly names was Kōshō [48]), commonly called Kūya Hall, still exists in Shijō, Kyoto, and the street itself is named Takaki-chō after his dancing style *hachi-tataki*. After his death his school became extinct, though the Ji School of Amita-pietism [49] revived it, honoring Kūya as the remote founder of the Ji School, which rules over 486 monasteries at present.

(3) Philosophical and Religious

Amita-pietism as represented by the Jōdo School [50] of Hōnen,[51] the Shin School [52] of Shinran [53] and the Ji School [54] of Ippen,[55] shows a unique aspect of Buddhism. While all other schools of Mahayana insist on self-enlightenment, these schools teach sole reliance on the Buddha's power. The Buddha of all other exoteric schools is Sakyamuni while the Buddha of these schools is Amita or Amitabha ('Infinite Light') or Amitayus ('Infinite Life') whose Land of Bliss (*Sukhavati)* is laid in the Western Quarter, often designated as the Pure Land (Jōdo).

The critical division of the Buddha's teaching adopted by Hōnen was into the two doctrines of the Holy Path and the Pure Land, originally proposed by Tao-ch'o [56] (Dōshaku) of China, c. 645. The former is the difficult way to traverse while the latter is the easy way to travel defined by Nagarjuna. There is another division which was proposed by Vasubandhu and elucidated by Tao-ch'o, that is, the ways of self-power and of another's power. Another's power here means the power of the Buddha Amitabha, not any other's power like that of Yūzūnembutsu. Those who pursue the Holy Path

---

[43] 十一面観音　[44] 平定盛　[45] 空也念佛　[46] 金叩　[47] 空也宗
[49] 光勝　[49] 峕宗　[50] 淨土宗　[51] 法然　[52] 眞宗　[53] 親鸞　[54] 時宗
[55] 一遍　[56] 道綽

can attain Buddhahood in this world, if they are qualified, while those who aspire for the Pure Land can attain Buddhahood only in Sukhavati, the Pure Land.

Now what is Sukhavati and who is Amitabha or Amitayus? We have seen that the Amitabha or Amitayus ('Infinite Light' or 'Infinite Life') is a Buddha idealized from the historical Buddha Sakyamuni. If the Buddha is purely idealized he will be simply the Infinite in principle. The Infinite will then be identical with Thusness. The Infinite, if depicted in reference to space, will be the Infinite Light, and if depicted in reference to time, the Infinite Life. This is *Dharma-kaya* (ideal). This *Dharma-kaya* is the *Sambhoga-kaya* (the 'Reward-body' or 'body of enjoyment'), if the Buddha is viewed as a Buddha 'coming down to the world.' If he is viewed as a Bodhisattva going up to the Buddhahood, he is a would-be Buddha like the toiling Bodhisattva (Sakyamuni). It is Sakyamuni himself who describes in the *Sukhavati-vyuha* the activities of the would-be Buddha, *Dharmakara*, as if it had been his former existence.

The vow, original to the would-be Buddha or even to Sakyamuni himself, is fully expressed in forty-eight items in the text. Items Nos. 12 and 13 refer to the Infinite Light and the Infinite Life. "If he cannot get such aspects of Infinite Light and Life he will not be a Buddha." If he becomes a Buddha he can constitute a Buddha Land as he likes. A Buddha, of course, lives in the 'Nirvana of No Abode,' and hence he can live anywhere and everywhere. His vow is to establish the Land of Bliss for the sake of all beings. An ideal land with adornments, ideal plants, ideal lakes or what not is all for receiving pious aspirants. The eighteenth vow which is regarded as most important, promises a birth in his Land of Bliss to those who have a perfect reliance on the Buddha, believing with serene heart and repeating the Buddha's name. The nineteenth vow promises a welcome by the Buddha himself on the eve of death to those who perform meritorious deeds. The twentieth vow further indicates that anyone who repeats his name with the object of winning a birth in his Land will also be received.

As to the interpretation of these three vows, there are certain differences among the schools. Generally speaking, the Jōdo School takes the vows as literally as possible, while the Shin School elucidates the intent of them rather freely to suit all parts of the text.

According to the Jōdo School these three vows should be taken separately as they are independent vows, though there are some differences in importance.

To the Shin School, however, they are interdependent. The eighteenth is the fundamental vow. The nineteenth and the twentieth are subordinate vows. Though the eighteenth vow expects sole reliance on the Buddha, the followers of the nineteenth and twentieth vows depend on their own actions, the former on meritorious deeds and the latter on repetition of the Buddha's name. They have no complete reliance on the Buddha's power. So their destiny cannot be the Pure Land itself. They must, according to Shinran, go through some purgatory which is called the 'secluded place' or the 'realm of neglect' referred to in other sections of the text. But they will be transformed and in the end admitted to the real Land of Bliss.

With regard to the appearance of Amita or Amitabha, their opinions are also at variance. It is said to have been ten *kalpas* (long periods) ago. The Jōdo School takes this literally, while the Shin School holds that the time 'ten *kalpas* ago' is something like 'ages ago,' and may refer to a second or third appearance. The original Buddha may be of much more remote age. Thus the 'Lotus' doctrine is here applied to the Amita-pietism.

The smaller text of *Sukhavati-vyuha*[57] is a résumé or abridged text of the larger one. The last of the three texts, the *Amitayurdhyana Sutra,*[58] tells us the origin of the Pure Land doctrine taught by the Buddha Sākyamuni. Ajatasatru, the prince heir-apparent of Rajagriha, revolted against his father King Bimbisara and imprisoned him. His consort Vaidehi too was confined to a room. Thereupon the Queen asked the Buddha to show her a better place where no such calamities could be encountered. The World-Honored One appeared before her and showed all the Buddha lands and she chose the Land of Amita as the best of all. The Buddha then taught her how to meditate upon it and finally to be admitted there. He instructed her by his own way of teaching and at the same time by the special teaching of Amita. That both teachings were one in the end could be seen from the words he spoke to Ananda at the

---

[57] 阿彌陀經
[58] *Taishō,* No. 365 觀無量壽經 See my English translation, *The Sutra of the Meditation on Amitayus,* Sacred Books of the East, Vol. XLIX, The Clarendon Press, 1894.

conclusion of his sermons. "O Ananda! Remember this sermon and rehearse it to the assembly on the Vulture Peak. By this sermon, I mean the name of Amitabha." From this we can infer that the object of the sermon was the adoration of Amita. Thus, we see that Sakyamuni's teaching was after all not different from that of Amitabha.

The principal difference of the Jōdo School from that of Shin is in the treatment of the repetition of the Buddha's name. With Jōdo the devotional repetition of the Buddha's name is a necessary action of the pious to deepen the faith, without which salvation will never be complete; while according to the Shin School it is simply an action of gratitude or an expression of thanksgiving, after one's realizing the Buddha's power conferred on one. The Shin School holds the exclusive worship of the Amitabha, not allowing even that of Sakyamuni, the strict prohibition of prayers in any form on account of private interests, and the abolition of all disciplinary rules and the priestly or ecclesiastical life, thus forming a community of purely lay believers, i.e., householders. As the orthodox Jōdo School with all kindred sects still conforms to the old priestly life, it differs extensively from the Shin School.

The Ji School of Amita-pietism is somewhat different. It was founded in 1276 by Ippen [59] (1238-1289). He set forth the rule of reciting the hymns of Shan-tao (Zendō) [60] six times every day, hence the name Ji (time). In theory he derived his idea from the *Lotus* as did Ryōnin of Yūzūnembutsu, but in practice he followed Kūya who invented a popular dance for the popularization of the Amita-faith. Thus the school has a totally different feature from the other schools of Amita-pietism. Ippen is said to have visited Kumano Shrine in Kii in 1275 where he was inspired by a holy verse of four lines, which he believed to have come from the deity of the shrine. Each of the first three lines was headed by a numeral, 6, 10, 10,000 and the last line by 'people,' altogether making up 'six hundred thousand people.' He at once made up his mind to save that number of people by a propagation of the Amita-faith. Now Amita-pietism with all its kindred schools taken together has more than one-half of the Japanese population as adherents.

Amita-pietism is of four aspects: 1. That of Tendai and Shingon, in which Amita is one of the five Wisdom Buddhas (Dhyani-

---

[59] 一遍　　[60] 善導 d. 681

Buddhas) governing the Western Quarters, having Mahavairo-cana [61] (the Great Sun Buddha) at the center. 2. That of Yū-zūnembutsu in which the value of one's faith in Amita is trans-ferable to another or vice versa, i.e., religion of mutual help with faith. 3. That of Jōdo in which Amita's faith is taught exclusively in accordance with the three *Sukhavati* texts of the school, especially based on the Buddha's vows. 4. That of Shin in which the faith is taught strictly in accordance with the eighteenth vow of the Bud-dha described in the larger *Sukhavati* text. In both Jōdo and Shin the Buddha Amita is more than one of the five Buddhas, although his Land is laid in the Western Quarter; instead, he is the one central Buddha. Of these four aspects, the first originated from mystics, the second was influenced by *Lotus* principles, the third was based chiefly on the three vows, and the fourth centered on one vow of the Amita.

Thus we see the ideas of the Amita schools concerning the Bud-dhological principle of Mahayana. According to the theory of ori-ginal immanence of Tendai and the duo-homoiousian (two essences in one) theory of Shingon, the principle of one-is-all and all-are-one will be readily admitted. Of the five Wisdom Buddhas, Amitabha of the West may be identical with the central Mahavairocana, the Buddha of homo-cosmic identity. Without reference to mysticism, Amitabha's original vows, his attainment of Buddhahood of Infinite Light and Life, and his establishment of the Land of Bliss are all fully described in the *Sukhavati* text. It is but natural that Sakya-muni, who hinted to his pupils in the *Lotus* not to regard him as a Buddha of eighty years of age with a small stature, for he is in reality a Buddha of remote ages and of world-wide pervasions, should be identified with the Buddha of Infinite Light and Life. A complete reliance on such a Buddha's power will be a reasonable outcome of this teaching. Shinran especially represents the last stage of this idea. He insisted on an absolute faith in Amita, not making any effort for enlightenment by oneself. One should rely exclusively and absolutely on Amita, faith alone being the cause of salvation. According to him, even the believing thought itself is the grace of the Buddha, and one's remembrance or repetition of the name of the Buddha is simply a token of free thanksgiving shown toward the Buddha.

---

[61] 大日如來

175

XIII. THE NICHIREN SCHOOL[1]
(NEW LOTUS)

(Lotus-pietism)
[Mahayanistic]

(1) Preliminary

Since the *Lotus of the Good Law* [2] was translated and expounded
by Kumarajiva,[3] it has been one of the most popular subjects of
Buddhist study along with the *Prajna* and *Nirvana* [4] texts. When
the philosophy of immanence or the phenomenological doctrine was
promulgated on the basis of the *Lotus* by Chih-i,[5] it was generally
known as the T'ien-T'ai [6] School. It was Saichō [7] (Dengyō Daishi,
767-822 A.D.) who went to China and received the doctrine from
this school and on his return in 804 A.D. founded the school in
Japan. His theoretical elucidation of the *Lotus* doctrine may not be
much different from the original Chinese school, but his practical
application of the doctrine to the national cult and synthetic treatment of all other Buddhist schools subordinate to his school seem to
be the new aspects added by virtue of his genius. Besides the *Lotus*
doctrine, he professed to teach mystic Shingon, Amita-pietism, contemplative Zen, as well as Mahayanistic Vinaya discipline. To him
these were subordinate doctrines to the *Lotus* or at any rate con-
current systems to complete the central doctrine. However, in the
course of time, there appeared among his followers some ardent
specialists in each of these systems and sometimes the result was
separation. In the Heian period (781-1183) the mystic rituals and
ceremonial performances promoted by this school in concert with
the Shingon School carried the day to satisfy the aristocratic taste
of the time. There arose in time a devotional school of Amita-pietism
which also flourished in the bosom of the school. Through the influence of the two streams of religious activities a great Buddhist

---

[1] 日蓮宗　[2] 妙法蓮華經
[3] 鳩摩羅什 during 383-406 A.D. in China　[4] 般若經, 涅槃經
[5] 智顗 Chih-kai, 531-597 A.D.　[6] 天台 Tendai in Japanese.
[7] 最澄, 傳敎大師

transformation took place in the national life and thoughts of Japan during the period.

The refinement of vernacular literature, mystification of fine arts, development of national architectural and industrial arts, and the graceful manners and customs of the refined class were all due to the influence of Buddhist culture. Probably the Japanese appreciation of universals, tolerance, and thoroughness in research owe a great deal to Buddhist training. But peace often ends in effeminacy. As a rule political corruption and social degeneration in general could not be checked in any way. An opportunity for a military power was now opened and perhaps hatred and struggle among courtiers, clans, territorial lords and partisans were more than we know from history. Already in the closing period of the Heian era all under heaven was weary of war and disorder. By the establishment of the military government at Kamakura, the people in general expected peace and order to be restored, but all in vain. Intrigues and strifes were going on more than ever. The arrival of the 'latter age' of religion was now felt in the public life of the nation. A general reformation in political as well as religious life seemed to be an urgent need. The authority of the two old schools of Tendai and Shingon was waning, or at any rate, was suffering the same fate with the aristocratic classes. The new Amita-pietism of Hō-nen,[8] though gaining ground among the people at large, had no marked influence over the ruling classes. The Zen School of the time, though it seemed appropriate for the knightly training of military people, had as yet no power over the political affairs. A man of keen observation and strong character like Nichiren[9] (1222-1282), if imbued with a firm religious conviction, could not remain without protesting.

To know Nichiren and his school we must first know the *Lotus* text on which all his ideas and arguments are founded. What is the *Lotus* text? A text-criticism shows that originally the *Lotus* text consisted of twenty-one sections and was later enlarged into twenty-eight sections by addition and division. The earliest translation was by Dharmaraksa[10] in 286 A.D., the second by Kumarajiva in 406 A.D., and the third (complete translation) by Jnanagupta and Dharmagupta in 601 A.D. Among them, the second was the

---

[8] 法然 1133-1212   [9] 日蓮   [10] 法護

177

best in Chinese composition and regarded as authoritative by the best *Lotus* authorities.[11] In spite of late translation, it represented an earlier form of the text than the first translation, judging from some internal evidences, e.g., a quotation by Nagarjuna [12] and the like. Besides, elements of the contents of the added or divided chapters were extant in the original form of twenty-one sections. Anyhow, the existing text in twenty-eight sections (Kumarajiva's translation) was used by Chih-i, Saichō and Nichiren himself. It is the only translation of the text used in Japan, either within or without the Nichiren School. Let us review the contents of the text and the standpoint of Nichiren in the *Lotus* doctrine.

(2) Historical

What is historical with the other schools of thought is personal with the Nichiren's Lotus-pietism, for it is Nichiren's personality that constitutes the feature of the school. It was not accidental that the school was called after the founder's name. Nichiren was born in 1222, the son of a fisherman of Kominato, Awa, the southeastern coast of Japan. He was sent to Kiyozumi, a hill near his home, to live as a novice in a monastery. He was ordained in his fifteenth year. His early problem, "What was the Truth taught by the Buddha?" was not solved there. He proceeded to Kamakura and later passed to Mount Hiei in search of the Truth. His study of ten years (1243-1253) on the mountain convinced him that a revival of Tendai philosophy alone was the nearest approach to the Truth.

By Tendai philosophy Nichiren meant not what he found there at hand but what was taught by Dengyō Daishi himself. The original T'ien-T'ai of Chih-i was chiefly theoretical, whereas the Japanese Tendai of Dengyō Daishi was practical as well as theoretical. But after the two great masters, Jikaku [13] and Chishō,[14] the practical sides of Tendai were either mystic rituals or Amita-faith; that seemed to them most important. The fundamental truth of the *Lotus* doctrine seemed to be laid aside as if it were a philosophical amusement. Nichiren could not accept this attitude and

---

[11] *Taishō*, No. 262 妙法蓮華經 English translations: *The Lotus of the True Law,* translated by H. Kern, Sacred Books of the East, Vol. XXI, The Clarendon Press, 1884; *The Lotus of the Wonderful Law,* translated by W. E. Soothill, Oxford, 1930.
[12] 龍樹 c. 100-200 A.D.   [13] 慈覺   [14] 智澄.

so returned in 1253 to his old monastery at Kiyozumi where he proclaimed his new doctrine that the *Lotus* alone could save the people of the depraved age, the essential formula being "Homage to the Text of the *Lotus* of the True Ideal." [15] It is *Dharma-smriti* (thought on *Dharma*) and not *Buddha-smriti* as was the Amita-formula. *Dharma* is the ideal realized by the original Buddha. All beings are saved through homage to the Lotus of Truth, and this alone, he declared, is the true final message of the Buddha.

The abbot and all others opposed him and he had to escape to Kamakura where he built a cottage and lived for a while. He preached his doctrine in streets or in parks, attacking the other schools as violently as ever. He wrote a treatise on the *Establishment of Righteousness as the Safeguard of the Nation*,[16] which he presented to the Hōjō Regent in 1260. His main arguments were against the Amita-pietism of Hōnen, which he considered to be chiefly responsible for the evils and calamities within and without the nation. In the treatise he condemned Hōnen as the enemy of all Buddhas, all scriptures, all sages and all people. It was the duty of the government, he said, to terminate his heresy even with the sword. His idea of the identification of religion with national life is manifest throughout the work.

Nichiren's classification of 'latter age' began with the year 1050, according to the generally accepted calculation of the date of Nirvana. The last of seven calamities, the foreign invasion, was predicted in it. He contended that national peace and prosperity could be attained only through the unification of all Buddhism by the doctrine of the Lotus of Truth. Later, he attacked the religious schools then extant and formulated his views as follows: Jōdo (Amita-pietism) is hell, Zen (meditative intuitionism) is devil, Shingon (mysticism) is national ruin and Ritsu (discipline) is traitorous. These four practically cover all existing schools of his time and were the doctrines that had been subordinate to Tendai.

As Amita-faith propagated by Hōnen, Shinran [17] and others was most influential among the people at large, the Zen trend of thought, specially appealing to the ruling military class of the time, was probably the second influential doctrine. Owing to the activities of Eisai,[18] Dōgen [19] and Enni [20] in Kyoto, and the Chinese teachers Rankei,[21]

---

[15] 喃嘸妙法蓮華經　　[16] 立正安國論　　[17] 親鸞 1173-1262　　[18] 榮西
1141-1215　　[19] 道元. 1200-1253　　[20] 圓爾 1235　　[21] 蘭溪

179

Sogen [22] and Ichinei,[23] in Kamakura, the Zen School was certainly asserting its position in the national life and culture. As to Shingon, the power of mystification which it cherished never lost its hold on the mind of the people; the Shingon School was influential all over Japan. The Ritsu was a school of discipline reformed by Eison [24] who prayed against the Mongol invasion at the Shinto shrine of Iwashimizu by an Imperial order, when Emperor Kameyama himself was present and vowed to sacrifice his life for the safety of the nation. Thus the Ritsu must have been quite influential at the Court.

Nichiren's attacks against these schools became more violent than ever when he was mobbed, attacked and banished to Izu in 1261. Even after his return to Kamakura and to his native place to see his ailing mother, he did not refrain from his violent protest against the government as well as the religion, and went so far as to say that Tokiyori, the Hōjō Regent who believed in Zen and wore a Buddhist robe, was already in hell and that the succeeding Regent Tokumune was on the way to hell. Upon the arrival of the Mongolian envoys demanding tribute, he again remonstrated the Regime to suppress the heresies and adopt the *Lotus* doctrine as the only way out of national calamities. In 1271 he was arrested, tried and sentenced to death. In a miraculous way he escaped the execution and was banished to the remote island of Sado at the end of the same year.

In spite of the hardships and troubles he experienced there, Nichiren wrote several works. In the *Eye-opener,*[25] his famous vows are found: "I will be the pillar of Japan; I will be the eyes of Japan; I will be the vessel of Japan." Here he became conscious of himself being the Bodhisattva Visistacaritra ('Distinguished Action') [26] with whom the Buddha entrusted the work of protecting the Truth.

After three years he was allowed to return to Kamakura in 1274. No moderation, no compromise and no tolerance could be extracted from him in spite of an ardent effort on the part of the government. He retired to Minobu, west of Mount Fuji, and lived peacefully. He died at Ikegami, near Tokyo, in 1282.

Nichiren's militant spirit was kept alive by his disciples, six of whom were earnest propagandists. One of them, Nichiji,[27] went

---

[22] 祖元　　[23] 一寧　　[24] 睿尊　　[25] 開目鈔　　[26] 上行　　[27] 日持

to Siberia in 1295 but no further report was heard of him. The
school, always colored by a fighting attitude, had many disputes
with other religious institutions. In 1532, for example, it had a
conflict with Tendai, the mother school, called the war of Tembun.
One of the Nichiren sects called Fujufuse Sect ('no give or take') [28]
refused to comply with the parish rule conventionally set forth
by the government and was prohibited in 1614 along with Christianity by the Tokugawa Shogunate. There are at present eight
Nichiren sects, two of which are important; 1. The Nichiren School
proper [29] with headquarters in Minobu, 3,600 monasteries under it.
2. The Kenpon-Hokke School,[30] otherwise called the Myōmanji School
which has 580 monasteries.

(3) Philosophical and Religious

Just as the personality of Nichiren constitutes the Nichiren
School, the essence of which is the *Lotus* formula "Homage to the
Lotus of Truth," so it is the personality of the Buddha that constitutes the *Lotus* doctrine. The whole *Lotus* text may be a drama
as Professor Kern imagined, but the Buddha is not only the hero
in the play. The Buddha is also the organizer or proprietor of the
drama. The Truth of the *Lotus* text is not an impersonal dead
truth; it is the ideal, the Truth blooming, fragrant and bearing
fruits as the lotus, the Truth active, the Truth embodied in the
Buddha, the Truth-body, the Enlightenment itself, the Enlightened
and Enlightenment and Enlightener all combined. So the real Buddha of the text is not that corporeal Buddha who got enlightened
under the *bodhi* tree, preached for the first time at the Deer Park
of Benares and entered Nirvana at the Sala grove of Kusinagara
at eighty-one years of age. He is the Buddha of immeasurable ages
past, ever acting as the Enlightener. By enlightening all beings he
exercises benevolence to all. Out of his mercy he teaches the doctrine
of expediency. He is in reality the organizer of the drama, yet he
himself acts as a hero in the play, leading all the dramatic personnel,
even with some of the inferior characters who in time will be able
to play a role. The three Vehicles, of course, as well as Devadatta
the wicked and Naga the serpent maid, all come under the Buddha's
illumination. The world of illumination of the remote Buddha is
called the 'realm of origin' [31] and the world of illumination by the

---

[28] 不受不施派   [29] 日蓮宗   [30] 顕本法華宗   [31] 本門

incarnate Buddha is called the 'realm of trace.'[32] I used the word 'realm' but it does not mean a separate division or place. It simply indicates the 'activity of the Buddha of original position' [33] or 'that of the Buddha of trace-leaving manifestation.' [34] 'Original position' [35] and 'trace-manifestation' [36] are the problems long discussed in the Lotus schools and all center on the Buddha's personality, a Buddhological question. When it is applied to the *Lotus* text, the question at the outset will be, "Which Buddha is revealing the Truth?"

It is generally accepted that the first fourteen sections of the text, with an introduction, a principal portion and a conclusion, refer to the realm of trace, while the last fourteen sections also with an introduction, a principal portion and a conclusion, relate to the realm of origin. The object of the *Lotus* on the whole is a revelation of Truth. In the former sections, chiefly in the section of *upaya* or 'expediency,' the Buddha reveals that what he taught before the *Lotus,* during forty or more years, was only an expedient; more definitely, the teachings for direct disciples (*sravakas,* i.e., *arhat-* teaching),[37] for the enlightened-for-self (*pratyeka-buddha* teaching) [38] and for lesser *bodhisattvas,* i.e., the teaching for the three Vehicles, was for expediency's sake, and indicated clearly that the 'one vehicle for all' *(ekayana)* is the Truth.[39] In the latter sections, chiefly in the longevity section, the Buddha speaks of his own personality, and reveals that the historical existence which he has now nearly completed is not his real body but shows clearly his Truth-body *(Dharma-kaya)* to be a true realization of remote ages past.[40]

The former sections refer to the doctrine in which the Truth is revealed; expediency is taught as expediency and Truth as Truth. The latter sections, on the other hand, refer to the personality in which the Buddha himself is revealed; the recent as the manifested person and the remote as the real original person. So far Nichiren agrees with Dengyō Daishi. Nichiren, however, standing on the doctrine of personality, asserts that all teachings before the *Lotus* and also the former sections of the *Lotus* are the 'trace doctrines of the Trace Buddha' [41] and that only the latter sections are the 'essential original doctrines of the Original Buddha.' [42] He estab-

---

[32] 迹門　[33] 本門本化　[34] 迹門迹化　[35] 本地　[36] 垂迹　[37] 聲聞
[38] 緣覺　[39] 開三顯一　[40] 開近顯遠　[41] 迹門迹化　[42] 本門本化

lished his school on the basis of the original *Lotus*. Thus his school is called either the Nichiren School after the founder or the Hommon-Hokke School [43] after the doctrine.

The difference of the tenets of Dengyō Daishi and Nichiren is further seen in the treatment of the substance of the *Lotus* text. The Lotus doctrine assumes ten regions, ten thus-aspects and three realms. Dengyō Daishi lays importance on the principle of the realm of trace. The realm of trace treats only the nine regions, teaching the causal states of culture [44] and therefore considering mind and thought as important factors of training, and finally attributing all the phenomenal worlds to the mere-ideation theory. The three-fold view of one mind and the 3,000 worlds immanent in one thought-instant are taught minutely. According to the Nichiren School, the Tendai is too much inclined to the theoretical side of the Truth, thereby forgetting the practical side of it. Nichiren holds that the realm of origin teaches the effective state of enlightenment [45] and the Buddha's person is the center of Truth; the reality of the phenomenal worlds centers in the personality of the Buddha; and all aspirants should be guided to realize the Ideal-body of the Buddha.

The *Lotus* text reveals the original Buddha whose principle and practice are fully explained in the original portions of the text. What the founder holds important is the Buddha's practice, not his principle. One who understands and practices the practical aspects of that Buddha is a devotee or realizer of the *Lotus*,[46] just as the *bodhisattva* of supreme action (Visistacaritra) [47] is placed in the highest position in the text. The Buddhahood (perfect enlightenment) of such an adept will be immediate in this very body.[48]

The original Buddha was like the moon in the sky and all other Buddhas of the *Wreath*, of the *Agama*, of the *Vaipulya* ('developed'), the *Prajna* ('wisdom'), the *Gold Light (Suvarnaprabhasa)*, the *Sukhavati* (Pure Land) and the *Great Sun (Mahavairocana)* were all moons in various waters, and merely reflections of the one central moon. It is only a fool who would try to catch a reflected moon.

---

[43] 本門法華宗　　[44] 從因門　　[45] 觀化門　　[46] 法華經行坐　　[47] 上行菩薩　　[48] 即身成佛

The title of the *Lotus of the Good Law* sums up all these principles and practice of the Buddhas of origin and trace, and, to Nichiren, is the only remedy to procure the reform of the depraved state of the 'latter age,' in spite of all counteractions from existing poisons. The fourfold watchword set forth by Nichiren, as we have seen above, was the renowned object of hatred by all the rest of the Buddhist schools of Japan, for it was against the Amita-pietism of Jōdo, the meditative intuitionism of Zen, the ritual mysticism of Shingon and the formalistic discipline of Ritsu. This was the wholesale denunciation of all existing Buddhist schools except the Tendai School of Dengyō Daishi, which he sought to reform and restore to its original form.

XIV. THE NEW RITSU SCHOOL
(THE REFORMED DISCIPLINARY SCHOOL)[1]
(Vinaya)

(Disciplinary Formalism)
[Mahayanistic]

(1) Preliminary

Vinaya (discipline) is the moral code of Buddhism and is invariably translated into Japanese 'ritsu' *(discipline)*. The whole code containing 250 articles for priests and 348 for nuns existed from the lifetime of the Buddha. A weekly convocation called 'fast' *(uposadha)* was held for the purpose of reciting the code, one article after another, to ascertain whether any member of the 'noble' community had committed any crime or sins described in it. Confession, repentance, surveillance, custody, excommunication or any other necessary means was taken after judgment was passed on the person in question. The nature of precepts (*sila*)[2] was twofold: 1. The positive precepts, the precepts for performance,[3] i.e., the rules that should be performed on such occasions as ordination for a novice *(bhikshu)*, convocation for weekly reading of the code, summer retreat for yearly study and training of the community, graduation ceremony; rules concerning residence, medicines, leathers; settlements of disputes in the congregation; and also the rules of council meetings, judicial court of discussion, voting and decision, treatment of contributions, confiscation of properties or the like. 2. The negative precepts of prohibition,[4] i.e., not to commit any sin or crime. The nature of prohibition was also twofold: 1. prohibition in order to safeguard one from crime or sin, like the prohibition of drinking an intoxicating liquor, which may lead to a sin or crime; 2. prohibitions of actual crimes, such as killing, stealing, lying, committing adultery, etc., which are themselves evil in nature. The entire prohibitive code is as follows: 1. crimes that incur expulsion (for the monks, there are 4; for the nuns there are 8); 2. crimes that re-

---

[1] Lü 律　　[2] 戒　　[3] 作持戒　　[4] 止持戒

quire suspension of priestly right (for the monks, 13; for the nuns, 17) ; 3. offences that require confession and ablution (for the monks, 90; for the nuns, 178) ; 4. offences requiring public confession (for the monks, 4; for the nuns, 8); 5. offences requiring forfeiture (for the monks, 30; for the nuns, 30) ; 6. actions that are indefinite as to whether they are offences or not (for the monks, 2; for the nuns, none); 7. minor prohibitive regulations of the order (for the monks, 100; for the nuns, 100); 8. judicial settlement of disputes (for the monks, 7; for the nuns, 7)—total for priests, 250; for nuns, 348.

The formalistic Hinayana was inclined to hold to letters, words and forms of the *Vinaya* discipline. Consequently, a schism arose as to the legality of the ten allowances (such as receiving money only if used for the order) of the rules, and the council of Vaisali met to discuss and decide them. The idealistic Mahayana laid more emphasis on the spirit of the rules rather than the letter. Though Mahayana seemed to be transgressing the rules, it would harmonize itself with the spirit of the Buddhas who had set forth the rules.

The recipient of a precept had to keep in mind the four aspects of discipline: 1. the elements of discipline; [5] 2. the essence of discipline; [6] 3. the action of discipline; [7] and 4. the form of discipline. [8] Among these, the most important was the essence of discipline, without which the acceptance of discipline would never be complete. The essence of discipline is the conscious energy ever active as a firm impression received at the faithful acceptance of discipline. This is, in fact, the result of the heart-felt vow taken at the solemn occasion of ordination. This energy ought to manifest itself in thought, word or action whenever a function is needed, and one will therefore act accordingly so as to conform to discipline. The essence of discipline is thus a moral force acting in the mind, like conscience.

There are two ordinations, that for the initiation of a novice receiving five disciplinary rules and that for a full qualification of a priest receiving ten. Both are the precepts of common-sense morality (not to kill, steal, lie, commit adultery, drink liquors, etc.). These two are the formal ordinations performed by both Hinayana and Mahayana and may be called a priest *(bhikshu)* ordination. There

---

[5] 戒法　[6] 戒體　[7] 戒行　[8] 戒相

is another informal self-vow ordination performed by the Mahayana only, which is set forth in the *Brahma-jala Sutra,* and may be called a *bodhisattva* (future Buddha) ordination. In the Nara period (710-794 A.D.) there was only the former, but during and after the Heian period (794-1183) the latter came to be generally followed.

(2) Historical

The Emperor Shōmu (724-748 A.D.) once intended to invite an able teacher from China in order to train the Japanese priests and nuns in the Ritsu (Vinaya) doctrine. He sent out two priests, Eiei [9] and Fushō [10] by name, to carry out this purpose. The then ruling Chinese Emperor, Hsüan-tsung,[11] however, was much in favor of Taoism and did not wish to send any Buddhist teacher to Japan. Consequently, negotiation with a much-famed *vinaya* teacher, Chien-chên (Ganjin),[12] failed. However, as the need of an instructor was imminent, Tao-hsüan (Dōsen),[13] one of the pupils of that teacher, was sent to Nara in advance. He arrived there in 735 A.D. and busied himself teaching the Ritsu, the Zen and the T'ien-t'ai doctrines while waiting for his teacher's arrival.

Meanwhile, Ganjin prepared secretly for his departure with the aid of the two students, Eiei and Fushō. He actually built ships five times with the help of the former prime minister Li Lin-fu [14] and others, but each time failed through shipwrecks. Finally, he embarked on the ship of the Japanese envoys returning home and arrived at Nara in 754 A.D. He was welcomed by the Court and a special monastery Tōshōdaiji as well as a sacred area for ordination was built for him. All of the Imperial family, headed by the ruling Empress, the ex-Emperor and ministers, received the first ordination from him. His discipline was that of the Four-Division tradition,[15] (Dharmaguptiya), otherwise called the Ritsu School of the South Mountain [16] founded by Tao-hsüan, a pupil of the famous Hiuen-tsang.[17]

Dengyō Daishi (Saichō, 767-822 A.D.) [18] received the ordination but afterwards rejected it, and started a new *bodhisattva* ordination based on the Tendai doctrine which was purely Mahayanistic and

[9] 榮睿　[10] 普照　[11] 玄宗　[12] 鑑眞 687-763 A.D.　[13] 道宣 596-667 A.D.　[14] 李林甫　[15] 四分律　[16] 南山律宗　[17] Hsüan-tsang　[18] 最澄, 傳教大師

informal, called the discipline based on 'round and abrupt' doctrine which is the Lotus doctrine, the round or perfect doctrine, the effect of which can be obtained abruptly.[19] A strong protest from Nara was raised against it. It was only after his death that Imperial permission was given for the establishment of the new ordination. A sacred hall of this ordination was built on Mount Hiei and became the basis of ordinations of all other schools, Zen, Jōdo and their sub-sects. Even Nichiren intended a special ordination hall of a similar type but he did not succeed.

In the Nara period there were three sacred areas of ordination: 1. Tōdaiji Temple, Nara; 2. Kwanzeonji Temple, Tsukusho; 3. Yakushiji Temple, Shimozuke. In the Heian period there was another ordination hall on Mount Hiei, originally planned by Dengyō Daishi. The Shingon School of Kōbō Daishi [20] had an anointment hall in Tōji, Kyoto, as a substitute for the ordination hall. Later, when the followers of Chishō Daishi [21] at the Mii Temple began to dispute with the followers of Jikaku Daishi [22] at Mount Hiei, the former could not receive ordinations on the mount and consequently built a new hall called Samaya Kaidan. Thus in the Heian period there were practically five ordination halls in Japan. Of these, the typical one was the 'round and abrupt' ordination hall which was based on the 'round and abrupt' doctrine of the 'Lotus Truth.'

The essence of discipline was considered to be an unmanifested moral force *(musa)* immanent in the recipient's mind.[23] We can thus realize that importance was here laid upon the spiritual effect of ordination rather than the ceremonial performance of the rite.

The Tōshōdaiji Monastery in Nara was built by the Court and was made the authorized headquarters of all Buddhist training in discipline. The founder of the Ritsu School of the South Mountain, Ganjin, was succeeded by his able pupils, **Fa-chin (Hōshin)**[24] from China, and Johō [25] from Arsak, East Persia, both of whom lived to the Heian period and took part in the Imperial ordination. The school exists even today as a separate school, but its formal discipline has never been popular in Japan, partly because of the introduction of the new Hinayanistic doctrine brought home by I-tsing [26] from

---

[19] 圓頓戒　[20] 弘法大師 774-835 A.D.　[21] 智澄大師 814-891 A.D.
[22] 慈覺大師　[23] 興心本具　[24] 法進　[25] 如寶 Ju-pao
[26] 義淨 I-ching, 635-713 A.D.

India and partly because of the rise of the Mahayanistic discipline of the Tendai School.

(3) Philosophical and Religious

The formality of the Ritsu School lies in the carrying out of the disciplinary code, both positive and negative, in letter rather than in spirit. To keep the discipline to letters and words was the chief concern of the schools of the Nara period when the Four-Division doctrine was introduced by Ganjin. It was Hinayanistic, but, since there was no other alternative, it was admitted as common to both Hinayana and Mahayana. Let us call it the Disciplinary School. In Japan, since the time of Prince Shōtoku [27] there has been the idea of a non-formal discipline, to maintain the original spirit of the Buddha's moral code. This non-formal discipline was the chief idea running through all schools of all ages in Japan. While the aspirants of formal discipline were chiefly priests, those of non-formal discipline were *bodhisattvas* or future Buddhas, without distinction of priests or laymen.

Generally speaking, the importance of discipline was laid on what we call the essence of discipline, i.e., spiritual force created in the mind on making a vow and vividly acting always against a violation of that vow. The Realistic (Kusha) School takes this to be one of the forms (*rupa,* matter),[28] i.e., a substantial element without manifestation *(avijnapti-rupa),*[29] while the Nihilistic (Jojitsu) School regards it as a special element—neither matter nor mind—in want of a function of both. Further, the Idealistic (Hossō) School treats it as a perceptive form conceived at ordination that really proceeds from the stored seed of thought *(cetana).* This is the unmanifested mental function that keeps one in accordance with his own pledge. It is the innermost impression which functions like conscience.

Self-vow Discipline [30]

In the formal discipline there should be a private tutor (*upadhyaya),* a ceremonial teacher *(karma-acarya)* and some witnesses. An ordination should be carried through by a convocation *(sangha).* When the article of a disciplinary code is read, the recipient makes a vow of obeisance. But in some cases when such formal require-

---

[27] 聖德太子 574-622 A.D.　　[28] 色　　[29] 無表色　　[30] 自誓大事之戒

ment cannot be fulfilled, one is entitled to make a self-vow informally. It can be designated as the self-vow discipline, as is gloriously exemplified by Queen Srimala in the *Srimala Sutra*.[31] Prince Shōtoku lectured twice on this text before the Throne. At the second time the Empress Suiko stood up before the Buddha and loudly repeated the Queen's vows as her own. This was the first example of the self-vow discipline ever practiced in Japan. The self-vow ordination is permitted in the *Brahma-jala Sutra*.[32] On failing to obtain the proper instructor in discipline one can accept the precepts by self-vow. It is a kind of *bodhisattva* ordination.

Self-immanent Discipline [33]

In opposition to the formal ordination, an ideal ordination was proposed by Dengyō Daishi. He called it the 'round and abrupt' ordination. As stated before, the 'round and abrupt' was the appellation of the Lotus doctrine, the perfect doctrine, the effect of which could be obtained suddenly. It is purely Mahayanistic and considered by the Tendai School as an ordination only for *bodhisattvas*. According to the Lotus doctrine, all the morals of discipline are originally immanent in one's own mind and not the products of a special effort. It can be called the self-immanent discipline and is special to the Tendai School.

Self-nature Discipline [34]

The Zen School of the Kamakura period (1183-1331 A.D.) had an ordination of a similar kind. According to this school the idea of moral discipline is originally innate in human nature. By introspective meditation one can draw it out and put it to practice. The formal side of discipline is now also carefully attended to by the Zen School, but the introspective nature of the Zen training makes the ordination ceremony very impressive and fascinating.

Besides this Zen ordination, there are the anointment ritual of the Shingon School of mysticism and the fivefold transmission of the Jōdo School of Amita-pietism. These take the place of the disciplinary ordination but can be left unnoticed here because of their somewhat different nature.

In the Ritsu School there was a new movement in this period, a departure from the Ritsu School of the South Mountain or the Four-

---

[31] 勝鬘經　　[32] *Taishō*, No. 21 梵網經　　[33] 自心本具之戒
[34] 自相本性之戒

Division School. The movement was started by Eison (1201-1290) [35] on the basis of self-vow discipline. It was a reformed doctrine, called the Reformed or New Ritsu or Reformed Disciplinary School [36] and was, in reality, a revival of the self-vow ordination of Prince Shōtoku, as performed by the Empress Suiko. Eison studied the Vinaya literature in the Tōdaiji Temple and, as he became aware of the idea of self-vow running through the *Srimala* and *Brahma-jala* texts and the Tendai and Zen schools, founded with a fellow-student this Reformed School of Self-vow Formalism. He meant to revert to the original idea of the Buddha and Prince Shōtoku, following the general tendency of Buddhism of the Kamakura age. However, it is regrettable that we do not have the details of his idea of training. His fame as a great Ritsu (Vinaya) reformer was far-reaching, and it was due to his influence that this disciplinary school saw the most flourishing age after the time of Ganjin of Nara. In 1281 the Emperor Gouda ordered Eison to pray in the Otokoyama Shrine against the invasion of Kubilai Khan. The storm which exterminated the 100,000 invaders was believed to have been an answer to his earnest prayer. The title, Kō-shō Bodhisattva ('promoter of righteousness') [37] was given to Eison in 1300 A.D. by the Court.

During the age of Buddhist Renaissance in the Tokugawa period (1603-1867 A.D.), the two branches of disciplinary formalism, the Myōhō-ritsu (discipline according to the Law) [38] School of Jōgon [39] in Yedo, and the Shōbō-ritsu (discipline of True Law) [40] School of Jiun [41] in Kawachi, had certain connections with Eison's new discipline, either directly or indirectly. The two branches of the Tokugawa period did not prosper much, but the founders of both schools were talented scholars of Sanskrit and revived the Indian study to a great extent.

---

[35] 叡尊　　[36] 新律宗　　[37] 興正　　[38] 妙法律　　[39] 淨嚴 1641-1704 A.D.
[40] 正法律　　[41] 慈雲 1718-1804 A.D.

191

XV. CONCLUSION

In conclusion, I should like to say something more about the metaphysical and dialectical questions of Buddhism, for in the foregoing pages I have been too occupied with describing the historical and technical details of the different Buddhist schools and have somehow neglected to consider the general problems of philosophy which concern special doctrines.

With regard to *cosmogonical* and *cosmological* questions, Buddhism has no special theory of its own and seems to have adopted the then-accepted theory of the world-system of Sumeru *(sineru)* and Chiliocosm *(sahassi-lokadhatu)*. However, it does have a definite theory of the world-periods or aeons *(kalpa)* which is substantially identical with that of the Sankhya and Jaina Schools of India. The Sankhya School might have been the originator of the *kalpa* theory as Garbe thinks,[1] and Buddhism as well as Jainism might have been indebted to it. Although evolution *(samvatta* and *samvatta-tthayi)* and devolution *(vivatta* and *vivatta-tthayi)* are equally described in all three schools, Buddhism gives minute details as to the Buddhas who appear and the people who live in each of the four world-periods.

Since the cycle of aeons repeats itself in due course, a story of creation or the Creator does not exist in Buddhism. Practically speaking, Buddhism has no cosmogony, no theology, no divinity. Brahma as a personal God in Buddhism is only a Being in the 'form-heaven' who comes and receives the Buddha's instruction. Thus a deification of the Buddha, as some suppose, is out of the question.

The universe, according to the Buddhist idea, is not homocentric. It is instead a co-creation of all beings. Moreover, everyone of us is self-created and self-creating. As long as all beings have common purposes, it is but natural that there be groups of similar types of beings. Buddhism does not believe in the doctrine that all have come out of one cause, but holds that everything inevitably comes

---

[1] Richard Garbe, *Die Sankhya Philosophie.*

out of more than one cause; in other words, all is mutually relative, a product of interdependence.

As to *ontological* questions, Buddhism rarely concerns itself, for 'thatness' *(tattva,* reality), which refers chiefly to matter, is not what Buddhism seeks. The theory of no-substance (selflessness) which Buddhism holds will not permit any discussion about things-in-themselves or real entity. Instead, Buddhism is concerned with 'thusness' *(tathatva, tathata,* state of being thus), a term which originally referred to form *(rupa)* or becoming *(sanskara)* and not to matter. It is not accidental that Buddhist Realism (Kusha) or Idealism (Hossō) begins with 'form' *(rupa)* and never speaks of matter or substance in the enumeration of their seventy-five or one hundred elements which 'have become' and 'have not become' *(dharma sanskrita* and *asanskrita).* Some may doubt whether 'selfless' was applied to things in general from the beginning, but the phrase 'all things selfless' *(sarva dharma nairatmana)* does not allow any such supposition.

The Realist School (Sarvastivada), assuming that all things exist, has an atomic theory, but the existence of the atom is only for a moment and nothing remains the same for two consecutive moments *(sarva sanskara anitya).* The theory of momentary destruction *(ksana-bhanga)* is also held by the Mahayana schools, which regard the world as in a constant state of flux.

Whether Buddhism has the idea of the One against the Many or the Absolute against the Relative is extremely doubtful. Buddhism certainly opposes dualistic ideas and often negates a pluralistic diversity in man's ascent of Self-Culture. However, it never advances a monistic view positively. Even the Mahayana doctrine of Asvaghosa,[2] as in the *Awakening of Faith,*[3] limits Thusness to the human mind, which ascends if conditioned by a pure cause and descends if polluted by an impure cause. Thusness is therefore something like a neutral state. In reality, the term means 'the state of being thus' or, ultimately speaking, Buddhahood. *Dharma-dhatu* (The Realm of Principle)[4] has a double meaning, signifying the actual universe and the indeterminate world (Nirvana); in the latter case it is identical with the Thusness of the Buddha. Nirvana ('flamelessness')[5] means, on the one hand, the death of the human

---

[2] 馬鳴   [3] 大乘起信論   [4] 法界   [5] 涅槃

body and, on the other, the total extinction of life-conditions (negatively) or the perfect freedom of will and action (positively). *Tathagata-garbha* ('Matrix of Thus-come or Thus-gone')[6] likewise has a twofold meaning: the 'Thus-come' or 'Thus-gone' (Buddha) concealed in the Womb (man's nature) and the Buddha-nature as it is. Buddha-nature, which refers to living beings, and *Dharma*-nature, which concerns chiefly things in general, are practically one as either the state of enlightenment (as a result) or the potentiality of becoming enlightened (as a cause). It is generally known that *Dharma-kaya*[7] has two senses: the 'Scripture-body' means that the Teaching remains as representative of the body after the Buddha's demise, and the 'Ideal-body' means the Enlightenment as a Formless-body. The same twofoldness applies to *Sunyata* or 'Void.'[8] 'Void' does not always mean an antithetical nothingness or emptiness. In a higher sense it indicates the state *devoid* of all conditions of life. Hence it is sometimes said that *sunya* is *asunya* (Void is non-void). More precisely, it is not the state in which nothing exists but is the state in which anything can exist. It is the world of perfect freedom of actions unconditioned by life. Exactly alike is the True Reality.[9] It is said that True Reality is no reality; or we may say that true characteristic is no characteristic. In such cases, the terms 'reality' and 'characteristic' should be interpreted in their ordinary literal sense while the adjective 'true' determines their real meaning.

Thus in Buddhism any word which represents something like the First Principle must always be interpreted in its twofold meaning, for Buddhism admits a worldly or common-sense truth and, by its side, sets forth a higher or absolute truth in order to elevate it.

The terms given above are all expressive, either subjectively or objectively, of the true principle of nature, universe and humanity, and point finally to perfect enlightenment or perfect freedom. Buddhism, after all, does not lose individuality or personality, for the result is nothing but the perfection of personality or the realization of the Life-Ideal. A loss of identity is not the question. One may think that there exists a world of super-individuality apart from the world of individuality into which one figuratively jumps in due course and all becomes one. The view of such a distinct world of non-individuality is but the assumption of a larger individual world.

---

[6] 如來藏　　[7] 法身　　[8] 空　　[9] 實相

194

Such a world is utterly inadmissible in Buddhist thought; but, religiously speaking, it is possible for the enlightened to speak partially of the world of indeterminateness (Nirvana) in his instructing descent to the world of determinateness.

With regard to the *psychological* questions, Buddhism does not admit the existence of a soul that is real and immortal. *Anatma* or non-self refers to all things (*sarva-dharma*), organic or inorganic. In the case of human beings, there will accordingly be no soul, no real self that is immortal, while in the case of things in general, there will be no noumenon, no essence which is unchangeable. Because there is no real self spatially, i.e., no substance, there will be no permanence, i.e., no duration. Therefore no bliss is to be found in the world.

There are no ordinary *eschatological* questions in Buddhism because all beings are in the eternal flux of becoming. One should note, however, that birth incurs death and death again incurs birth. Birth and death are two inevitable phenomena of the cycle of life which ever repeats its course. The end of self-creation is simply the realization of the Life-Ideal, that is, the undoing of all life-conditions, in other words, the attainment of perfect freedom, never more to be conditioned by causation in space-time. Nirvana is the state of perfect freedom.

Concerning *epistemological* questions, Buddhism has much more to say than any other philosophy. As sources of cognition Buddhism recognizes the world of sensation *(pratyaksa-pramana)*, the world of inference *(anumana)* and the world of pure intuition *(dhyana)*. Thus sense data, reason and inner experience resulting from intuition will all provide the content of knowledge. Besides these we can appeal in every case to the Word that has been uttered from the world of perfect enlightenment *(bodhi)*, i.e., the Buddha (the 'Enlightened').

Without purity of conduct there will be no calm equipoise of thought; without the calm equipoise of thought there will be no completion of insight. The completion of insight *(prajna)* means the perfection of intellect and wisdom, i.e., perfect enlightenment. It is the result of self-creation and the ideal of the self-creating life.

The Buddha, as a man, taught men how to become perfect men. The central principle of self-creation is the gradual development of intellect and wisdom, the object being the perfection of personality. The realization of the Life-Ideal is Buddhahood. But there will be

195

no objective enlightenment apart from the Enlightened One. There exists only the inner experiencer, no absolute otherness.

The doctrine of the Middle Path means in the first instance the middle path between the two extremes of optimism and pessimism. Such a middle position is a third extreme, tending neither one way nor the other. The Buddha certainly began with this middle as only one step higher than the ordinary extremes. A gradual ascent of the dialectical ladder, however, will bring us higher and higher until a stage is attained wherein the antithetic onesidedness of *ens* and *non-ens* is denied and transcended by an idealistic synthesis. In this case the Middle Path has a similar purport as the Highest Truth.

The above statements refer chiefly to the metaphysical and intuitive problems of Buddhist thought. Now as to the *dialectical* questions. Nagarjuna's [10] method of argumentation is particularly notable. Following the Buddha's practice, he started from an evaluation of the worldly or common-sense truth and termed it 'closed truth' *(samvritti-satya)*. Without denying the common-sense truth he set forth beside it a highest-sense truth *(parama-artha-satya)*. 'Highest-sense' does not mean the highest-sense truth at the beginning, but is only the highest at any particular time. It is, in fact, only a higher-sense truth, as the term *lokottara* ('above the world') indicates. Gradually the common-sense world will reach the higher-sense truth then set forth, which latter has now become the common-sense truth. By the side of it Nagarjuna would set forth a still higher-sense truth which again will become a common-sense truth in time. Thus the standard of common-sense truth will be raised higher and higher until it attains pre-eminently the Highest-sense Truth, which can be taken as the Absolute in the Western sense of the word. But in fact, it is not the Absolute nor is it the One because any one can reach that stage of perfect freedom.

The Highest-sense Truth has been made dialectically and positively by Nagarjuna without using any antithetic and negative method such as expounded by Hegel. In addition to the six fundamental principles of Buddhist thought which I have described in Chapter III, I might add this Principle of Appreciation of Common-sense Truth. This was the attitude the Buddha himself took during his teaching career and was not altogether Nagarjuna's invention.

---

[10] 龍樹 c. 100-200 A.D.

A thorough-going negative method was also used by Nagarjuna in his famous Eightfold Negation. With it all the phases of becoming or life-conditions have been negated. "Production and extinction, permanence and annihilation, unity and diversity, coming and going" are the refuted examples in four pairs and eight items. If there be any views or attachments he would deny them at once as they come forward. The final result of Nagarjuna's negation is the Void which is not an actual emptiness but is instead the state *devoid of* special conditions of the world of life.

In passing we must not overlook Nagarjuna's important method of demonstrating Truth from all possible viewpoints. It is called the Discrimination of the Fourfold Thesis, as I have already referred in Ch. VII: 1. positive *(ens)*; 2. negative *(non-ens)*; 3. both positive and negative *(both ens and non-ens together);* 4. neither positive nor negative *(both ens and non-ens negated)*. These four are considered to be all the possible viewpoints which can be advocated. All the intellectual groups of the Buddha's time were not satisfied by the simple answer of "yes" or "no," for almost every one of his opponents used this fourfold viewpoint, and the Buddha used it carefully in refuting any erroneous thesis of his opponents. For example, when the First Cause is questioned: 1. Is it caused by self? 2. Or is it caused by another? 3. Or is it caused by both? 4. Or is it caused by neither? Similarly, if Being is the thesis: the first view will affirm it *(ens);* the second will deny it *(non-ens);* and the third will conditionally affirm the above two, as does the Buddhist idealist (affirming the inner world but denying the outer world). The fourth view, however, will negate both *ens* and *non-ens*. The application of this method to any disputation will exhaust all possibilities of an argued question. I should like to call it the Principle of Exhaustive Demonstration of Truth, and might add it also to the above-mentioned Fundamental Principles of Buddhist thought.

I shall not discuss here the details of the Buddhist logic of Nagarjuna, Vasubhandu,[11] and Dignaga (Dinnaga) [12] for which I shall refer the reader to Stcherbatsky's excellent work, *Buddhist Logic*.[13]

---

[11] 世親 c. 420-500 A.D.   [12] 陳那
[13] Th. Stcherbatsky, *Buddhist Logic*, 2 Vols., Leningrad, 1932. Vidyabhusana's exhaustive work entitled *A History of Indian Logic* should also be consulted among other studies.

Let it suffice here to say that Buddhist logic is not a formal logic of thought, but is rather a logic of dispute or debate which lays stress on the investigation of cause, relations and possibility and is therefore an art of argumentation and refutation. The science of cause (*hetu-vidya*) is the name given to Buddhist logic; the Buddha himself was sometimes called '*vibhajya-vada*' (the 'discriminative'), meaning a logician.

The aim of the Buddha was the establishment of the Kingdom of Truth. The foundation of such a Kingdom was, in case of a sovereign whose title was 'Turning the Wheel' *(cakra-vartin)*, laid by throwing a wheel into the air. The golden wheel thus thrown, going around in the sky, would come back to the original place in seven days. The circle-line drawn by the motion of the wheel in seven days would determine the sphere of the Kingdom to be ruled by the sovereign.

'Turning the Wheel of Truth' *(Dharma-cakra-pravartana)* would practically mean 'preaching the Buddha's Ideal' or the 'realization of the Buddha's Ideal in the world,' i.e., the 'foundation of Kingdom of Truth.'

The Buddha's Ideal, that is, the Truth he has conceived, would be difficult to be understood without reference to the fundamental principles of Brahmanism. The attributes of Brahman, the universal principle, were, according to the Upanishads, 'saccidanandam,' that is, 'being' (*sat*), 'thinking' (*cit*) and 'joy' (*anandam*). In the case of Brahman, the First Cause, these would be 'Self-extant,' 'All-knowing' and 'Blissful.'

The time-honored Buddhist principle was threefold:

1. *Sarva-dharma-anatmata,* 'Selflessness of all elements,' i.e., 'No substance.'

2. *Sarva-sanskara-anitya-ta,* 'Impermanence of all component beings and things and elements,' i.e., 'No duration.'

3. *Sarvam duhkham,* 'All in suffering,' i.e., 'No bliss.'

To these sometimes another *Nirvanam sukham,* "Nirvana is Bliss,' is added. These are generally called the 'Three or Four Signs' of Buddhism, which distinguish Buddhism from any other school. The Buddha's first theory that all beings have no abiding self is opposed to the Brahmanic theory of 'permanent being' *(sat)* and is against the immortality of an individual soul and the existence of the universal soul or spirit or Creator *(Maha-atman)*. It is the theory of no real substance. A denial of an immortal being is a denial of immortality. The Buddha's second theory that all beings or things are impermanent is directed at this point. All existence is temporary or transitory. Nothing will remain the same for two consecutive moments. Life is an eternal flux of change, that is, the wave of life. A continuity of flowing waves might give an appearance of permanence but it is an illusion. It is the theory of no duration.

Since the world has no abiding substance and no enduring permanence, we shall have no enjoyment in this world. One should accept suffering as suffering and not be deceived by a disguised joy. One should not be optimistic because all ends in suffering; nor should one try to shun it because there is no final escape. One should go against it with all bravery and perseverance and overcome it. This is the theory of no bliss and is directly opposed to the Brahmanic theory of bliss *(anandam)*.

As to the second Brahmanic theory of 'thinking' or 'knowing' *(cit)* which is later summed up as the 'knowledge' section *(jnana-kanda)* of the Upanishads, the Buddha proposed his theory of ignorance *(avidya)*, i.e., the 'blind will to live,' as the root-principle of the Twelve-Divisioned Cycle of Causations. The way of undoing one's ignorance is his religion of Self-Creation based on knowledge and wisdom. The perfection of fullness of insight is the perfection of personality, i.e., perfect Enlightenment *(Bodhi)*.

Accordingly, the Buddha first taught the way of Life-View *(darsana-marga)*. The Four Noble Truths on suffering and its extinction, the Twelve-Divisioned Cycle of Causations of Life and the principle of indeterminate nature of beings and things show his view of life. The indeterminate nature of men is to be determined by Self-Creation. The Buddha next taught the way of Life-Culture *(bhavana-marga)*. Here he trained his pupils either by dialectic argument or by intuitive meditation in order to awaken their intellect or insight. In course of time, Buddhist schools developed their own methods of attaining Enlightenment. Nagarjuna's negative rationalism [14] and Bodhidharma's [15] pure intuitionism [16] are the most developed examples. As a result of Life-Culture by these methods, the principles of Reciprocal Identification, True Reality and Totality

---

[14] 三論宗 The Sanron School   [15] 菩提達摩   [16] 禪宗 The Zen School

as described in Ch. III are arrived at. Finally, as the way of No More Learning, the principle of Nirvana, that is, perfect freedom, in which the state of undifferentiated indeterminateness is attained. This is the realization of Life-Ideal in Buddhism.

INDEX

Entries in the index conform, of course, to the style of the text. It is to be noted that Professor Takakusu has employed variations in transliteration of the Sanskrit in order to agree with general usage; for example, such equivalents as *r* and *ri*, *n* and *m*, and *sh* and *s* are both used. The editors have not considered it imperative to make changes for the sake of consistency. Capitalization also conforms to the usage in the text. To avoid unnecessary repetition and complexity, not all entries are indexed in both Sanskrit and English. For the convenience of those who are not familiar with the Sanskrit terms, however, many basic items are given double entry. [Editors' note.]

realm of, 138, 139; three aspects of, 141; Three Bodies, *see* Buddha-nature, Buddhahood; two aspects of, 149-150; Vehicle of, 106, 134; Wisdom Buddhas, 174-175; World of, 27; *see also* Gotama

Buddha-in-me, 149

Buddha-nature, 52, 194; in all men, 41; as Dharma-dhātu, 47; in Idealism, 91; in Jōdo, 167; in Tendai, 127-128; as Thus-come, 38; in Totalism, 115, 117, 123; in Zen, 163; *see also* Buddha, Buddhahood

Buddha-smriti, 179

Buddha-svabhāva, 47, 128

Buddha-tā, 47

Buddhabhadra, 110

Buddhadeva, 65

Buddhahood, 26-28, 115; in all men, 127-128; attainable in this world, 149, 172, 183; as Life-Ideal, 195; in Mysticism, 148-149; in Pure Land, 166-167, 172, 175; as Three Bodies, 141; as Thusness, 193; *see also* Buddha, Buddha-nature

Buddhapālita, 98

Buddhaśānta, 81, 110

Buddhism: Chinese, 9, 13-17, 62-63, 75, 78, 81, 99, 114, 128, 145-146, 156, 167-168, 187; classification of, 10-19, 114-117, 131-134, 143; cosmology of, 192; epistemology of, 195-196; eschatology, 195; fundamental principles of, 29-56, 198; ideal of, 25-26, 198; Indian, 9, 20, 61-63, 74-75, 81, 98, 144, 167; Influence of, 165, 177, 180; Japanese, 9-10, 17-19, 63, 76, 84-85, 100, 130-131, 142-147, 153-154, 160-161, 168, 178-179, 187-188; Life-Creation in, 199; Life-Culture in, 199; Life-View of, 199; logic of, 196-198; ontology of, 97, 193-195; periods of, 98; psychology of, 195; as religion, 22, 27, 162, 171, 181, 189, 199; schools of, 12, 17, 18, 19; Tibetan, 9, 142

Buddhist Logic, 11, 64n., 66n., 197

Buddhist logic, 197-198

Bushidō, 164

Butsugen, 161

Caitasika, 69, 72a, 78, 87, 94a; *see also* Mental Functions

Calmness, 157; and insight, 156, 157; *see also* Insight

Candrakīrti, 96n.

Caste, 25

Catvāri-ārya-satyāni, 25

Causal Origination, *see* Pratitya-sam-utpāda

Causation, 23, 24, 26, 53-56, 88, 92, 94, 95, 106, 135, 137, 139, 141, 157, 192, 193, 195, 198; by Action-influence, 30-36; Chain of, 29-43, 78; 199; Cycles of, 34, 199; Four Sub-causes, 70-72; in Idealism, 95, 97; by the Ideation-store, 36-38; in Negativism, 106; Principle of, 29-43; in Realism, 70-72; realm of cause, 149; Six Chief Causes, 70-71; Ten Causes, 70-72; by Ten Theories, 124; in Tendai, 129; by Thusness, 38-39; in Totalism, 113-124; by the Universal Principle, 39-41

Ceremony, 148, 151-153, 176, 185, 188

Chain of Causation, *see* Causation

Ch'an, 9, 15; *see also* Zen

Chan-jan, 130

Change, *see* Becoming, Impermanence

Character (Characteristic), 68, 80, 83, 85, 86, 91, 92, 94, 102, 106, 107, 118, 130, 194; *see also* Conditioned existence, Dependence, Dharma-nature, Indeterminateness, Void

Cheerfulness, *see* Muditā

Chên-hsiang, 113

Chên-yen, 16; *see also* Shingon

Ch'êng-kuan, 112, 113

Ch'êng-shih, *see* Jojitsu

Ch'i-an, 160

Chi-tsang, 14, 75, 99, 100, 101

Chia-hsiang Ta-shih, 99

Chien-chên, 187

Chigen, 113

204

Desire, 24, 26, 42, 52-55, 78, 79, 94a, 101, 129, 136, 157, 197; in Chain of Causation, 30-36; dharma of, 69; World of, 54-55
Determinate, 70
Determinism, 41-43
Deva, 35, 38; see also Deity
Devadatta, 127, 181
Devaprajña, 111
Devaśarman, 60
Devolution, 192
Devotion, 176; see also Faith
Dhamma-pada, 42, 51
Dhāraṇā, 155
Dhāraṇī, 144, 148
Dharma: character of, see Dharma-lakṣana; Circle of, 151; Created, 68, 72a, 93, 94a; as elements, 11, 12, 73, 102; as Ideal, 48, 51-52, 125, 127-128, 148, 163, 179, 198; in Idealism, 80, 82, 85, 86, 87, 91, 92-95; Idealistic School list of, 87, 91-94, 94a, 94-95; Literature, 48-50; meaning of, 57; in Negativism, 106; in Nihilism, 76-78; Nihilistic School list of, 77; in Realism, 64-68; Realistic School list of, 67-72, 72a, 73-77; in Tendai, 134-137, 140; in Totalism, 117, 123; in Zen, 158; see also Dharma-body, Dharma-dhatu, Dharma-nature
Dharma-body, see Three Bodies
Dharma-cakra, 105
Dharma-cakra-pravartana, 198
Dharma-dhātu, 27, 108, 124; Causation by, 39-41; Principle of, 47-48; realms of, 52-55, 193; in Totalism, 113-114; as Universal Principle, 39-41; see also Universal Principle
Dharma-dhātu-samāpatti, 27
Dharmakara, 172
Dharma-kāya, see Three Bodies
Dharma-lakṣana, 80, 83, 91, 115
Dharma-maṇḍala, 151
Dharma-megha, 125
Dharma-nature, 52, 76, 80, 91, 106, 123
Dharma-skandha, 60
Dharma-smriti, 179

Dharma-svabhāva, 80, 91, 106
Dharma-tā, 76
Dharmagupta, 14, 144, 177
Dharmaguptiya, 187
Dharmakīrti, 144
Dharmapāla, 83, 84, 86, 88
Dharmarakṣa, 177
Dharmatrāta, 59, 60, 62, 65, 67
Dharmottara, 59, 60, 62, 67
Dhātu-kāya, 60
Dhyāna, see Meditation
Dialectic, 18, 97, 100, 105, 106, 192, 196, 199
Diamond Cutter, 99
Diamond doctrine, 152
Diamond Element, 149, 150
Diamond Head, 148
Diamond Realm, 151
Diamond Vehicle, 142, 143
Dichotomy, 140
Differentiation, see Identification
Difficult way, 171
Dignāga (Diñnāga), 83, 88, 98, 197
Diligence, 22
Disciplinary Formalism, see Ritsu
Discipline, 48, 50, 82, 124, 127, 131, 154, 174, 176, 185-191; essence of, 186, 188, 189; four aspects of, 186; Literature, 58, 144; as part of Three Learnings, 21, 79, 157; Self-immanent Discipline, 190; Self-nature Discipline, 190; Self-vow Discipline, 154, 187, 189-190; see also Ritsu
Discourse on the Ultimate Truth, 17
Discrimination, 82, 104
Discrimination of the Fourfold Thesis, 197
Distinct Doctrine, 117, 133, 134
Distinction, 55, 120, 129, 132
Divākara, 111
Diversity, 103, 104, 122, 197
Divya-avadāna, 108
Dōan, 167
Doctrine Common to All, 133
Doctrine of Maturity, 116
Doctrine of Pitakas (Scripture), 133
Doctrine of the Small Vehicle, 114
Dōgen, 19, 154, 160, 161, 179
Dōji, 100

205

Harmony, 40-41, 117-123, 134, 136, 140, 149
Heaven, 27
Heavenly Beings, 138
Hedonism, 22, 80
Hell, 139
Hellish beings, 139
Hetu, 70
Hetu-pratyaya, 71
Hetu-vidyā, 198
Hijiri, 170
Hīnayāna, 88, 97, 101, 125, 142, 143, 188; compared with Mahāyāna, 9, 21, 28, 43, 46, 52, 86, 127, 131, 156, 157, 158, 186, 189; origin of the term, 166; periods of, 12, 14-16, 114, 131-134, 143; schools of, 12, 14-16, 57, 74-75, 114-115, 189; see also Vehicle
History of Buddhism, 75n.
History of Indian Logic, 197n.
Hiuen-tsang, *see* Hsüan-tsang
Hōjō, 168
Hokke, 126
Holy Path, 169, 171
Hommon-Hokke, 183
Hōmyō, 169
Hōnen, 19, 154, 168, 169, 171, 177, 179
Hōshin, 188
Hosshō, 91
Hossō, 11, 12, 15, 16, 18, 63, 80-95, 97, 98, 100, 115, 119, 124, 143, 144, 155, 156, 163, 189, 193, 197; Buddha-nature, 91; causation, 95; dharmas, 85-87, 91-95; eightfold consciousness, 82, 87-91; Five Species of men, 91; four functional divisions of consciousness, 88; history of, 81-84; literature of, 81, 84-85; Middle Path, 80, 94-95; philosophy of, 85-95; seeds, 90; three aspects of reality, 92, 94; Three Bodies, 82; three species of external world, 89; Thusness, 91, 94; vehicles, 91; Void, 95; wisdom, 95; *see also* Idealism, Vijñaptimātratā, Yogācāra

Hōtan, 112
Hōzō, 113
Hsien-shou, 100, 112
Hsiu-jan, 131
Hsüan-ch'ao, 146
Hsüan-tsang (Hiuen-tsang), 16, 61, 63, 75, 83-86, 100, 119 155, 187
Hsüan-tsung, 187
Hua-yen, *see* Kegon
Huai-kan, 168
Hui-ch'ung, 167
Hui-k'o, 159
Hui-kuan, 100, 101
Hui-kuang, 14, 110
Hui-kuo, 146
Hui-nêng, 16, 159
Hui-pien, 130
Hui-ssu, 130
Hui-tsê, 147
Hui-wên, 128
Hui-yüan, 112, 168
Human nature, 190
Humanity, 194
Hung-jên, 159
Hungry spirits, 139

I-ching, *see* I-tsing
I-hsiang, 111
I-hsing, 145, 146, 152
I-in-Buddha, 149
I-lin, 146
I-ning I-shan, *see* Ichinei Issan
I-ts'ao, 147
I-tsing (I-ching), 58, 111, 142, 144, 155, 188
Icchantika (Ecchantika), 91, 127, 128
Ichigyō, 145, 146
Ichijitsu, 144
Ichinei Issan (I-ning I-shan), 160, 180
Idea, 94a
Ideal, *see* Dharma
Ideal-body, *see* Three Bodies
Ideal world, 119, 120, 124
Idealism, 11, 12, 15, 16, 18, 97, 197; *see also* Hossō
Ideation, 53, 72a, 98, 118, 123; Ālaya-store, 81-83, 89-94, 94-95, 94a, 97-98, 110; Causation by

208

Joy, 124, 198
Jungyō, 146

Kakushin, 19, 154, 161
Kāla, see Time
Kalpa, 173, 192
Kamakura, 153-154
Kammaṭṭhāna, 158
Kaniṣka, 59
Kanjin, 131, 168
Kapilavastu, 38, 145
Kāraṇa-hetu, 71
Karma, 42, 48, 69, 73, 87, 90, 95,
113, 114, 115, 130, 151, 152,
157, 158; Causation by, 30-36;
Karma Circle, 151; Karma-sthāna,
157; see also Action
Karma-ācārya, 189
Karuṇā, 156
Kaśmīra, 58, 61, 63
Kathāvatthu, 58, 75
Kātyāyaniputra, 59, 61
Kegon, 9, 15, 19, 40, 41, 46, 99, 105,
108-125, 128, 131, 133, 143,
183; Causation, 113-124; Classi-
fication of Buddhism, 114-116;
Dharma-dhatu, 113-124; Five as-
pects of teaching, 114; fourfold
universe, 119; history of, 109-113;
Matrix of Thus-come, 113-114,
116; meaning of "Avataṅsaka,"
108-109; mutual penetration and
mutual identification, 119, 124;
New Profound Theories, 121;
Northern Path and Southern Path,
110; philosophy of, 113-125; Six-
fold Specific Nature, 121-123;
ten doctrines, 114, 117-118; Ten
Profound Theories, 120-123; Ten
Stages, 124-125; texts of, 108-
111; Thusness, 113-116; Ti-lun
School, 109-110; Universe of
One-Truth, 124; see also Avataṅ-
saka, Totalism, Totality, Wreath,
Wreath
Keikwa, 146
Kenpon-Hokke, 181
Kern, H., 126n., 178n., 181
Ki, see K'uei-chi

Kleśa, 69, 72a, 94a; see also Defile-
ment, Evil, Passion
Kleśa-mahābhūmika, 69, 72a
Knowledge, 18, 21, 22, 45, 79, 82,
88, 94, 94a, 95, 107, 129, 149,
163, 195, 199; see also Conscious-
ness, Enlightenment, Ideation, In-
sight, Learning, Wisdom
Kōan, 164
Kōbō Daishi (Kūkai), 142, 143,
146, 147, 188
Kośa, see Kusha
Kōshō, 171
Kōshō Bodhisattva, 191
Kōyasan, 52
Kōzen Gokoku-ron, 161
Kṣaṇa-bhaṅga, 193
Kṣānti, 125
Kuan-ting, 130
K'uei-chi (Ki), 16, 61, 63, 84, 86,
100, 119
Kūkai, see Kōbō Daishi
Kumārajīva, 14, 75, 81, 96, 99, 100,
126, 176-178
K'ung, 106
Kuo-i, 112
Kuśala-mahābhūmika, 69, 72a, 94a
Kusha, 12, 16, 18, 57-73, 74, 76, 78,
79, 80, 81, 92, 95, 97, 101, 102,
115, 117, 119, 139, 143, 189,
193; Aggregates, 72; branches of,
60; dharma, 57; Four Elements,
72; history of, 61-63; list of
dharmas, 66-70; literature of, 59-
63; Nirvāṇa, 73; origin of, 58-59;
P'i-t'an, 60-63; Self, 66-67, 72;
Six Causes, 70-71; Sub-causes, 70-
72; theory of time, 64-65
Kūya, 170, 171, 174
Kūyanembutsu, 171
Kwannon, 171

La Siddhi de Hiuen-tsang, 84
La Vallée Poussin, 57n., 62, 84n.
Lakṣaṇa, 80, 86; see also Character
Lakṣaṇa-bhāga, 88
Lamaism, 9
Laṅkāvatāra Sūtra, 101n.
Larger Sukhāvatī, 99
Laukika-satya, 86

Law, 158, 159
Law-body, see Three Bodies
Laymen, 189
Learning, 18, 21, 28, 79, 157, 200; see also Knowledge
Lévi, S., 85n.
Liberation, see Mokṣa
Lieo-chi, 83
Life, 30-36, 45, 53, 54, 70, 72a, 79, 94a
Life-culture, 18, 28, 125, 199
Life-Ideal, 18, 28, 194, 195, 200
Life-View, 18, 28, 124, 199
Logic, 163, 197, 198; see also Anumāna
Lokalakṣaṇa-nityatā, 137
Loḥottara, 118, 196
Lotus Doctrine, 130-135, 169, 174-184, 188, 190; see also Lotus Sūtra
Lotus-pietism, 19, 154, 169, 176-184; see also Lotus Sūtra, Nichiren, Tendai
Lotus School, see Nichiren, Tendai
Lotus Store, 40, 47, 124
Lotus Sūtra, 17, 79, 99, 105, 126, 127, 130-135, 174-184; see also Lotus Doctrine
Lü, see Ritsu

Madhyamā-pratipad, see Middle Path
Mādhyamika, 14, 18, 46n., 96, 97, 115, 144, 155; see also Sanron
Mādhyamika Śāstra, 96, 99, 102, 103, 128, 136n.
Madhyānta-vibhāga, 145
Mahā-maṇḍala, 151
Mahā-parinirvāṇa Sūtra, 52, 55, 79, 99, 115, 127, 132, 134, 176
Mahā-prajñā-pāramitā Śāstra, 97, 134; see also Prajñā-pāramitā Sūtra
Mahā-vairocana-garbhakośa, 145
Mahābhūmika, 69
Mahākāśyapa, 158-159
Mahākauṣṭhila, 60
Mahāsaṅghika, 64, 118
Mahātman, 155, 199
Mahāvairocana, 108, 112, 143, 149, 150, 175
Mahāvibhāṣā, 60, 61, 65

Mahāyāna, 39, 47, 50, 78, 96, 97, 98, 101, 115-116, 118, 119, 120, 125, 128, 135, 142, 171, 175, 187, 190; compared with Hinayāna, 9, 21, 28, 43, 46, 52, 86, 127, 131, 156, 157, 158, 186, 189, 193; in Japan, 17-19; origin of the term, 166; periods of, 98, 131-134, 143; relation with Nihilism, 75; schools of, 12, 14-16, 79, 80, 96-97, 108, 109, 126, 142, 153, 155, 166, 176, 185, 189; six general principles of, 29-55; ten special characteristics of, 81-82, see also Vehicle
Mahāyāna-samparigraha, 16, 81, 84
Mahīśāsaka, 64
Maitreya, 98
Maitreya Sūtra, 99
Maitrī, 156
Majjhima-Nikāya, 51n.
Man, 23, 24, 72-73, 115, 122, 139, 194, 195; see also Personality, Self
Manas, see Thought
Manas-vijñāna, 37, 87, 93, 94a
Mandala, 41, 124, 150-151
Manichaeism, 167
Manifestation, 37, 39, 40, 43, 53, 70, 86, 87, 90-93, 114, 120-122, 123-124, 127, 135, 137, 139, 148-150, 182, 189
Mañjuśrī, 109, 111
Mano-vijñāna, 37, 87, 93, 94a
Manoja, 93
Manomaya, 93
Mantra, see Shingon
Mantrayāna, 142
Materialism, 23, 73
Matériaux pour l'étude du système Vijñaptimātra, 85n.
Matrix Repository, 149-152
Matrix of Thus-come or Thus-gone, 38-39, 47, 113-114, 116
Matter, 21n., 27, 155, 189, 193; as member of Aggregates, 72, 76, 118, 139; or dharmas, 67-70, 77-79, 80, 102; and mind, see Mind
Maudgalyāyana, 60
Mean, see Middle Path

211

Meditation, 18, 21, 64, 70, 82, 84, 94a, 111, 116, 125, 130, 162, 163, 173, 190, 195, 199; as a way of learning, 21, 79, 157; Calmness and Insight as phases of, 157-158; Method of, 155-158; Patriarchal Meditation, 158-160; religion of, 18; School of, *see* Zen; sign of, 149, 164; sitting and meditating, 164; Tathāgata Meditation, 157-158; Worlds of Being attainable by, 27

Menandros (Milinda), 166

Mental Function, 67-68, 69 70, 72a, 77, 87, 94a; *see also* Caitasika

Mercy, 125, 156, 157

Mere-Ideation, *see* Hossō

Merit, 159

Metaphysics, 192, 196

Middle Path, 12, 18, 22, 23, 46-47, 69, 80, 94-95, 96, 128, 136, 196; in Idealism, 12, 80, 94; meaning of, 196; in Negativism, 12, 96-106; in Realism, 12; in Tendai, 128, 133-136

Mikkyō, 9

Milinda, *see* Menandros

Mind, 27, 66, 72a, 94a, 124, 130, 137, 140, 157, 158, 163, 183, 193; of Buddha, 162; in Chain of Causation, 30-34; as dharma, 77-80, 87, 92-95; and matter, 12, 21, 42, 46, 53-55, 66, 70, 72-73, 87-93, 140; *see also* Consciousness, Ideation, Thought

Minor Functions, 72a, 94a

Miscellaneous Mystics, 144

Mittlere Lehre des Nāgārjuna, 96n.

Mittlere Lehre, nach der tibetischen version, 96n.

Mokṣa, 128; *see also* Salvation

Momentariness, *see* Impermanence

Monism, 11, 64, 96, 153, 193

Monks, 186

Moral force, 188

Morality, *see* Ethics, Good, Sīla

Motion, 44, 46, 103, 104, 118

Muditā, 156

Mudrā, 144, 148

Mutual Penetration, 119-124

Myōe, 112

Myōmanji, 181

Mystical verses, 144, 148

Mysticism, 9, 16, 131, 133, 142, 144, 147, 148, 163, 175, 190; *see also* Shingon

Nāga, 181

Nāgabodhi, 145

Nāgārjuna, 11, 12, 13, 96-103, 129, 134, 166, 167 171, 178, 196-197, 199

Nāgasena, 166

Nālanda, 63, 83, 86, 88

Nāma mātra, 118

Name, 72a, 94a, 102, 106, 118, 129, 137

Name-Form, 30, 32, 34

Nanda, 84

Nara, 169

Nature, 21, 41, 154-156, 194

Nature of elements, 80, 85, 86, 91, 92, 94, 135, 139, 140

Negation, 12, 44, 97, 100, 101, 103, 105-107, 115, 136, 197

Negativism, 11, 12, 17, 18, 74; *see also* Jōjitsu, Sanron, Void

Neti, neti, 101

New Lotus, 19, 176; *see also* Nichiren

New Profound Theories, 121

New Ritsu, *see* Ritsu

Nichiji, 180

Nichiren, 19, 154, 176-184, 188; expediency, 182; Fujufuse Sect, 181; history of, 178-181; Ideal-body, 183; Kenpon-Hokke Sect, 181; life of Nichiren, 178-181; Nichiren's attack on other sects, 179; Original Buddha, 182, 183; phi'osophy and religion of, 181-184; realm of origin, 181; realm of trace, 182; Trace Buddha, 182

Nieh-p'an, 15

Nihilism, 12, 14, 18, 74, 102; *see also* Jōjitsu, Negativism

Nirmāṇa-kāya, 141

Nirodha-samāpatti, 27, 72a, 79n., 94a

Nirodha-satya, 76

212

213

219

Vajrabodhi, 16, 144-146, 152
Vajrapani, 149
Vajrayana, 142
Vak, 70
Valabhi, 63, 81, 84
Vallée Poussin, see La Vallée Poussin
Vassilief, 75n.
Vasubandhu, 11, 12, 13, 57, 61, 62,
    65, 66, 67, 68, 70, 74, 75, 80-81,
    83-86, 97, 98, 109, 110, 145, 155,
    167, 171, 197
Vasumitra, 60, 65
Vatsiputriya, 117
Vattagamani, 50

Vedanta, 98n.
Vedanta Sutra, 155
Vehicle, 91, 105, 124-125; in Mysti-
    cism, 143; in Negativism, 105-
    106; in Nichiren, 181, 182; in
    Pure Land, 166; in Tendai, 132-
    134; in Totalism, 114-119; see
    also Bodhisattva, Ekayana, Hina-
    yana, Mahayana, Pratyeka-Buddha-
    yana, Sravaka-yana, Triyana, Vaj-
    rayana
Vibhajya-vada, 198
Vibhasa, 59, 60, 63, 66
Vidhi, 148
Vidyabhusana, M. S., 197n.
Vijnana, 34, 82, 87, 93, 94a; see also
    Consciousness
Vijnana-kaya, 60
Vijnanavada, 98
Vijnapti-matrata-siddhi, 84, 86, 145
Vijnapti-matrata-trimsika, 85
Vijnaptimatrata, 84, 145
Vijnaptimatrata, 12, 16, 46n., 84,
    155; see also Hosso
Vikramasilas, 142
Vimala, 124
Vimalakirti, 17, 99, 116
Vimalakirti-nirdesa, 17n.
Vimsatika, 87n.
Vinaya, see Discipline
Vipaka-hetu, 71
Virya, 22, 72a, 94a, 125
Visaya, 89; see also External World
Visistacaritra, 180, 183
Visuddhi Magga, 158

Vivatta, 192
Vivatta-tthayi, 192
Void, 11, 12, 43-44, 115, 118, 124,
    194, 197; in Idealism, 95; mean-
    ing of, 46-47, 106; in Negativism,
    97, 100-107; in Nihilism, 76-79;
    in Realism, 66; in Tendai, 129,
    132-133, 135-137; see also Char-
    acter, Relativity, Self
Volition, 37, 72, 76, 94a, 118, 139;
    see also Will
Vow, 125, 151, 172, 173, 175, 180,
    186, 187, 189-191

Walleser, Max, 96n.
Wên-ku, 146
Watanabe, K., 10n.
Way, see Eightfold Path, Middle
    Path
Way of Life-Culture, 18; see also
    Bhavana-marga
Way of Life-View (Insight), 18; see
    also Darsana-marga
Way of viewing, 162
Way of walking, 162
Wei-shih, see Hosso
*Wei Shih Er Shih Lun or The
    Treatise in Twenty Stanzas on
    Representation-only*, 87n.
Wei-shih-shu-chi, 84
Wheel of Life, 30-36, 39; see also
    Becoming, Impermanence, Sansara
Whole and parts, 132
Will, 34, 36, 42, 69, 72a, 127, 139,
    194; see also Volition
Will to Live, 31, 33, 36, 50
Wisdom, 28, 57, 79, 82, 94a, 107,
    125, 128, 129, 157, 163, 167,
    195, 199; fourfold, 95; in Mysti-
    cism, 149-150; see also Prajna
Wisdom Buddha, 174-175
Wisdom-fist, 149
Woodward, F. L., 59n.
Word-teaching, 102
World, 139, 193, 194-195; see also
    External world, Ten Realms, Three
    Bodies, Universe
World of all realities or practical
    facts interwoven, 119

220